The Wonderful "Aha!"

At some time in your life, you have probably wrestled with a problem, tried to solve a puzzle or struggled to understand some intellectual truth, but with little success. After a time of grappling, the wonderful "Aha!" takes place when the solution is realized, the puzzle is solved or the truth is understood. Suddenly it all comes together as you experience a moment of enlightenment.

In this course, *Christ B.C.*, you and your group members will experience many moments of "Aha!" as you discover Christ in the stories, events, prophecies and spiritual truths of the Old Testament. These hidden pictures are sometimes called types, foreshadowings, prefigures or symbols. And they all point to Christ—His birth, ministry, redemptive work and future reign.

This course by Lloyd H. Ahlem and the Regal devotional book, *Christ B.C.*, by Bill Myers, blend together to especially enrich the Bible students' understanding of doctrinal truths relating to the redemptive work of Christ. You and your group members will be spiritually *enlightened* as you examine Christ in the pages of the Old Testament.

Other Adult Bible Studies in This Series

How to Be a Christian and Still Enjoy Life
(Philippians)
> Regal book by Fritz Ridenour

Joseph
(Biographical study)
> Regal book by Gene A. Getz

Issues in Focus
(Topical Study)
> Regal book by 13 different authors

Psalms of Faith
(Psalms)
> Regal book by Ray C. Stedman

Walking What You're Talking
(James)
> Regal book by Harold L. Fickett

God, I've Got a Problem
(Topical Study)
> Regal book by Ben Ferguson

How to Be a Christian Without Being Religious
(Romans)
> Regal book by Fritz Ridenour

God's Way Out
(Exodus)
> Regal book by Bernard L. Ramm

Contents

EDITORIAL STAFF

Annette Parrish	Managing Editor
Margaret Rosenberger	Editor
Judith L. Roth	Assistant Editor
Hope Deck	Editorial Coordinator

CONTRIBUTING EDITORS

Don Pugh
John Whitman

CONTRIBUTING WRITER

Lloyd M. Ahlem

Scripture taken from the HOLY BIBLE: *NEW INTERNATIONAL VERSION.* Copyright © 1973, 1978, 1984 International Bible Society. Used by permission of Zondervan Bible publishers.

Other translations used:
KJV—*King James Version.*

The publishers do not necessarily endorse the entire contents of all publications referred to in this Leader's Guide.

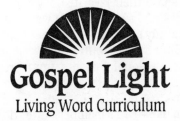

Gospel Light
Living Word Curriculum

How to Use the Regal Book *Christ B.C.*

The Regal book, *Christ B.C.*, is a devotional book that supplements this Leader's Guide. Authored by Bill Myers, popular Christian book-and-film-writer and producer, the Regal devotional book replaces, with this course, the often used paperback commentary.

Christ B.C. is designed to assist your group members in their personal daily devotions. Each day's devotion is based on a key word taken from the previous week's lesson. The first day's devotion views the key word as it relates to the lesson theme. Devotions for succeeding days focus on the key word as it pertains to other related topics and passages of Scripture. For example, the theme for Session 3 is "Noah Finds Refuge in the Ark." The key word is "refuge." The first day's devotion views the word *refuge* as it relates to Noah and the ark. Devotions for succeeding days are based on the theme of *refuge* as it pertains to worry, fear, self, etc.

Christ B.C. is not only an easy to use devotional book, but it adds a dimension of rich spiritual input to learner's devotional times with the Lord. Here are several ways you and your group members may want to use Bill Myers' book as part of your study:

● **Presession sharing**—You can take a few minutes at the beginning of your Bible study session to allow your learners to share their favorite daily devotions for the previous week and the blessing it was to them.

● **Midweek study sessions**—Consider getting together with your Bible study group in between sessions just to reflect on personal insights from previous devotions. You may want to prepare a few key questions on the devotions to guide the sharing.

● **In-session use**—Draw members' attention to various devotions for the coming week that will especially reinforce a truth of the lesson you wish to emphasize.

● **Caring group devotional material**—Many churches have small caring groups to complement the ministry of adult Sunday School classes and/or Bible study groups. *Christ B.C.* can be used to lead a devotional time for caring groups while classes or Bible study groups follow the Leader's Guide study plan.

● **Build a Bible study library**—Every Regal book that is Bible based can become a valuable addition to a growing personal library for your members. For years after this devotional book is read and used, each learner will enjoy having it in his or her personal library for review and reflection and for lending to friends.

● **Members buy personal copies**—Ask learners to buy their own copies at the start of the course. The personal investment will stimulate them to be faithful in their daily devotions. If they are not already involved in a daily devotional time, it could be the means of getting them started.

● **Church supplies copies**—Often a church will include in the curriculum budget enough funds to supply adult Bible study groups with copies of the Regal book for all group members. Churches like these are making an investment to provide tangible resources for nurture and growth.

● **Church and individuals share costs**—Sometimes churches will supply books to the learners at a minimal cost that does not reflect the total purchase price. Such an arrangement makes the book more accessible to a greater number of learners while at the same time inviting individuals to make a less demanding personal investment.

The objective of Gospel Light's Bible study and devotional materials for adults is to help the leader and learners "in all things grow up into. . .Christ" (Eph. 4:15). As you and your group members faithfully read and participate in daily devotions, you will find that the Regal book is one of the practical tools designed to help the entire group accomplish this goal.

Christ B.C.
Course Overview

Christians today, like everyone else, are feeling a time crunch. Urgent activities and must-do duties crowd the schedule. New technology, instead of fulfilling the dreams of lightening the work load, has actually substantially increased it.

In this hectic environment, moderns look to streamline the demands on their time. Priorities are hot; trivialities are not.

Because of this, Christians may seek Bible studies that seem to provide a quick route to understanding. Or they may concentrate their efforts in certain sections of the Bible, avoiding those that seem more difficult or obscure. Unfortunately, study of the Old Testament may be neglected.

It is ironic that the Old Testament is one of the most efficient tools for understanding the truths of the New. The Old Testament is rich with figurative illustrations, pictures and prophecies that were fulfilled by Jesus. Fundamental doctrines such as atonement, substitution and the value of the blood are more clearly understood when the Old Testament is taught in connection with the New.

The reverse is also true. The deeper meaning of the New Testament cannot be fully understood unless it is related to the Old. Jesus confirmed this when on the road to Emmaus "beginning with Moses and all the Prophets, he explained to them what was said in all the Scriptures concerning himself" (Luke 24:27). The Scriptures spoken of in this verse are those in what is now known as the Old Testament.

Besides deeper understanding, a study of prophecy, types, pictures and symbols of the Old Testament has many other benefits, such as: It provides evidence of one Spirit inspiring the whole Bible; it demonstrates God's intervention in history; it provides a rebuttal to the misconception that Bible stories are only allegories; it builds faith and diminishes doubt; and it presents an interesting, intriguing way to explore the Bible.

You will find this course, *Christ B.C.*, to provide that deeper understanding as well as the benefits just mentioned. Each session examines an Old Testament foreshadowing or prophecy of Jesus and its fulfillment in the New Testament.

The following overview of *Christ B.C.* provides a brief synopsis of each of the 13 sessions in this course.

Session 1, The Road to Emmaus: Members learn that Christ is the key that unlocks full understanding of all Scripture. And they discover that it is God's will that they have a proper understanding of His Word.

Session 2, God Covers Adam and Eve's Nakedness: In this session learners examine, in the light of Scripture, the futility of people's efforts to cover their sin. Members discover that Christ's blood is the only remedy for sin's cleansing.

Session 3, Noah Finds Refuge in the Ark: As God provided a place of refuge for Noah and his family during the Flood, this study reveals how believers can find refuge in Christ during life's storms.

Session 4, Melchizedek: Bible students learn that the Levitical priesthood was inadequate to bring salvation to the world. Learners discover how Jesus is both King and High Priest in the order of Melchizedek and, as such, is the only one who can offer the world complete redemption.

Session 5, Abraham and Isaac: This session's study reveals God's provision of a sacrifice in the place of Abraham's son Isaac. Members see God providing, several centuries later, the ultimate substitutionary sacrifice in the death of His Son Jesus for our sins.

Session 6, Joseph: Joseph's obedience to God under difficult circumstances is examined in this session. Learners are encouraged to obey God in all circumstances, as well, and thus fulfill His ultimate goals for their lives.

Session 7, The Passover: This momentous event in Israel's Old Testament history is explored. Members discover how Christ is seen in the Passover and how His shed blood can deliver from the bondage of sin today.

Session 8, The Tabernacle Curtain: Bible students learn that the Israelites were separated from God's presence by this curtain. And they discover that Christ's death on the cross caused the curtain in the Temple to be torn in two, symbolizing that through Him sinners are made acceptable to God.

Session 9, The Ark of the Covenant: This session study reveals a loving God who desired to dwell among a people who were unworthy of His presence because of their sin. God's mercy was extended to them through the blood that was sprinkled on the atonement cover.

Learners discuss how God's glory and presence is now available to all who put their faith in Christ.

Session 10, **The Bronze Snake:** Members examine how Christ was the fulfillment of the bronze snake, and they discover how unbelievers can receive salvation as they look to Christ for spiritual healing. Also, members learn how God alone is worthy of our worship.

Session 11, **Prophecies of the Messiah:** Learners explore Old Testament prophecies concerning Christ and their fulfillment in New Testament Scripture. They learn that the Bible is not just history or literature, it is truth.

Session 12, **The Suffering Servant:** This study focuses on several of Isaiah's prophecies concerning Christ's sufferings. And because Christ understands pain and suffering, Bible students can be assured that He understands their needs and suffering.

Session 13, **The Victorious King:** As members explore what Scripture says about the end of history, they receive hope in the truth that it is the beginning of a glorious eternity with Christ as their victorious King.

SUPPLEMENT MATERIALS

1. *Leader's Guide Sheet* is provided with each lesson. This handy fold-over sheet may be used to record your personal planning notes. Tuck it in your Bible as a guide for leading each lesson study.

2. *Lesson Handout* is provided for each member of the study group that includes a "Lesson Outline" on which he or she may take notes of the Bible lesson as it is presented during the session. Also included on this handout is a "Further Application and Study" section that provides direction for additional Bible study during the week as well as guidance to learners to apply the truths of the lesson to their lives in the days ahead. Permission is granted to reproduce for Bible study use only.

ADAPTING THIS COURSE
FOR FEWER SESSIONS

Perhaps your time schedule does not allow for a full 13-session study of *Christ B.C.* This course can be easily adapted to fit a group study schedule of as few as eight sessions. Consider the following suggestions for shortening the length of this course:

1. **Combine complementary sessions:** Each of the following combinations will reduce the session count by one. When combining sessions, choose a prevailing theme and then support that theme with input from the complementary sessions:

● Combine Sessions 1 and 12 that focus on Christ as the theme of all Scripture and on prophecies that foretell His suffering and death.

● Combine Sessions 2 and 7 on the theme of Christ's blood that delivers us from the bondage of sin.

● Combine Sessions 5 and 10 on the theme of Christ as the perfect sacrifice who died on the cross to bring salvation to all who put their trust in Him.

● Combine Sessions 8 and 9 on the theme of mercy that is extended to all who come to Christ in faith, thus being made acceptable to God.

● Combine Sessions 11 and 13 on the theme of the accuracy of prophecies that foretell Christ's birth, ministry and death and on prophecies that foretell His future, victorious reign.

2. **Create your own "highlights" course:** Carefully read the Session Focus and Session Goal from each session in this Leader's Guide. Select only those sessions that you feel are most pertinent to your Bible study group at this time.

ADAPTING THIS COURSE FOR
DISCUSSION AND RESEARCH GROUPS

If your group meets in the church sanctuary or small chapel with pews for seating accommodations, it is next to impossible to move your members into groups of four to six as suggested in many of the session plans. But before you eliminate discussion groups altogether, follow this plan:

Form groups of two to four by asking members seated in one pew to turn around and form a group with those seated behind them. Or you could limit groups to a one-on-one discussion situation.

By implementing these suggestions, you will discover that even small group discussion will make meaningful contributions to the success of the session's study. Group discussion *can* work for you!

Bible Learning Activities to Supplement the Session Plan

As you begin your lesson preparation for *Christ B.C.*, you will notice a new format for *this* course. In response to requests from many Bible study leaders, we have focused on Bible exposition with a one-page Lesson Outline handout for each lesson on which your Bible students may take notes.

In the event that your group requires a variety of learning activities, we are suggesting the following Bible learning activities (from the Gospel Light Adult Resource, *How to Do Bible Learning Activities*). These activities can be easily adapted and incorporated into the Session Plans:

Role-play: The purpose is to encourage learners to spontaneously act out given emotions and roles in specific true-to-life situations in order to emphasize the lesson goal.

Individuals are presented with a biblical or life-related situation and specific roles and/or feelings within the situation to be acted out. Players study briefly their assigned roles in preparation for spontaneous drama. Next, participants play their roles for one to five minutes or until the leader feels the goals of the role-play have been met. Observers and participants discuss the role-play in light of the lesson goals.

For variety, a role-play may be repeated after discussion, changing the roles or emotions to be played by the main characters. Or role-plays may be done as pantomime, making participants express their roles through actions rather than words.

Open-ended Story: The purpose is to encourage everyone to use scriptural principles to solve a specific true-to-life dilemma as presented in an unfinished story.

Learners discuss scriptural principles that will be involved in the open-ended story. Next, individuals or groups working together read the unfinished story and then write a conclusion to the story, based on their application of scriptural principles to the story situation. Participants share their open-ended story completions with each other.

For variety, open-ended story completions may be written on poster paper for classroom display. Also, members may act out their written story completions for the rest of the group or role-play may be substituted for open-ended story completion with the same goal being accomplished.

Buzz Groups: The purpose is to allow small groups to discuss a given subject for a brief period of time.

Small groups of four to six form circles. A written statement of the subject to be discussed is handed out. Next, a time limit is set for the discussion—usually 3 to 20 minutes. Each group chooses a recorder to record the group's results.

For variety, buzz groups can be used to develop some ways of coping with a problem, describing a concept or subject or developing a project. Also, they can be used to study a particular Scripture to discover a meaning, list items, or develop an application.

Hymn/Song Writing: The purpose is to provide members the opportunity to participate in creating an original hymn or song that reflects the scriptural principles of the lesson or unit studied.

Learners read a pre-selected passage of Scripture, looking for main ideas relating to lesson theme. Next, they summarize their discoveries and use their summaries to compose lyrics that capture the essence of the Scripture passage. Lyrics may be written to a familiar tune (hymn, Christian song, secular song, etc.). Persons then share their original composition with other groups or the entire congregation.

For variety, everyone may compose the song over two or more weeks of a unit of study, completing the song on the final meeting. Outside-of-session work may also be done on the song. Or key Scripture verses may be set to music to aid in memorization.

Interview: The purpose is to encourage learners to (1) relate the details of a Bible event and/or the feelings and insights of a Bible character through the medium of an imaginary interview of one or more Bible characters; (2) interview present-day people concerning topics being studied.

Everyone reads a pre-selected Bible narrative, noting the key events and characters. Groups of learners work together preparing an imaginary interview of one or more of the principal characters by one or more interviewers. Next, persons present their interview of the group and discuss the concepts presented.

For variety, members may record their interviews on audio or videocassette for presentation as a simulated radio or TV interview. Also, interviews may be used in a contemporary setting as learners apply Bible principles to life situations.

The Road to Emmaus

SESSION VERSES

"The secret things belong to the Lord our God, but the things revealed belong to us and to our children forever." Deuteronomy 29:29

"And beginning with Moses and all the Prophets, he explained to them what was said in all the Scriptures concerning himself." Luke 24:27

SESSION FOCUS

Jesus is the key that unlocks full understanding of all Scripture.

SESSION BASIS

Luke 24:13-35

SESSION GOAL

● Discuss ways the Word of God is illuminated to people today.

INSIGHTS FOR THE LEADER

Unlocking the Scriptures Today

This course, *Christ B.C.*, is a study of Old Testament Scriptures that reveal God's historical and eternal plan for salvation through His Son, Jesus. A study of types, symbols, pictures and prophecies of Christ in the Old Testament will unlock the Scriptures for us, as Jesus unlocked the Scriptures for two travelers on the road to Emmaus following His resurrection—the theme of today's study. Each of the succeeding sessions in this course will explore an Old Testament prophecy, symbol or event that points to Christ. But before we begin this study, a good understanding of what types, symbols and prophecies are and how they function is necessary.

Types and Symbols

Augustine said, "The New is in the Old contained; the Old is by the New explained." Jesus is the key to the riddle of the Old Testament; the translator for the code. Many Old Testament events, although impressive in their own right, have spectacular meaning and bring us light when we see them as types of Christ and His work. Deuteronomy 29:29 tells us, "The secret things belong to the Lord our God, but the things revealed belong to us and to our children forever." We are to study and understand the Scriptures. In them

God has revealed His plan for a Savior and has given this knowledge to us as a gift.

The types of Christ in the Old Testament have several characteristics. A type is a person or experience that is symbolic of the nature of Christ and His work. It represents Him accurately with respect to some important character trait or deed. It will not represent every aspect of His character or purpose. When the Israelites painted blood on their doorposts so the angel of death would not enter their households, it was symbolic of the fact that salvation comes only by the shedding of blood (see Exod. 12:13; Lev. 9:7-9; Heb. 9:22).

A type is often symbolic of God's initiative to reconcile humankind to Himself. God always makes the first move. God commanded Abraham to sacrifice his son Isaac—an event that seems only a test of Abraham's obedience until we see that it was a picture of the sacrifice of Christ (see Gen. 22:2,7,8; John 1:29; 3:16; Rom. 8:32). Man would never initiate such a thing, but God, in His divine wisdom, created a foundation upon which we can understand Jesus' substitutionary sacrifice. As God provided a ram as a substitute for Isaac, He also provided His only Son as a substitutionary payment for our sins.

A type may be symbolic of revelation yet to be realized. As such, the typical characters became creatures of faith and not just performers of ritual. Hebrews 11 is a great litany of heroes of faith who believed, even though they had not seen, and had their faith regarded by God as righteousness.

Prophecies

One of the strongest arguments for the validity of the Word of God is fulfilled prophecies concerning the birth, death and resurrection of Jesus Christ. The Old Testament is replete with prophecies concerning Christ, as foretold not only by the prophets, but by King David as well (see Ps. 22). A prophecy could foretell (predict) a future event, or forthtell (admonish or exhort) concerning a present situation. In both cases the Old Testament prophets either warned or offered encouragement; they were speaking for God, declaring His divine will and purpose. The prophecies concerning Jesus that are recorded in the Old Testament are all foretelling in nature with some prophecies concerning Him yet to be fulfilled.

Although looking for references to Jesus in the Old Testament is not a new way to study the Bible, it may be new to some of your learners. Reassure them that it is a method that has the New Testament stamp of approval (see Luke 24:27; 1 Cor. 10:1-4; 1 Pet. 3:18-22). It is a faith-building exercise that strengthens the Bible student's belief in the divine inspiration of God's Word and that also points again and again to God's plan of salvation through Jesus Christ. Jesus truly is the key that unlocks all Scripture. Today's study bears this out.

A Long Walk Home

The story in Luke 24:13-35 has been described by scholars and critics as one of the immortal short stories of the world. Within a single page, the minds of two devout Jews are moved from utter confusion, to a clear understanding of Christ's purpose as described in Scripture, to total enthusiasm and dedication. The Jews had recently witnessed a crucifixion—dirty work done at the hands of religious leaders they had believed and trusted. The victim was a prophet whose deeds and words carried love and authority and compelled their confidence. A good man had died, horribly punished by men who claimed to be doing God a favor. The two travelers on the road to Emmaus were at a loss to understand what had happened. Either they had to believe in the utter wrongdoing of the authorities or in the righteousness of their act; in the complete innocence of the victim or in his guilt as a blasphemer. There was no middle ground, no comfortable explanation for the sentence. Their confusion was evident by the downcast expressions on their faces and the intensity of their discussion of the events that had just taken place in Jerusalem (see vv. 13-18).

Sense Out of Confusion

In the midst of their discussion, Cleopas and his companion were joined by Jesus, whose identity was divinely hidden from them until the time was right (see vv. 16,31). Jesus' simple questions concerning the travelers' discussion reveal the depth of their struggle. When He asked, "What are you discussing together as you walk along?" (v. 17), they answered, "About Jesus of Nazareth. . . .The chief priests and our rulers handed him over to be sentenced to death, and they crucified him; but we had hoped that he was the one who was going to redeem Israel" (vv. 19-21). There was no way the travelers could keep their beliefs intact without blocking out the reality of the events they had witnessed and the hope they had placed in Christ as the Messiah. Their minds were about to be forced into a new understanding of all they held dear concerning the Scriptures and God's plan to provide a Messiah.

Have you ever witnessed the dramatic changes that take place when someone discards false beliefs? I have. I once counseled with a teenager who was perpetually in trouble with his parents, school authorities and the law. In three years of high school, he had little more than one semester's credits. He was the product of a divorced family, a strained family economy and some badly chosen friends. A juvenile officer told me that this boy would end up either shooting or being shot by a police officer.

"I'm stupid!" he would bark, as we talked. "Let's test that out," I finally replied. "Believing you're stupid doesn't make it so!" So we administered a Wechsler Adult Intelligence Scale to get the truth. The result? The boy's I.Q. was in the superior range, similar to that of college professors and physicians. I explained this to my client, and he would not believe it—at first. But as the truth of the matter sunk in, he realized this information explained his intense interest in reading and other things about himself he could not explain while believing that he was stupid. Eventually, his old, misconceived self-image changed. It would not stand in the light of truth. He would never be the same again. The reason for the dramatic change? Sense and hope had come out of confusion.

The Emmaus story demonstrates the ability of Jesus to bring sense out of confusion. The travelers had "hoped that he was the one who was going to redeem Israel" (v. 21). Before Jesus enlightened the travelers' understanding, they admitted to Him, in regretful, bewildered tones, that their dreams and hopes had seemed shattered. The rabbinic teaching they had learned to trust had let them down. They had expected Jesus, as the Messiah, to bring a great political victory for Israel over her oppressors. Messiah, you see, was more than just a religious idea to devout Jews. The rabbis of Jesus' day were teaching (and many still do today) that the Messiah would come and overturn the existing political and military order. Jews were taught four characteristics of Messiah's coming: (1) He would come cataclysmically; (2) Jerusalem would be the seat of His power; (3) Israel would be restored to full political and military dominance in the world; and (4) the essential character of Messiah's reign would be full justice with retribution for all of Israel's enemies. The hopes of Jews who expected Jesus to fulfill this image of the Messiah were dashed to pieces in the Crucifixion.

Jesus responded to the disappointment of His companions by cutting through the misconceptions of rabbinic teaching and opening their eyes to the insight of the ages! "Beginning with Moses and all the Prophets, he explained to them what was said in all the Scriptures concerning himself" (v. 27). We do not know the particular points Jesus made. But the phrase "Moses and all the Prophets" is believed by many Bible scholars to indicate that *all* of the Old Testament not only records the history of God's interaction with His people, but it also testifies concerning His Son. From Genesis to Malachi the Old Testament cannot be fully understood without using God's key: Jesus Christ.

Jesus brings order out of chaos. Although Cleopas and his friend did not at first realize that it was Jesus who was teaching them, they were, nevertheless, greatly impressed by His words. In retrospect they observed, "Were not our hearts burning within us while he talked with us on the road and opened the Scriptures to us?" (v. 32).

At this point of enlightenment concerning the Scriptures, the story takes a new turn. Jesus acted as if He would go on, not obligating His companions to extend hospitality on His behalf. True to His character, He would not force Himself upon His potential hosts. They obviously had spent a long time discussing the Scriptures, and the time was ripe for His companions to extend themselves to Jesus personally, not just academically. Jesus' attitude was characteristic of the Holy Spirit; never coercive, never pounding His way into lives. This attitude is illustrated by His words in

Revelation 3:20: "Here I am! I stand at the door and knock. If anyone hears my voice and opens the door, I will come in and eat with him, and he with me." Jesus creates the opportunity. But we must open the door.

The Wonderful "Aha!"

The Emmaus travelers did not know Jesus' identity but felt in their hearts the authority of His words. As a result they reached out to Him personally, urging Him to stay the night (see Luke 24:29). They listened to the voice and opened the door. In doing so they met the resurrected Christ, the true Messiah.

This meeting took place through the breaking of bread. Once Jesus had entered the house and the bread had been brought to the table, He assumed the role of master or father of the household. Jesus did this by performing the tasks of giving thanks and breaking the bread for His hosts. As Cleopas and his companion viewed Jesus in this role, "Their eyes were opened and they recognized him" (v. 31). Their enlightenment was complete, and Jesus' purpose for that situation was fulfilled. At this point Jesus "disappeared from their sight" (v. 31).

It was an ordinary meal, in an ordinary home, with common bread being divided. This situation reminds us that He is Christ in very common, ordinary situations to very common, ordinary folks.

Most of us prefer persuasion in spectacular settings, with great miracles and stereophonic sound announcing the Christ. No quiet, noncoercive voices for us. Deafening noise, rhythmic pounding and a star-studded performance by folk heroes making Him known is our style. No wonder we often miss Him! But the Emmaus travelers didn't miss Him. Their experience stirred an excitement in them that, despite the late hour, they had to share with the disciples back in Jerusalem. Jesus had personally unlocked all the Scriptures and had shown how they all pointed to Him. Cleopas and his companion had vaulted from utter disappointment to utter elation. No wonder they beat a hasty retreat back to Jerusalem to share their excitement with the disciples and those gathered with them (see v. 33).

The understanding of Cleopas and his companion had an additional twist. It was that wonderful "Aha!" that comes when something begins to make sense. Educational psychologists call this kind of understanding insight learning. It is that sudden burst of comprehension that comes when the answer to a complex puzzle is finally figured out. The solution is obvious when it appears. As such, we can assume that it is almost immune to forgetting. Cleopas and his friend, even when they reached old age, had no trouble recalling their encounter on the Emmaus road. It was sudden, dramatic and made sense of the confused mix of rabbinic teaching and Scripture. Furthermore, it was life-changing, and such an event is never forgotten.

Emmaus and Principles of Learning

We, like the Emmaus travelers, will benefit from searching the Word of God "beginning with Moses and all the Prophets" to discover "what was said in all the Scriptures concerning himself" (v. 27). The result of our study could be like that of the Emmaus travelers. We could have the opportunity to see God's plan of salvation woven throughout Scripture, have our faith strengthened and experience an excitement to share what Christ has done with others.

Before you begin unfolding the story of Jesus, told throughout the Scriptures, consider the following principles of Bible learning and understanding, some of which were displayed in the experience of Cleopas and his companion. Use these principles to prepare yourself, as a teacher and as a learner, to make the most of your opportunities. Then use these principles to foster growth in the lives of the group members.

1. Jesus did not leave His followers alone in their struggle for deeper understanding. Although He is no longer physically present to teach us as He did Cleopas and his companion on the Emmaus road, we do have the Holy Spirit who is now present to teach us all things (see John 14:26; 16:13; 1 Cor. 2:9,10). As Jesus unlocked the Scriptures to Cleopas and his friend, the Holy Spirit continues to illuminate the already revealed Word of God to us today to enable us to make right decisions and to realize growth in our Christian experience.

Also, the travelers on the Emmaus road were being taught by the greatest Teacher the world has ever known. The interpretation of the Old Testament Scriptures that they received from Jesus was a correct one. When Jesus ascended into heaven, He did not leave the Church without teachers, but placed gifted teachers in the Church (see Eph. 4:7,11-14). As we consistently come under their teaching, we receive a steady and healthy diet of God's Word that results in spiritual maturity and that protects us from "every wind of teaching" (see vv. 12-14). It is then that we are assured of receiving sound doctrine (see Titus 1:9; 2:1).

2. Another significant and helpful means of learning is tutored learning. This is learning in a one-to-one relationship, close up, directly given. It is why Barna-

bas took the recently converted Paul under his wing (see Acts 9:27,28; 11:25,26). In turn, Paul served as mentor to Timothy (see 1 Tim. 1:1,2,18). This is why doctors have internships and residencies. This is the reason prospective teachers are assigned to student-teaching roles, or why apprentices learn their trades from master craftsmen. Was there tutorial teaching in the Emmaus experience? Of course. It was short, to be sure, but divine energy was present and the result was lasting. In the same way, you and your learners can benefit from a tutorial relationship. Seek out people whose knowledge of the Scriptures and personal maturity you respect. Ask those persons to interact with you and work through questions you have as you study the Bible. Share truths being discovered and discuss application of those truths. This personal discipling will enrich your life and will spur you on to growth beyond that which can be accomplished in the study session.

3. Learning achieved in a social situation stays with us longer. The sociality experienced by the two travelers with Jesus on the seven-mile walk to Emmaus and the meal shared together, created an important atmosphere for learning. And remember that Jesus not only taught but also lived with His disciples (see Luke 8:1-3). We learn better in the presence of others. Truth not only can be taught, it also can be modeled in the lives of mature Christians (see 1 Cor. 11:1). Others keep an eye on us, and we feel accountable to each other (see Acts 14;26,27; Gal. 2:11).

4. Sharing reinforces our beliefs. I have often said that I learned more psychology in my first year of college teaching than I did in all the years of my graduate and undergraduate study. As a leader, have you ever felt that you learned more from the lessons you prepared and taught than your group of learners? This is a common occurrence.

The scriptural idea that what we believe with our hearts we need to confess with our lips is a great and valid learning principle (see Rom. 10:9,10). Once we have shared our learning, we imply that we are ready to defend what we have said. Look again at the Emmaus travelers. Once the great insight had occurred, they rushed back to Jerusalem to share what they had learned (see Luke 24:33-35). They were no longer passive about their knowledge, for they had found the answer to their lives' greatest question and were not going to sit and wonder. Their doubts were overcome, and they went public with their information. Your group members can do the same with what you share in the study session. Convey to them the sense of excitement that comes from sharing God's truth with others.

5. Meaningful learning often comes at the end of times of pondering, after many trial answers to problems, after much wondering and committed study. Then the great "Aha!" happens. In the case of our Emmaus folks, insight was preceded by lengthy training in the Scriptures. It is safe to say that when Jesus opened the Scriptures to them, they knew what He was referring to. These travelers had probably been through years of instruction. Similarly, a Bible passage that has been read often will sometimes "open up," revealing deeper truth or understanding of divine principles. The work of the Holy Spirit, our reading and applying knowledge from other points of Scripture and our pondering the meaning of the passage all contribute to this common experience.

6. Don't cloud the truth, and it will do a remarkable job of presenting and defending itself. God's truth has great capacity to survive manipulations. Truth is highly reinforcing. Jesus said, "If you hold to my teaching, you are really my disciples. Then you will know the truth, and the truth will set you free" (John 8:31,32). The more we immerse ourselves in the Word, the more clearly truth will reveal itself to us. Note how Jesus based His teaching to the Emmaus travelers on Scripture (see Luke 24:27). So bare the truth; unsheathe the Word; let truth do its own arguing in the hearts of men. It is "powerful, and sharper than any two-edged sword" (Heb. 4:12, *KJV*).

7. In the experience of faith, it is always God who takes the initiative. Our coming to faith is not some original adventure or great mental invention. It is our response to a thrust already made (see Luke 19:10). God has been at work before we ever dreamed He existed (see Eph. 1:4; 1 Pet. 1:18-21). Faith is the expression of a loving Father who is tenderly seeking His children (see Rom. 2:4). So it was at Emmaus. It was not the travelers who overtook Jesus while looking for an answer to their quandary. It was the Savior coming to those whose minds had already been prepared—through their discussion with each other—to believe His Word (see Luke 24:13-15).

In contrast, all other religions are humankind's attempt to find God. As such, they become the extension of people's intellectual futility. Human thought systems are always limited to one's imagination and do not flourish with the glory of God-given revelation. When Jesus revealed Himself to Cleopas and his partner, their hearts warmed strangely within them—a common experience of those who come to understand truth. Our understanding of spiritual truth is a personal matter. No one can do our learning for us. As we continue in the study of this course, may we share the desire of the psalmist, "Open my eyes that I may see wonderful things in your law" (Ps. 119:18).

A B C PLAN FOR THE SESSION

Materials needed:
- Your Session 1 Leader's Guide Sheet (Use this handy fold-over sheet to record your personal session planning notes. Then tuck it in your Bible as a guide for leading the study);
- Sufficient copies of the Regal book, *Christ B.C.*, by Bill Myers, for group members to purchase;
- One copy of the three Session 1 handouts for each group member;
- Large sheets of paper (newsprint or shelf paper), felt pens and masking tape;
- Blank sheets of paper;
- Index cards or Post-it Notes with Scripture references;
- A *King James Version* of the Bible;
- Chalkboard or overhead projector with transparencies;
- Overhead projector transparency of the Session 1 Lesson Outline (optional);
- Name tags for group members (optional).

Advance preparations:
- Read the information under "Advance preparations" for Session 2 in order to make a needed advance assignment for next week's session;
- Prepare several posters by printing the title "Christ B.C." across the top of large sheets of newsprint or shelf paper. Tape the posters to various walls in the room;
- List the following numbers and respective Scripture references on seven index cards or Post-it Notes—one per card: (1) Luke 24:27; John 14:26; 16:13; 1 Corinthians 2:9,10; Ephesians 4:7,11-14; Titus 1:9; 2:1; (2) Luke 24:27; Acts 9:27,28; 11:25,26; 1 Timothy 1:1,2,18; (3) Luke 24:15,29,30; 8:1-3; Acts 14:26,27; 1 Corinthians 11:1; Galatians 2:11; (4) Luke 24:33-35; Romans 10:9,10; (5) Luke 24:14,15; Psalms 119:15,16; Proverbs 2:1-5; (6) Luke 24:27; John 8:31,32; Hebrews 4:12, *KJV*; (7) Luke 24:13-15; 19:10; Romans 2:4; Ephesians 1:4; 1 Peter 1:18-21.

NOTE: For additional activities that you may care to incorporate into the following Session Plan, refer to the article, "Bible Learning Activities to Supplement the Session Plan," in the opening pages of this Leader's Guide.

A PPROACH (10 minutes)

As you begin a new course of study, there may be those who are joining your group for the first time. Allow several minutes for the group to get acquainted with new members. (You may want to consider wearing name tags for the first session.) Ask learners to give their names and to share something of interest about themselves.

Next ask the question, *What events or things in the Old Testament foreshadow something that took place in Jesus' life or ministry, or that is yet to take place?* Allow everyone a few moments to think about the question. Then invite the group to list the events they have thought of, and their fulfillments or future fulfillments, on any one of the posters displayed in the room. If group members seem stumped, give the example of the Passover lamb foreshadowing Christ's sacrifice (see Exod. 12:21-23; 1 Cor. 5:7) or Psalm 22 foreshadowing Christ's suffering and triumph on the cross (see Matt. 27:35,39,43,46; John 19:23,24,28; Heb. 2:12). Mention that it is not necessary to list

Bible references. Allow several minutes for writing.

Quickly review the events that everyone has listed on the posters and then move to the Bible Exploration by saying, *In this course of study, we will explore Old Testament people, things, events or prophecies that prefigured events in Jesus' life, ministry and future reign.* Add that today's study will reveal how Jesus explained these types, symbols and prophecies concerning Himself to two of His disciples who were in a state of confusion following His death.

Alternate Approach (5 minutes)

Write the question listed under the Approach on the chalkboard or overhead transparency. Next, encourage learners to form clusters of three and then discuss the question together. Distribute paper to one person in each cluster, who will record suggestions made by his or her group.

After several minutes of brainstorming among clusters, ask for feedback from recorders. Move to the Bible Exploration by sharing the closing statements made under the Approach.

B IBLE EXPLORATION
(35-45 minutes)

Step 1 (5-10 minutes): Distribute the three Session 1 handouts to everyone. Point out that the "Bible Chronology" and "Word List" handouts are to serve as additional information and resource material that they may refer to throughout this course of study. Mention, further, that the Lesson Outline is designed so that they may take notes of the lesson as it progresses throughout the session.

Also inform learners that a Lesson Outline will be made available for their use in succeeding sessions. It will help them to review the main points of the lesson during the week. You will, likewise, want to take notes of the lesson on the chalkboard or Lesson Outline transparency as it is presented throughout the session.

Next, share Augustine's quote, "The New is in the Old contained; the Old is by the New explained." Ask, *How is the New in the Old contained?* Responses should include the various events, types, symbols and prophecies that are mentioned in the Old Testament that are fulfilled in the New Testament. Explain the meaning of types and symbols (see "Insights for the Leader" under the heading "Types and Symbols"). Refer to the suggestions listed on the posters that were used in the Approach for examples.

Next say, *Prophecies play an important role in the study of Jesus in the Old Testament.* Ask, *How would you define a prophecy?* Allow time for responses. Be sure learners understand that a prophecy may be foretelling (predicting) a future event, or forthtelling (admonishing or exhorting) concerning a present situation (see "Insights for the Leader" under the heading "Prophecies" for added information). Point out that some prophecies recorded in the Old Testament, as well as the New, are yet to be fulfilled.

Invite a member to read aloud Deuteronomy 29:29. Follow by saying, *God desires that we study and understand the Scriptures. In them God has revealed His plan for a Savior and all that salvation includes. He desires that we might experience salvation in all its fullness and then share with future generations the rich truths of His Word.*

Step 2 (10-15 minutes): Ask the group to open their Bibles to Luke 24:13-35. Invite several people to share in reading verses 13-27 as other members follow along in their Bibles. Then ask the following questions (see "Insights for the Leader" for added information to inject into the discussion):

- How would you describe the mood of the setting of this event? (see v. 17).
- What were the reasons for this mood? (see vv. 19-24). Share the rabbinic teaching concerning the coming Messiah that Cleopas and his companion had no doubt embraced concerning Jesus (the Messiah would bring a great political victory for Israel over her oppressors).
- Had you been one of the travelers, would you have experienced similar feelings? Why or why not?
- Jesus chided them for their failure to understand the Old Testament Scriptures concerning Himself (see v. 25). Why should they have understood? Would Jesus have reason to chide us today for failure to understand certain Scriptures? Why or why not?

Invite several learners to read aloud verses 28-32.

- Read aloud Revelation 3:20 and refer back to Luke 24:28. What principle about our relationship with Jesus can be derived from these two verses? (Jesus creates the opportunity; we must open the door. He waits for us to invite Him in.)
- How did Jesus assume the role of master/father of the household in this setting? (see v. 30). What were the results? (see vv. 31,32). How do we deprive ourselves of spiritual enlightenment and God's rich blessings?
- Share the comments of Dr. Lloyd Ahlem, writer of the leader's commentary, regarding the receiving of spiritual truth in ordinary circumstances (see "Insights for the Leader" under the heading "The Wonderful 'Aha!'"). Why are we so prone to look to spectacular settings for spiritual enlightenment? After several responses are received, invite several members who have experienced moments of enlightenment in ordinary circumstances to share at this time.

Invite several learners to read aloud verses 33-35.

- Why do you think Cleopas and his companion went at once to Jerusalem?
- What effect do you think the telling of their experience had on their faith? On the faith of the Eleven?
- Why is it important to reaffirm spiritual truth? (see vv. 9-11,34,35; also see Rom. 10:9-11).

Move to Step 3 by stating that there are many lessons to be learned from the story of the Emmaus road travelers. Add, *Some we have already considered. But there are also some important principles of learning and understanding that are displayed in this narrative. Let's consider several of them at this time.*

Step 3 (10 minutes): Move members into small groups of four to six. Appoint group leaders and distribute one or more numbered index cards or Post-it Notes listing Scripture references to each group. (The group with the Number 6 card or note should be given the *King James Version* of the Bible.) Direct groups to research the Scripture passages they have been assigned, to discover a principle of learning and understanding displayed in this story and/or other related Scriptures. Point out that the first reference listed deals with the Emmaus story. Ask them to list their respective group's discovery in the corresponding number on their Lesson Outline handout (under *D*). Encourage learners to draw from their own Bible knowledge or use their Bible concordances to include additional Scriptures.

Step 4 (10 minutes): Regather as one large group and ask for feedback from small group leaders. Some groups may suggest principles not mentioned in "Insights for the Leader." Be sure, however, to include the suggested principles in the responses. Also ask the suggested questions and include the following information in the discussion:

Principles of Learning and Understanding

1. As Jesus is no longer physically present to teach us, God has provided the Holy Spirit (see Luke 24:27; John 14:26; 16:13; 1 Cor. 2:9,10) and teachers appointed in the Church (see Eph. 4:7,11-14; Titus 1:9; 2:1).

2. Another effective way to learn is in a one-to-one, close relationship—tutoring, mentoring or discipling (see Luke 24:27; Acts 9:27,28; 11:25,26; 1 Tim. 1:1,2,18). What examples of the effectiveness of this learning principle are demonstrated in the professional or business world today? (Medical internships, student-teacher and apprenticeship positions are examples.)

3. We often learn better in a social situation where more mature Christians provide role models and hold us accountable (see Luke 24:15,29,30; 8:1-3; 1 Cor. 11:1; Acts 14:26,27; Gal. 2:11). Why does this kind of learning stay with us longer?

4. Sharing reinforces our beliefs (see Luke 24:33-35; Rom. 10:9,10).

5. Insights often occur after times of pondering (see Luke 24:13-32; Ps. 119:15,16; Prov. 2:1-5). Is it wrong to question our beliefs? Why or why not?

6. The truth of God's Word does a remarkable job of presenting and defending itself (see Luke 24:27; John 8:31,32; Heb. 4:12, *KJV*). How can one cloud the truth?

7. Realize that God always takes the initiative (see Luke 24:13-15; 19:10; Rom. 2:4; Eph. 1:4; 1 Pet. 1:18-21). The two travelers did not overtake Jesus; He overtook them. How does God seek men and women today?

C | ONCLUSION (5 minutes)

Through today's study we see the shattered hopes and dreams of Cleopas and his companion restored, as the risen Savior explains the Scriptures concerning Himself to them. As we find Christ throughout all of the Bible, our understanding of God's Word will be in proper perspective.

Today's study also revealed that it is God's will that we have a proper understanding of His Word. As we have explored several principles of learning and understanding, we need to apply these principles to our lives so that we might experience the fullness of His salvation. This may include the initial step of accepting Christ as personal Savior, the restoration of a shattered dream, healing of a damaged area in our lives, or the strengthening of our spiritual experience.

Close the session by leading in a corporate prayer, asking God to create a desire in our hearts for a greater understanding of His Word and for His help in applying a needed principle of learning and understanding to our lives.

Encourage members to read chapter 1 of the Regal book, *Christ B.C.*, which will assist them in their time of daily devotions. Each day's devotion is based on the theme of *understanding*.

God Covers Adam and Eve's Nakedness

SESSION VERSES

"Blessed is he whose transgressions are forgiven, whose sins are covered." Psalm 32:1

"The law requires that nearly everything be cleansed with blood, and without the shedding of blood there is no forgiveness." Hebrews 9:22

SESSION FOCUS

Adam and Eve's attempt to cover their nakedness was insufficient; only the animal skins provided by God were adequate. In the same way, our attempts to cover our own sinfulness are insufficient. Through the shed blood of His Son, Jesus, God provides a covering of righteousness and forgiveness for our sins.

SESSION BASIS

Genesis 2:1—3:1-21

SESSION GOAL

Identify ways people endeavor to cover their sins today.

INSIGHTS FOR THE LEADER

This session examines a familiar Bible event—the Fall. Pay special attention to the element of the story that is focused on a foreshadowing of Christ. That element is the animal skins God provided to cover Adam and Eve's nakedness.

Back to the Beginning

Upon completion of creation, it was as if God had written a beautiful symphony; trees, flowers, animals, resources, scenic wonders all in harmony waiting to be explored, placed under the stewardship of humankind. God said to Adam and Eve, "Be fruitful and increase in number; fill the earth and subdue it. Rule over the fish of the sea and the birds of the air and over every living creature that moves on the ground" (Gen. 1:28). All that God required of Adam and Eve was obedience to one simple requirement: "You are free to eat from any tree in the garden; but you must not eat from the tree of the knowledge of good and evil, for when you eat of it you will surely die" (2:16,17). God's generosity to Adam and Eve and the freedom He allowed them

were beyond compare. They were truly free. Their innocence was complete; there was no blemish of sin in their lives. Their innocence and obedience to God's commands are symbolized by the fact that in their nakedness "they felt no shame" (v. 25). God made them like Himself—they were independent in will, capable of loving relationships and in perfect harmony with all of creation.

But having been made free, Adam and Eve were also given the opportunity to obey or disobey the divine order God had created. They could experience the fulfillment of divine design, or they could choose to conduct the symphony their own way. They could squawk away on their own little horn, moved by disintegrated impulses that produce only noise, concentrating on their own selfish interests and ignoring the wishes of God. God made them free to rebel, and this they chose.

Satan's Methods

In Genesis 3:1 we discover several interesting lessons about Satan's character and methods. Satan, or the serpent (see Gen. 3:1; Rev. 12:9) is described as very crafty or subtle—more so than any other creature. The fact that "the serpent was more crafty than any of the wild animals the Lord God had made" (Gen. 3:1) is a good warning to us to remember our limited awareness and gullibility in spiritual matters.

Our first clue revealing how Satan works comes with his questioning of God's command. Satan asked, "Did God really say, 'You must not eat from any tree in the garden'?" (v. 1). That question was enough to catch Eve's attention. Satan began with a truth that Eve knew came from God and placed a big question mark after it. With a seed of doubt planted in Eve's mind, Satan moved from questioning God's truth to presenting a reasonable half-truth. "'You will not surely die,' the serpent said to the woman" (v. 4). Cunningly, the serpent blended the lie that Eve would not die with the truth: "For God knows that when you eat of it your eyes will be opened, and you will be like God, knowing good and evil" (v. 5). Satan always appeals to human reason and pride and makes his suggestions seem plausible, even if they conflict with God's Word. After giving ear to Satan's words, Eve, looking at the tree in a new light, "saw that the fruit of the tree was good for food and pleasing to the eye, and also desirable for gaining wisdom" (v. 6). She was sold. She yielded to Satan's reasoning and "she took some and ate it" (v. 6).

Who wouldn't want to learn and understand? Who isn't mystified by the hidden, tantalized by the unseen? On the basis of Satan's half-truth, Eve allowed herself to ponder the possibilities. The tree was, after all, pleasant to the eye, would make one wise and was good for food. The most basic needs and wants of humankind were dangled before her, packaged in a way that allowed her to meet these needs and wants on her own power.

We also find that Eve did not sin alone. "She also gave some to her husband, who was with her, and he ate it" (v. 6). She shared the temptation and opportunity with Adam. We may feel sympathy for Eve when we recognize our humanness in her. We may even desire to justify what she did. Shared disobedience makes sin feel so much safer, much more acceptable.

Sin is almost always shared, and its effects ripple through friendships and relationships. But sin is a faulty basis for relationships. It does not build; it destroys. The results are aloneness and isolation.

Loss of Innocence

Adam and Eve lived physically to experience the eye-opening that Satan had promised, but they died spiritually, as God had promised. Innocence was lost. For the first time in their experience, they perceived evil. It is also likely that for the first time they perceived the character of Satan as well. God had made everything good, and Adam and Eve had been shielded from the only evil that existed by the command not to eat (see Gen. 2:16,17). God wanted to continue to shield them. But Adam and Eve bolted from behind His protection and faced evil on their own. Immediately their disobedience ushered in shame and they became aware of their need for covering. "Then the eyes of both of them were opened, and they realized they were naked; so they sewed fig leaves together and made coverings for themselves" (Gen. 3:7).

Genesis 3:7 strikes me as one of the most ludicrous, ineffectual and senseless efforts of humankind. Adam and Eve broke a perfect relationship with a perfect God. They exposed themselves to Satan, whose wisdom and power, although exceeding anything known to humankind, is totally devoted to evil. Then Adam and Eve tried to cover themselves and their shame with fig leaves. Their efforts were hopelessly inadequate. Had we been Adam or Eve, we would no doubt have done the same. Our nakedness being upmost in our minds, we would have probably headed for the nearest fig tree and tried to cover ourselves, too. But how can the guilty fend off the indignation of an insulted God with only fig leaves as a covering?

One way people try to avoid confronting their sinfulness and need for repentance is rationalization. And one of the great rationalizations for humankind's sin is that people are just acting the way "nature" made them, therefore they are not to be blamed. Sinful actions are dubbed "impulses that evolved over time." They are even given the positive tone that sometimes in history they served as self-protective devices. When people act out these impulses, they are merely doing what nature intended, or so goes the argument. The language of the *New Bible Commentary* clarifies this point. "The Bible nowhere provides a philosophical or speculative account of the ultimate origin of evil. As the book of redemption, it describes the mode by which sin made its entry into the sphere of human experience. This is an historical account of the fall of man. . . .The important theological point in this record is that it teaches that temptation came from without and that sin was an intruder into the life of man. Sin cannot be regarded, therefore, as 'good in the making': rather did it spoil a world made 'good'." [1] Evil exists because two free people made a terrible choice:

to play God for themselves, to determine good and evil for themselves and to exempt themselves from the need for God's loving protection. Evil did not just happen to them without their consent.

Lost Bearings

In Genesis 3:8 the story takes an interesting turn. Adam and Eve hear a familiar, once welcome, but now fearful sound. "Then the man and his wife heard the sound of the Lord God as he was walking in the garden in the cool of the day" (v. 8). Their response? "They hid from the Lord God among the trees of the garden" (v. 8). Then God called out what seems to be a strange question: "Where are you?" (v. 9). Doesn't it seem that God should have asked, "What have you done?" But in a sense, these questions are one in the same. God knew where Adam and Eve were. He was simply confronting them with the result of their sin: their lostness. This is how sin works. When we sin, we lose our bearings. We lose our sense of place and rootedness. We become disoriented as to where we are and where we belong. Adam illustrates this point in his response to God's question. He said, "I heard you in the garden, and I was afraid because I was naked; so I hid" (v. 10).

Before Adam and Eve's experience with sin, they belonged in God's presence, walking in the garden with Him during the cool of the day. After they sinned they did not know where they belonged. Their relationship with God had been redefined and they were confused. They were afraid; they were not willing to take responsibility for their sin.

Along with covering their nakedness with fig leaves, Adam and Eve tried to cover their guilt with excuses. Both attempts were inadequate. God questioned them further, and their responses became more desperate. "Who told you that you were naked? Have you eaten from the tree that I commanded you not to eat from?" God asked (v. 11). Adam, unwilling to admit his sin, passed the buck to Eve—and to God as well: "The woman you put here with me—she gave me some fruit from the tree, and I ate it" (v. 12). God questioned Eve, and she also denied responsibility saying, "The serpent deceived me, and I ate" (v. 13).

Following this interrogation of Adam and Eve, the judgment of God upon both humankind and Satan is described. All of Adam and Eve's excuses and attempts to cover their guilt and shame did not shield them from experiencing the consequences of their sin. Creation is cursed, Adam and Eve's sorrows multiply and life becomes a sweaty struggle for existence ending in death (see vv. 16-19). This is a clear signal that our attempts to cover and justify ourselves are inadequate. Yet just like Adam and Eve, people still try.

During the 1960s I was a member of an academic senate in a system of colleges and universities. Campus disturbances were common, sometimes violent. One of my colleagues on the senate, a political moderate in those days, was badgered by professional radicals to join in a destructive demonstration on his campus. The consequences of not joining would be injury to his family and home. He thought it easier to go along with the idea than to risk these losses. So he participated, only to be shown on television while engaging in very foolish, unprofessional behavior.

When the melee subsided, he had to explain why he had allowed himself to be caught up in such foolishness. But he had no way to cover himself. His misbehavior was a matter of public record. Instead of apologizing and risking further threats from the radicals, he began to rationalize his behavior. In a few weeks he became a ranting revolutionary, more out of the need to cover himself than from any well-thought-out change of philosophy. He really needed forgiveness, but he knew no way to obtain it except to embarrass himself in public and risk further threat. He was not willing to do this, so he altered his belief to match his behavior. His new belief made his behavior seem acceptable and his conscience was temporarily salved.

To those who saw through his experience, he was merely doing a fig-leaf job on a bad act. And like Adam he lost his place and his bearing about life. He became a campus sorehead and shortly gave up his professorship to follow radical causes. I don't know where he is today, but he is probably wandering a good deal and doing a lot of repair on his apron of fig leaves.

Our own efforts to cover our sin aren't much better. Like Adam, Eve and my former colleague, we are equally ludicrous when we justify and cover ourselves with silly rationalizations and maskings. The greatest self-deception in all the world is a belief that we can shield ourselves from the consequences of knowing evil and experiencing sin. Yet social science textbooks and self-help literature are full of gimmicks that encourage us to attempt just that. Popularized religion (Science of Mind, Dianetics, Erhard Seminars' Training), humanistic philosophy and cult ritual still sell the theory that some form of fig leaves will take care of our need for forgiveness and our relationship problem with God.

God's Covering Foreshadows Jesus

In Genesis 3:21 God addresses humankind's lostness and their need for adequate covering, or forgiveness. God did not abandon the man and woman, leaving them alone to struggle with their guilt and shame. "The Lord God made garments of skin for Adam and his wife and clothed them" (v. 21). There are two characteristics of the covering God provided for Adam and Eve that are significant. The first is the fact that God "provided" it. This presents a picture of God's grace toward all humanity. The initiative God took to reach out to Adam and Eve foreshadowed another event in which God reached out to all the people of the world. "But God demonstrates his own love for us in this: While we were still sinners, Christ died for us" (Rom. 5:8. Also see John 3:16.) This event is mentioned for the first time in Genesis 3:15.

The second significant characteristic of God's covering provided for Adam and Eve is the nature of the covering: skins. There is no cost involved in using fig leaves as a covering. A fig tree can simply grow new leaves to replace those taken. A covering of skins, however, involves the death of an animal; it involves the shedding of blood. This is the beginning of the sacrificial system among God's people. The shedding of blood is the only means by which humankind's sins can be covered and forgiveness can be obtained. As Hebrews 9:22 says, "the law requires that nearly everything be cleansed with blood, and without the shedding of blood there is no forgiveness." From the beginning of the presence of sin, the need for cleansing by blood has been restated throughout history.

The story of Cain and Abel presenting their sacrifices to God suggests this point. Abel's offering—"fat portions from some of the firstborn of his flock" (Gen. 4:4)—was accepted by God (see v. 4), while Cain's offering—"fruits of the soil" (v. 3)—was rejected (see v. 5). Although the text does not refer to a sin offering that required an animal sacrifice, most commentators feel that Abel's sacrifice was accepted because of a spirit of unworthiness and helplessness that he demonstrated. Abel realized that he needed forgiveness for his sins, which could only come through a blood sacrifice. Hebrews 11:4 supports this argument by stating, "By faith he [Abel] was commended as a righteous man, when God spoke well of his offerings." Thus, Abel's sacrifice was based on some knowledge of what God required to make him acceptable (see Rom. 1:17). Cain, on the other hand, did not bring his offering in the right spirit—that of faith—as did Abel. Cain demonstrated a self-sufficiency when he brought merely of what he had acquired and not a firstfruits offering.

Leviticus describes in more detail God's requirements concerning sacrifices. Those sacrifices whose purposes include atonement or forgiveness of sins require the shedding of blood of some animal (see Lev. 1; 4:1—6:13). Yet this means of obtaining forgiveness was imperfect. This shedding of blood had to be repeated "again and again, the way the high priest enters the Most Holy Place every year with blood that is not his own" (Heb. 9:25).

In putting the sacrificial system in place, God did more than provide a temporary means by which people, like Adam and Eve, could receive pardon from sin (see Lev. 16:15; Heb. 5:3). God created a picture, a reference point, from which His obedient people could recognize His provision of an eternal, once for all, sacrifice of atonement—Jesus Christ. "We have been made holy through the sacrifice of the body of Jesus Christ once for all" (Heb. 10:10). This picture has been displayed for us to see throughout history that means of receiving forgiveness through Jesus Christ's sacrifice is now available to everyone. And this forgiveness is more than a covering of our sin as was offered in the animal skins (see Gen. 3:21; Heb. 10:4,11). Through Christ's shed blood, we receive a covering of His righteousness (see Rom. 3:22; 13:14; 2 Cor. 5:21). It is now complete forgiveness (see Heb. 10:12-17)—our sins to be remembered against us no more (see Ps. 103:12; Jer. 31:34).

Fig Leaves or Forgiveness?

So where does this leave those of us who are disoriented and lost in sin? We must recognize that we have fallen short of God's expectations. At this point we have two choices: forgiveness or fig leaves. We can receive genuine forgiveness for our mistakes and straighten out our bearings, or we can dress in elaborate gowns and robes of fig leaves, deceiving ourselves into believing nothing has gone awry. When I meet older people who have opted for a lifetime of fig-leaf coverings, I discover whole gardens and arboretums of clipped, shaped, trellised and fertilized fig leaves. The path to repentance for these people is so difficult. It takes major stress or sometimes catastrophe for them to uncover themselves, admit their sin and receive God's forgiveness.

We all have a tendency, like Adam and Eve, to run for the fig tree rather than seek God's forgiveness. Our personal bouquets of fig leaves consist of all our excuses, rationalizations, blaming of others or any other device we may use to cover a sin. Or our fig leaf arrangements may be elaborately constructed philosophies of self-fulfillment that keep us from yielding to

God's direction for our lives. When we hide behind a brand of psychology, philosophy or an alteration of God's truth, we are investing in fig leaves. Our society is drenched in the human potential movement, in self-actualization psychology, even moral legalism and reinforcement that prevent people from dealing with their spiritual need for genuine, complete forgiveness. Anything less than submitting to God's provision of forgiveness through Jesus Christ will not produce jus-tification (declared righteous and acceptable before God; see Rom. 5:1) and eternal life for us. Only Christ, through His death and resurrection, can adequately cover us—a covering that surpasses that provided for Adam and Eve.

Note
1. Davidson, Stibbs and Kevan, *The New Bible Commentary* (Grand Rapids: Wm. B. Eerdmans Publishing Co., 1963), p. 79.

[A] [B] [C] PLAN FOR THE SESSION

Materials needed:
- Your Session 2 Leader's Guide Sheet (Use this handy fold-over sheet to record your personal session planning notes. Then tuck it in your Bible as a guide for leading the study);
- One copy of the Session 2 Lesson Outline for each group member;
- Small index cards or Post-it Notes, with Scripture references;
- Chalkboard or overhead projector with transparencies;
- Overhead projector transparency of the Session 2 Lesson Outline (optional).

Advance preparations:
- Read the information under "Advance preparations" for Session 3 in order to make a needed advance assignment for next week's session;
- Write the following Scripture references on nine small index cards or Post-it Notes—one per card: (1) John 8:44; (2) 1 Peter 5:8; (3) Revelation 12:10; (4) Revelation 20:3; (5) Matthew 4:3; (6) 2 Corinthians 11:14; Mark 4:15; (7) 1 Thessalonians 2:18; (8) John 12:31; 2 Corinthians 4:4; (9) Acts 10:38;
- Enlist a group member to present the lesson material to be given in Step 4 of the Bible Exploration. To assist in his or her preparation, make a copy of the lesson guidelines listed in this step for his or her use. Also suggest that this person use a Bible commentary as an added resource.

[A] PPROACH (5 minutes)

Distribute the index cards or Post-it Notes with Scripture references to different learners. Ask them to be prepared to read the Scripture(s) listed on their respective cards when called on during Step 1 of the Bible Exploration.

Write the following statement on the chalkboard or overhead transparency: *Sin is almost always shared.* Mention that this statement is made by Dr. Lloyd Ahlem, writer of the leader's commentary. Ask everyone to think about the statement for a few moments. Then invite members to neighbor-nudge the person next to them and discuss the statement. Ask the group to consider if the statement is true, and if so, in what way. After several minutes regain the attention of the learners and ask for feedback. Responses could include: By our influence upon those around us (example, role modeling, enlisting others' participa-tion); by others realizing the consequence of sin with us (our families, other relationships and associates).

Move to the Bible Exploration by stating, *In today's Bible study we will examine the sharing and consequence of humankind's initial sin known as the Fall, as well as God's provision of the animal skins to cover Adam and Eve's nakedness. We will also see how God's act was a foreshadowing of a greater provision to be made centuries later.*

[B] IBLE EXPLORATION (40-50 minutes)

Step 1 (5-10 minutes): Say, *Satan played a major role in humankind's initial sin, and he continues to play such a role up to the present day. His characteristics and activities are varied.* Add, *Several members will read aloud Bible verses about Satan. Iden-*

tify, from these Scriptures, some of his characteristics and activities. Members read aloud their assigned Scriptures. List characteristics and activities on the chalkboard or overhead projector as they are identified by learners.

Move to Step 2 by stating, *Our Bible lesson will reveal Satan in action. We should be able to recognize several of his traits we have just identified.*

Step 2 (10-15 minutes): Distribute the Lesson Outline to everyone. Encourage members to take notes on their outlines as the study progresses. Do the same on the Lesson Outline transparency or on the chalkboard.

Next invite members to open their Bibles to Genesis, chapter 2. Present a brief synopsis of this chapter. Point out that at this point in their lives, Adam and Eve knew complete freedom. Add, *They were free to enjoy their innocence and their stewardship over God's creation. They felt no shame regarding their nakedness* (see v. 25).

Invite a learner to read aloud verses 16 and 17. Mention that Adam and Eve were given the opportunity to obey or disobey the divine order God had created. Also state that they were given a will; they could choose to obey or disobey.

Next, ask several people to share in reading aloud Genesis 3:1-6, with the group following along in their Bibles. Incorporate the following questions into the discussion of this passage (refer to information in "Insights for the Leaders" for additional lesson helps):

- What characteristics of the serpent or Satan do you recognize in this passage that we previously identified in other passages of Scripture? (Tempter; deceitful; liar; thief.)

- How did Satan undermine God's command in verse 3? (He questioned what God had said, thus planting a seed of doubt in Eve's mind.) How does Satan seek to undermine God's Word today? (In the same way—by causing people to question and doubt what God has said.)

- How did Satan appeal to human reason and pride in Eve's life? (By the lie that she would not die and the truth that she would be as God, knowing good and evil.) Can you think of another instance in Scripture when pride resulted in someone's fall? (see Isa. 14:12-15; 2 Sam. 24:1-4,9,10). Where do we see Satan mixing a lie with the truth of God's Word today? (In the cults. There is a measure of truth in every cult. The truth is the hook, but the end result of cultic lies is bondage and spiritual death.)

- What three mistakes did Eve make in Genesis

3:6? (She looked, took and gave.) With sin flaunted in today's media, is it an impossibility to refrain from *looking*? Why or why not? How can today's Christian deal with this temptation? (see 2 Cor. 7:1; Phil. 4:8). How was sin shared in Genesis 3:6? (Review comments made in the Approach to the lesson.)

Invite a learner to read aloud verses 7-11.

- What do you think Adam and Eve immediately learned about Satan? Do you think people recognize Satan's tactics as quickly today? Why or why not? Do they realize their sinful state today as did Adam and Eve? Why or why not?

- What did Adam and Eve lose by disobeying God's command, and what did they gain? (They lost their innocence and gained the knowledge of good and evil. See 2:17; 3:7,22.)

- What all is implied in Adam's reasons for hiding from God? (His shame, guilt and a disorder in his spirit that he had not known. Share Lloyd Ahlem's comments from "Insights for the Leader" under the heading "Lost Bearings" about humankind's lostness.) In what ways are people running from God today?

Step 3 (15 minutes): Mention that even as Adam and Eve endeavored to cover their sin with fig leaves, people continue today to hide and gloss over their sin, improvising many coverings through human effort. Announce that the group will research Genesis 3, verses 12 and 13 to discover and list on the Lesson Outline excuses Adam and Eve made for sinning when they were confronted by God. They will then list the excuses people make in covering and/or dealing with their sin today.

Move members into small groups and appoint a leader over each group. Announce that they will have about seven minutes for research. Move among the groups and offer guidance where needed. When time is up, regather the group and ask for feedback from small group leaders. Write responses on the chalkboard or Lesson Outline transparency. Responses could include the following suggestions (see "Insights for the Leader" for added lesson information):

- Blaming others. (Adam blamed God and the woman God gave him—see v. 12; Eve blamed the serpent—see v. 13.)

- Rationalizing. (Acting how "nature" made us; blaming our parents or our environment.)

- Inherited characteristics (short tempered, stubborn, impatient, outspoken, etc.).

- Popularized religion (Science of Mind, Dianetics,

Erhard Seminars' Training, New Age).
- Humanism (the belief that salvation is within man; good works).
- Cultic religions (endeavoring to gain one's salvation through a system of works).
- Right moral conduct (endeavoring through good works and good morals to become acceptable to God).

Move to Step 4 by stating that as Adam and Eve's efforts to cover their sin were inadequate, even so humankind's efforts today are inadequate. Say, *But God provided a covering for Adam and Eve's sin and He has made provision for our sin as well.*

Step 4 (10 minutes): Member assigned this portion of the lesson—verses 14-21—makes presentation. It should include the following main points:
- The results of Adam and Eve's sin (see vv. 14-19).
    -The serpent and the ground cursed (see vv. 14,15,17).
    -Eve would experience pain in childbearing and Adam would rule over her (see v. 16).
    -Adam would experience a life of painful toil (see vv. 17-19).
- God's provision for the sin of Adam and Eve (see v. 21).
    -Covering made from the skins of animals.
    -An animal had to be slain, blood had to be shed in order to provide this covering. This was the first incident of death in the world.
    -Their sin was covered, and they were forgiven (see Neh. 4:5; Heb. 9:22).
- God's full provision for humankind's sin (see Gen. 3:15).
    -Christ shed His blood on the cross; He gave His life (see Rom. 3:25; Phil. 2:8; Rev. 1:5). The skin coverings were a type or a foreshadowing of this ultimate sacrifice.
    -We are clothed with Christ's righteousness (see Rom. 3:22; 13:14; 2 Cor. 5:21).
    -We are now justified. This means to be declared righteous and acceptable, as if we had never sinned; our sins will never be remembered against us (see Ps. 103:12; Jer. 31:34; Rom. 3:24; 5:9; Heb. 8:6,7; 10:4-17).
    -We receive eternal life (see John 3:16,36).

Follow this presentation by a time of brief discus-

sion. As time will not allow a thorough exposition of all we receive in the salvation provided through Christ's death, suggest that those desiring additional study during the week, may want to do a more complete study of this subject. Point out the "Further Study and Application" section on the Lesson Outline.

 ONCLUSION (5 minutes)

Our study today began in a beautiful garden—the garden of Eden. But this perfect setting was soon tarnished as Adam and Eve listened to the lies of the serpent and disobeyed God's command not to eat of the tree of the knowledge of good and evil. Their human efforts to cover their sin with fig leaves was futile; they needed a Savior.

Adam and Eve's fall did not catch God off guard. The Scriptures state in 1 Peter 1:18-20 that Christ was chosen before the creation of the world to redeem us with His precious blood. The skins prepared by God for Adam and Eve's covering (that resulted in the shedding of blood of the slain animal and ultimately the forgiveness of their sin) was a foreshadowing of a greater redemption—the shedding of Christ's blood on the cross for all humankind.

Today men and women continue to improvise fig-leaf coverings for their sin instead of accepting the forgiveness and cleansing that comes only through faith in the shed blood of Jesus Christ. We have discussed a number of ways they are endeavoring to do this. Ask, *As believers, are we appropriating Christ's blood to our lives for daily cleansing, or are we refusing Christ's forgiveness and endeavoring to cover our sins by excusing them or by blaming others?* For those in the group who may not know Christ as their Savior, this would be a good time to afford them the opportunity to accept Him and His forgiveness.

Close the session by asking, *Will it be fig leaves or forgiveness?* Add, *Let's pray and ask God to help us accept His greater provision—the cleansing and removal of our sins from our lives through His shed blood.* Suggest that learners form clusters of three members and pray for one another.

Encourage members to read chapter 2 of the Regal book, *Christ B.C.*, which will assist them in their time of daily devotions. Each day's devotion is based on the theme of *righteousness*.

Noah Finds Refuge in the Ark

SESSION VERSES

"You are my hiding place; you will protect me from trouble and surround me with songs of deliverance." Psalm 32:7

"Come to me, all you who are weary and burdened, and I will give you rest. Take my yoke upon you and learn from me, for I am gentle and humble in heart, and you will find rest for your souls. For my yoke is easy and my burden is light." Matthew 11:28-30

SESSION FOCUS

Just as God provided refuge for Noah and his family in the ark, God has provided Christ as our refuge during stormy experiences.

SESSION BASIS

Genesis 6:1—9:17

SESSION GOAL

Explore ways Christ can be a refuge to us during times of trial and adverse circumstances.

INSIGHTS FOR THE LEADER

The story of Noah and his family finding refuge in the ark during the Flood is a symbol of God's grace extended to humankind in many ways. In this session we will focus on a few of the many types and pictures from this well-known narrative that were fulfilled in Christ.

The Days of Noah

From the day that Adam and Eve were denied residence in Eden, the character of humankind declined into moral and spiritual bankruptcy. Genesis 6:5 declares that the evil of man was great; it had saturated his thoughts and his heart: "The Lord saw how great man's wickedness on the earth had become, and that every inclination of the thoughts of his heart was only evil all the time." Humankind's behavior had become so bad that God was sorry for having made them: "The Lord was grieved that he had made man on the earth, and his heart was filled with pain" (v. 6). Such language does not indicate that God made a mistake. His perfect creation had gone foul by the free will of people, and God was repulsed by it. The following words of Scripture express the response of an insulted

God: "I will wipe mankind, whom I have created, from the face of the earth" (v. 7). Only a new start would be sufficient to renew hope for humankind and their relationship with God.

But even when insulted by sin, God gives grace. One man found favor in God's eyes. One man had not surrendered to all the evil impulses in which others indulged. This man was Noah (see vv. 8,9). Noah's character was above reproach. He was not sinless, but he sought to do God's bidding and was regarded by God as righteous. Noah would be preserved from the deluge God had planned for the destruction of the human race (see Heb. 11:7).

Like Noah, many men and women throughout history have refused to take on the life-styles of their respective cultures, choosing rather to obey God and live righteous lives, whatever the cost. Joseph is a prime example of such a one when he refused the advances of Potiphar's wife and as a result was sent to prison (see Gen. 39). Shadrach, Meshach and Abednego were thrown into a fiery furnace because they refused to fall down and worship the image that Nebuchadnezzar set up (see Dan. 3). And Esther put her life on the line when she went before the king to plead for the lives of her people, the Jews (see Esther 3:8—5:8; 7:1—8:14). All of these people were living in pagan cultures, surrounded by men and women who were not serving the living God. Although members of a minority group, their examples prove to us today that it is possible to live a life pleasing to God, even when one is not surrounded by a strong support system of believers. Noah was such a person.

The Ark Is Built

Upon choosing Noah, God told him of His plan "to put an end to all people, for the earth is filled with violence because of them" (Gen. 6:13). Then God gave Noah specific instructions to build an ark (see vv. 14-17). God told him what size to make it, where to put the door, how to lay out the interior and what materials to use. Finally God told Noah exactly what to put in the ark (see vv. 19-21). There would be a plentiful supply to begin again—both physically and spiritually. Noah's immediate family would be included (see v. 18), animals for repopulating the earth (see vv. 19,20), as well as for burnt offerings (see 8:20) and enough food for all (see 6:21).

Noah's response to God's instructions stress his obedience and faith in God. Verse 22 states, "Noah did everything just as God commanded him." Noah's response also set him further apart from the rest of his generation. His construction project must have boggled the minds of most who watched him. Imagine seeing a huge boat being built without a sail or rudder, and on dry land so far from the water that you could never haul it to sea. Furthermore, it had no prow or stern; just a big box made of wood and sealed up tight with pitch. This was no Chris-craft for waterskiing. This was a barge with only one purpose in mind: to protect as much cargo as could be loaded aboard. No provisions were made for navigation or for seaside loading or docking. Noah's neighbors must have laughed at him.

The Preacher of Righteousness

During this time Noah could possibly have been occupied with more than building. As a "preacher of righteousness" (2 Pet. 2:5), he, perhaps, split his time by preaching also. It appears that Noah's preaching did not meet with much success, for the apostle Peter wrote that only Noah and his family were spared God's judgment (see 1 Pet. 3:20, 2 Pet. 2:5). Nobody heeded Noah's preaching. The ancient historian Josephus says that he prodded his audience so insistently that

they wearied greatly and threatened to kill him if he didn't stop. I surely hope your preacher gets off better than that. It's tough to share a message that must be told, only to have people refuse to listen. Jesus experienced this, as well as an attempt on His life, when He preached to the people in His hometown (see Matt. 13:53-58; Luke 4:16-30). I wonder how many times Noah went back to his work of building the ark just to get away from surly audiences.

But Noah was a man of character. God says of him, "I have found you righteous in this generation" (Gen. 7:1). Only a man of character could have persisted in such a mission. Noah lived out the purpose for which he was intended. If we live as God intends, we can persist through rejection. And we can find our way in God's will without a lot of cheering or back-patting.

In evil times such as Noah's, evil people are unable to see their sin. So long have excuses been made, motives rationalized and consequences overlooked that the mind can no longer comprehend the evil done. This is evident in the fact that no one listened to Noah. Satan influenced people's reasoning then, just as he did Eve's in the garden of Eden (see Gen. 3:1-5). His purpose remains the same—to undermine and create doubt concerning what God has established. I imagine that the people of Noah's day had the same rationalizing capacities as Eve had and as we have in our time. It is clear that Satan is just as active in pursuing his evil interests in the world today as he was in the days of Eve and Noah (see 1 Pet. 5:8,9).

I remember counseling a young college student who was feeling terribly depressed. His moods were starting to interfere with his studies as well as his social life. As we unraveled his story, some reasons for his depression became obvious. He had been raised on good moral principles, but without the structure and reinforcement of sound biblical understanding. Without a solid base he began to think he could make up his own standards. He decided he would not do anything that was without his or his friends' consent. He entered into a life-style of pleasure and sexual indulgence that he and his friends condoned. But when his girlfriend became pregnant and badgered him for a promise of support, he could not understand why the problem was being handed to him. It wasn't really his fault, he thought; she had consented to being sexually involved. She did not protect herself and therefore she could just as well face the consequences on her own.

But those old standards he had been raised with were gnawing at him. Although he could not understand why, his conscience had long ago been formed by these standards; now they were telling him he was a moral failure. As with most failure, depression was the result. The solution to resolving his depression was to face up to his sin and find the biblical basis behind the moral standards imprinted on his conscience. But he would have none of it. The pleasure of his indulgence was too gripping. Instead, he began an intellectual assault upon his conscience, rationalizing his impulses as good in themselves and his behavior as in keeping with modern standards. Furthermore, he had plenty of help from teachers who saw him as a youngster liberating himself from old structures that hampered his freedom and life-style. But his depression remained. He was being devoured by his rationalizations (with Satan's help, I'm sure). His situation was probably similar to the hardheartedness of the people of Noah's day.

Noah Finds Refuge in the Ark

The trying days of preaching to spiritually deaf ears and hardened hearts and the physical toil of building ended with the completion of the ark. "The Lord then said to Noah, 'Go into the ark, you and your whole family'" (Gen. 7:1). And Noah, still persisting in obedience to God, "did all that the Lord commanded him" (v. 5). After Noah and his family entered the ark, the famous parade of animals began. It is interesting to note that Noah did not have to round up the animals on his own. "Pairs of clean and unclean animals. . .came to Noah and entered the ark" (v. 8,9). Noah had done what God had asked, and now God was intervening to complete the job. When all was secure in the ark, "the Lord shut him in" (v. 16). God Himself closed the door of the ark.

Then God unleashed the forces of nature (see vv. 11,12). The restraints imposed on the waters on the second and third days of creation were relaxed for the destruction of sinful man (see 1:7-10,13). The "springs of the great deep burst forth" (7:11) and rain came and drenched the earth from above. For approximately one year's time, Noah and his family survived (see 7:6,11; 8:13,14), and only because God Himself preserved them.

Finally, in accordance with God's timing, the waters receded. "God remembered Noah. . .and he sent a wind over the earth, and the waters receded" (8:1). God's last recorded conversation with Noah had been, "Go into the ark" (7:1). Now God said to Noah, "Come out of the ark" (8:16). Noah would now begin humankind's story again. And he began by giving honor to the Lord. He did not build a house but first "built an altar to the Lord and. . .sacrificed burnt offerings on it" (v. 20). God was pleased by Noah's act of worship and sacrifice of praise. Following the sacrifice God established a covenant with Noah and with "all life on the earth" (9:17). Genesis 9:8-17 gives the details of the first covenant between God and humankind. A covenant is an agreement, a pledge irrevocably taken and marked by a sign. The sign God provided for Noah was the rainbow. The agreement God made was, "'Never again will all life be cut off by the waters of a flood; never again will there be a flood to destroy the earth'" (v. 11).

Noah and Types of Christ

The story of Noah is much more than an account of a catastrophic event. It is a collage of pictures that illustrate God's grace and salvation through Jesus Christ. Let's isolate the individual pictures and see what they teach us about Jesus.

First, we see Noah as a singular, righteous person. He was the only one through whom God could redeem humankind from the judgment of the Flood. God used Noah as a singular instrument to affect that redemption. This points to Christ as the only means God has provided by which we can be saved from our sin (see Acts 4:12).

Second, Noah's character illustrates an important point concerning Christ's character. Only a righteous individual could be God's agent of salvation. Likewise, only a clean, unblemished animal could be offered as a sacrifice by the priests for sin (see Lev. 4:3). Like Christ, whatever offering was used to make atonement for a person's sin, it had to be a clean, unblemished animal. These are the terms Peter used to describe Christ: "For you know that it was not with perishable things such as silver or gold that you were redeemed from the empty way of life handed down to you from your forefathers, but with the precious blood of Christ, a lamb without blemish or defect" (1 Pet. 1:18,19). Peter goes on to say in verse 20 that "He was chosen before the creation of the world, but was revealed in these last times for your sake." God had planned a way of salvation for man from the very beginning. It isn't by chance that He chose Noah to save humankind from the flood; it was by design and for our sake.

The third picture we will examine is one of God's grace and provision through Jesus Christ. It is this picture that will be the focus of your time with your Bible students. In this picture we see that God provided a refuge for Noah. Having heard God and obeyed Him, Noah was exempted from the judgment that befell his unrepentant generation. In the midst of the upheaval when "all the springs of the great deep burst forth, and the floodgates of the heavens were opened" (see Gen. 7:11), Noah was preserved by God. Like Noah we are provided a refuge during times of turmoil if we obey and believe God's Word. This refuge is found in a right relationship with Jesus Christ. Psalm 32:7 declares, "You are my hiding place; you will protect me from trouble and surround me with songs of deliverance." Psalm 91 is a beautiful hymn that further describes God's gracious provision for the godly, "I will say of the Lord, 'He is my refuge and my fortress, my God, in whom I trust'. . . .He will cover you with his feathers, and under his wings you will find refuge; his faithfulness will be your shield and rampart. You will not fear the terror of night, nor the arrow that flies by day" (vv. 2,4,5). The Old Testament is full of descriptions such as these. Take time to read Psalm 57 as well. As you do, notice that it is in the *midst* of disaster and distress that God provides refuge. He does not always remove disaster from around us. Like Noah, He often provides a way for us to survive, protected by our trust in Him, in spite of the storms of life.

This message continues into the New Testament. Here Jesus identifies Himself as the one who can provide rest and rejuvenation. Matthew 11:28-30 is Jesus' invitation to share the burden of life with Him. It says, "'Come to me, all you who are weary and burdened, and I will give you rest. Take my yoke upon you and learn from me, for I am gentle and humble in heart, and you will find rest for your souls. For my yoke is easy and my burden is light.'" It is by coming to Christ, submitting to Him, learning from Him and giving Him our burdens that our souls can find rest.

The rich young ruler deprived himself of this rest by refusing to submit to the Lordship of Jesus (see Matt. 19:16-22; Luke 18:18-23). Mary, a follower of Christ who later anointed His feet with expensive perfume and wiped them with her hair (see John 12:1-3), discovered the secret of realizing Christ's rest in day-to-day circumstances. While her sister Martha was pressed to the point of impatience by her own desire to extend hospitality to Jesus and His disciples, Mary chose to sit peacefully at Jesus' feet and receive from His teaching (see Luke 10:38-42).

As New Testament believers were not exempt from trials and everyday stresses (see Acts 14:22; Rom. 5:3; 1 Thess. 3:4), we, too, will share in life's difficulties. But God has provided for these times of stress and trial by making available to us the rest and peace that only Christ can give (see Matt. 11:28-30; John 14:27). Peter exhorts us to "Cast all your anxiety on him [Christ]

because he cares for you" (I Pet. 5:7).

The biblical message is generously punctuated with many other promises of rest, refuge and peace for children of God who seek solace in Him (see Deut. 33:27; Pss. 23:1-3; 28:7; 37:7 (*KJV*); Isa. 43:2; Phil. 4:7). There is no man-made belief system or philosophy that is so personal and mindful of highly individual human needs as the gospel of Christ.

Considering the many invitations in Scripture to enter into the peace of God and find refuge in Him, I wonder at my efforts to go it alone and take all the bruises I do when I'm in trouble. I also wonder at the places of refuge chosen by so many that only add to their troubles. I am thinking of a college freshman who was in my class in introductory psychology. She was cute, verbal, intelligent and experimenting with all the nonsensical ideas and activities the world made available to her. As I got to know her, I found the force of guilt heavily upon her. She had been molested by her father, introduced to drugs by her high school English teacher and scolded by her priest for not taking her religion seriously. Furthermore, she felt helplessly guilty for having allowed herself to be exploited and abused by all these people. The refuge she chose was the deadening numbness of alcohol and deceptive euphoria of drugs.

Happily, not every person's search for refuge manifests itself in this way. On Monday evenings my wife and I began opening our living room for students who wanted to talk about personal concerns. No agenda was necessary, there was no admission charge and no barriers restricting any subject. My wife and I simply listened. We listened from about 8:30 P.M. when our small children went to bed until about 10:30 P.M. when we served refreshments. Most went home then, but some had not completed their agendas. So we sat up longer, often past midnight, with one or two who carried burdens they could hardly bear. Then we gently tried to point them to Christ, not coercively or with guilt, but with the message of the refuge God wanted to provide for them. By the time the last of them left, the coffee cups had been filled many times, then stuffed with ashes from innumerable cigarettes. The house stunk and our clothes smelled like a tobacco bonfire, but peace began to come and over a couple of years we were heartened by a number of students who found peace and refuge in Christ.

In time we left that area of the country for other duties in the Midwest. As we were leaving, one young woman who had spent many evenings with us, but who had shared little of herself, came and said, "I'm sorry you are going. Your living room is the safest place I have ever known in my life. No one accused me, and I could think through the assaults made upon my weak values. God was there with me. Thank you for making me feel safe." I felt more than paid for all the long nights we had spent.

But if the needs of these students were so great, so are the needs of so many others. What is happening to those who have no refuge in Christ, and no home to enter to feel a little sensation of His comfort? What is your favorite refuge that you run to? Is it to the loving arms of Jesus and His followers or some self-chosen substitute? Are you facing the world without the help of God's protection? Even though I have known the good news of God's comfort for many years, I am still constructing little refuges that fall short of the grace of God. I would still rather rationalize certain of my errors than seek forgiveness and peace in Christ. But when the heat is on and my stress is high, I run quickly to the presence of God. It's the little things that still tempt me to "go it alone"—the tiny arenas of struggle where pride wants a foothold and I want to dictate the outcomes and settle the issues. But I am learning that I don't have the power to effectively protect myself. I've discovered that Jesus is more able than I.

A final lesson we can learn from Noah is this: In seeking refuge in God we, like Noah, are provided with an opportunity to begin again (see 1 Pet. 3:18-21). This is like the experience of people newly regenerated in Christ (see 2 Cor. 5:17). Noah was an old man in his new beginning. This illustrates for us that there is always hope. In Christ it is never too late for a new beginning. In Christ there is always relief from spiritual debt and moral fault (see 1 John 1:9; 2:1). In Christ there is rest for your souls. For many this comes in the form of forgiveness. People, by their own resources and wits, accumulate debts they cannot pay and sins they cannot forgive or have forgiven. They wonder if there is any way out. Not until they come to terms with their sin and seek refuge and forgiveness through Jesus Christ will they find a way out. In receiving forgiveness through Christ, they are set free to begin again (see Ps. 37:23,24; 1 John 2:1).

Christ, the perfect Sacrifice that redeemed humankind from the penalty of sin and God's judgment, is ever present to provide rest and peace to our troubled souls during times of trial. And He is present to offer forgiveness and cleansing to our hearts when we sin and fall short of His righteousness. These acts represent a perfect picture of the refuge that Noah found during the Flood and the new beginning he experienced as he disembarked from the ark.

A B C PLAN FOR THE SESSION

Materials Needed:
- Your Session 3 Leader's Guide Sheet;
- One copy of the Session 3 Lesson Outline for each group member;
- Small index cards or Post-it Notes with Scripture references;
- Chalkboard or overhead projector with transparencies;
- Overhead projector transparency of the Session 3 Lesson Outline (optional).

Advance preparations:
- Invite a member to prepare a five-minute report on the specifications of Noah's ark. Refer member to a Bible dictionary and commentary for resource material. Pictures may be available in a Bible dictionary or Bible atlas from which simple sketches could be made on an overhead projector transparency.
- Write the following Scripture references on nine small index cards or Post-it Notes—one per card: (1) Romans 6:18,23; 1 John 1:9; (2) 2 Samuel 22:1-3; Psalm 91:9,10; 1 John 5:18; (3) Matthew 6:6; Acts 12:5-7; Philippians 4:6; Hebrews 4:14-16; (4) Proverbs 3:5,6; Matthew 6:31-33; (5) Matthew 11:28-30; Hebrews 4:10,11; 1 Peter 5:7; (6) Isaiah 40:29-31; Ephesians 6:10-17; (7) Acts 2:46; 1 Corinthians 12:12,13 27; Hebrews 10:25; (8) John 14:16,17; Romans 8:26; (9) Isaiah 26:3; Philippians 4:7; Colossians 1:19,20; 2 Thessalonians 3:16.

 A PPROACH (5 minutes)

Begin the session by stating that there is much talk today about the high stress and fast pace of living that people are experiencing in our present technological age. Ask, *How do people without Christ deal with this stress, and how do they cope with the difficulties they face from day to day?* Write responses on chalkboard or overhead transparency. They could include: Taking drugs and consuming alcohol; burying themselves in their work; keeping busy with hobbies and pleasurable activities; positive thinking; etc.

Move to the Bible Exploration by saying, *Sometimes believers respond to stress in the same way unbelievers respond. Our Bible study today, about Noah finding refuge in the ark during the Flood, will help us to discover where we can find rest and refuge during the storms in our lives.*

 IBLE EXPLORATION
(45-50 minutes)

Step 1 (10-15 minutes): Distribute the Lesson Outline to everyone. Encourage members to take notes on their outlines as the lesson progresses. Do the same on the chalkboard or Lesson Outline transparency.

Next, invite the group to open their Bibles to Genesis 6. Ask several learners to share in reading aloud Genesis 6:1-7,11-13. Follow by reading Luke 17:26,27. Lead a discussion of these passages and inject the following questions and comments (include further lesson material from "Insights for the Leader"):

- What were the moral conditions of the people at the time of the Flood? (Do not become involved in a discussion of the "sons of God" marrying the "daughters of men" as found in Genesis 6:2,4. The interpretation of this passage varies among Bible commentators and is not the focus of the lesson. To the person who may show an interest in the subject, suggest that he or she make an independent study of the passage.)
- What similar conditions are seen in today's society? Point out that God hates sin (see Ps. 95:10; Prov. 6:16-19; Isa. 43:24; Ezek. 6:9; Zech. 8:17), and we should hate it, too. Add, *As God wanted to destroy humankind because of their sin, even so we should want to destroy sin in our lives* (see Rom. 8:12,13).

Invite several persons in the group to share in reading aloud Genesis 6:8,9.

- In what ways do you think Noah was blameless? (He pleased God; he did not walk in the ways of sinful men.)
- What other Bible characters lived godly lives in an ungodly society and were not afraid to stand up for righteousness? (Joseph—see Gen. 39; Shadrach, Meshach and Abednego—see Dan. 3; Esther—see Esther 3:8—5:8; 7:1—8:14.) What can we learn from their examples? (Although they were members of minority groups, living in

pagan cultures, they demonstrated that it is possible to live godly lives when one must stand alone and not have the encouragement of support groups. Joseph is a prime example of this.)

Present a brief synopsis of Genesis 6:14-22.

Step 2 (5 minutes): Ask the group member who agreed to do research to present his or her report on the specifications of the ark and any displays, sketches or pictures he or she may have.

Step 3 (15 minutes): Say, *We see God providing for humankind's escape from the judgment of the Flood by instructing Noah to build an ark. Let's consider other ways God extended His mercy to humankind.*

Ask several learners to share in reading aloud Hebrews 11:7; 1 Peter 3:18-20 and 2 Peter 2:5.

- What do you think was the content of Noah's preaching? (Some commonly-held views are that Noah preached about God's righteousness and the coming judgment of the Flood because of the people's sins. Also, he may have offered an invitation to enter the ark.)
- Are we responsible to warn people today of God's coming judgment on their sin? Why or why not? (see Ezek. 3:17-19; 2 Cor. 5:10,11,18.)
- Many commentators feel that the earth prior to the Flood was still watered by mists as mentioned in Genesis 2:6. If you had never seen rain, what would your thoughts have been to see the building of such a large boat, especially so far from water?
- Why do you think the people did not respond to Noah's preaching? Present the information concerning the writings about Noah by Josephus from "Insights for the Leader" under the heading "The Preacher of Righteousness." Point out that although Noah did not receive the favor of the people, he did receive the favor of the Lord (see Gen. 6:8).
- Can we always expect to receive the favor of people? Why or why not? (see John 15:18,19).
- In what ways are people's rejection of the gospel today similar to those of the people in Noah's time?
- How does sin deaden one's conscience? (see Rom. 1:21-24,28; Eph. 4:18,19; Heb. 3:8-12).

Invite several persons to share in reading aloud Genesis 7:6-12,15,16. Share the following lessons from this passage:

- The animals came to Noah on their own; he did not have to seek them out (see v. 15). Point out that when Adam named the animals, God brought the animals to Adam (see Gen. 2:19).

- The Lord, not Noah, shut the door of the ark (see 7:16). What lesson can we learn from this? (We must leave open the door of opportunity for people to receive Christ; only He knows when the door is to be closed.)

Read aloud Genesis 8:6-14 and share the following lessons:

- The dove, returning with an olive branch, is the basis of the modern symbol of peace. This told Noah that God's judgment was over and the waters were receding. Also, the dove is a type of the Holy Spirit (see John 1:32).
- Of what does Noah's act of reaching out his hand to return the dove to himself and into the ark speak to us? (Christ, reaching out to humankind, will receive all who come to Him. See Matt. 11:28-30; John 6:37.)

Invite several members to share in reading aloud Genesis 8:15,20,21.

- What lessons can be learned from Noah's actions? (Noah put first things first—he worshiped and offered a sacrifice. Before he built a house, he built an alter. Our worship should come before our needs or desires.)

Draw learners' attention to Genesis 9:8-17. Point out that this passage gives the details of the first covenant between God and humankind. Also, the sign of the covenant—a rainbow—made its first appearance in the skies at this time.

Mention briefly how Noah is a type of Christ. Noah was righteous and the only one God could use to provide a way of escape from the Flood. Christ, the *perfect* One, is the only means God has provided by which we can be saved from our sins (see Acts 4:12). Also point out that as Noah was offered a new beginning after the Flood, even so we are offered a new beginning when we receive Christ as our Savior (see 2 Cor. 5:17). Add, *And new beginnings are ours when we fail or fall in our Christian walk. When we repent, Christ forgives us and picks us up so that we might continue on our walk* (see 1 John 1:9; 2:1).

Ask, *How is the ark a type of Christ?* (Through Christ, Christians are safe from God's just condemnation; see Rom. 5:9. And they find rest and refuge in Him, amid their daily testings and trials; see Matt. 11:28,29. Noah was saved from the destruction of the Flood—God's judgment upon Noah's unrepentant generation. The ark was his refuge. Inside its walls he found shelter from the storm that raged on the outside.)

Move to Step 4 by stating, *There are many types that can be drawn from Noah and the ark. We will focus on the ark as a type of Christ as our rest during times of stress and as our refuge from life's storms.*

Step 4 (15 minutes): Ask everyone to form groups of four to six members and appoint group leaders. Next, distribute one or several index cards or Post-it Notes to each group.

Ask groups to look up the Scripture references on their respective card(s) to discover specific ways Christ can be a refuge to us and provide rest during stormy times and periods of stress. Encourage learners to list their findings on their Lesson Outlines. Also, announce that they will have seven minutes for research and writing.

When time is up, regather into the larger group and ask for feedback from the small group leaders. Be sure the following ways are included in the findings (allow time for discussion of the various points and jot down responses on the board as reports are given):

1. Romans 6:23; 1 John 1:9—He saves us from sin and death;

2. 2 Samuel 22:1-3; Psalm 91:9,10; 1 John 5:18—He protects us from sinfulness in the world;

3. Matthew 6:6; Acts 12:5; Philippians 4:6; Hebrews 4:14-16—He provides access to God through prayer;

4. Proverbs 3:5,6; Matthew 6:31-33—He affirms our trust in God's promises;

5. Matthew 11:28-30; Hebrews 4:10,11; 1 Peter 5:7—He provides rest for the weary;

6. Isaiah 40:29-31; Ephesians 6:10-17—He provides strength and the armor of God;

7. Acts 2:46; 1 Corinthians 12:12,13,27; Hebrews 10:25—He has provided the refuge of the Church so that even in hostile cultures we may have fellowship with other believers;

8. John 14:16,17; Romans 8:26—He has provided the Holy Spirit to counsel and comfort us;

9. Isaiah 26:3; Philippians 4:7; Colossians 1:19,20; 2 Thessalonians 3:16—He provides lasting, perfect peace.

Move to the Conclusion by stating, *From your discoveries we can see that God has more than provided for life's storms or testings. We do not need to take the escape routes that many in the world take to cope with their stresses and trials* (refer to suggestions made in the Approach to the study). *Our rest and refuge can be found in Christ.*

C ONCLUSION (5 minutes)

The story of Noah finding refuge in the ark is filled with types that find their fulfillment in Christ. He is our righteousness, our salvation from the penalty of sin and our rest and refuge in life's storms. We are offered a new beginning when we receive Him as our Savior and succeeding beginnings when we fail.

Ask, *How are you coping with day-to-day stresses or critical trials and storms in your life? Are you responding the same way many unbelievers respond by taking escape routes that offer only temporary rest*

and peace? Let's take God's route of escape and look to Christ for our rest. Refer to the list of suggested ways Christ can be our rest and a refuge to us. Ask, *Which one do you need to apply to your life? Which avenue will bring you rest and peace in your trial?*

Close the session by encouraging members to form small groups of four and pray for one another. Some may want to share specific needs with their respective group members. Allow this to be an option. Encourage members to read chapter 3 of the Regal book, *Christ B.C.*, which will assist them in their daily devotions. Each day's devotion is based on the theme, *refuge*.

TEACHING TIP
Considering Your Adults' Needs

Adulthood is the widest age range of any of the defined periods of life. Once a person becomes an adult, he remains in that classification until death. But adulthood is not static. Changes take place and characteristics emerge at different periods.

Because of these changes, adulthood is divided into three periods. Keep in mind the needs and responsibilities of your learners as you prepare to teach an adult class.

Young Adults (approximately 18-35)

Young adults of college age (age 18-23) have adult responsibilities which are new to them and are broadening rapidly. Within this age group some people may be attending college, some may be working at a job, and others may be doing both. Most retain some measure of dependence on parents, but are anxious to attain economic, social, and emotional freedom.

Young adults age 24-35 are often urban and mobile. They are very independent and searching for identity and values. Their responsibilities include involvement in relationships; selecting a mate, if they choose to marry (learning to live with a marriage partner; starting a family; rearing children are major concerns for married young adults); managing a home; finding a social group; and launching a career.

Middle Adults (approximately age 35 to 60)

Responsibilities for middle-aged people include civic and social responsibility; establishing and maintaining economic stability; guiding children to adulthood; involvement in leisure activities; accepting and adjusting to physical changes; changes in the marital relationship once children leave the home; and relating to one's own aging parents.

The years of middle age are a time of change and challenge. They can be a time of growth and leadership—what some refer to as the prime years of life.

Older Adults (age 65 and up)

Older adults comprise an increasing segment of our population. They differ in some needs and abilities from any other age group.

Older adults often experience a number of adjustments (changes in vision, hearing, bodily functions, and so on); economic adjustment and retirement; adjusting to loss of loved ones; and becoming a part of the older adult society.

As we teach adults, we need to keep their age-related, and unique, needs in mind, that our ministry may be what God wants it to be.

Melchizedek

SESSION VERSES

"The Lord has sworn and will not change his mind: 'You are a priest forever, in the order of Melchizedek.'" Psalm 110:4

"Therefore, since we have a great high priest who has gone through the heavens, Jesus the Son of God, let us hold firmly to the faith we profess." Hebrews 4:14

SESSION FOCUS

Jesus is our High Priest in the order of Melchizedek. As such, only He can offer us complete redemption.

SESSION BASIS

Genesis 12:1—14:20; Hebrews 5:5-10; 7:1-28

SESSION GOAL

List ways Jesus is our High Priest in the order of Melchizedek and why this superior priesthood is needed.

INSIGHTS FOR THE LEADER

Melchizedek's appearance in Scripture has a mystery about it. Only a few verses are devoted to him, but within these verses a clear type of Christ emerges. We also find reference to Melchizedek in the New Testament—Hebrews, chapters 5 through 7.

The Setting

Genesis 12 through 14 describes the circumstances in which Abraham (at this time he was called Abram) and Melchizedek met. Abraham had followed God's call to leave his home in Ur of the Chaldeans and go to Canaan (see 12:1,5; Acts 7:2-4). Because of the severe famine afflicting Canaan, Abraham proceeded to Egypt where he set up temporary residence (see Gen. 12:10). While in Egypt his wealth and numbers increased greatly. "Abram acquired sheep and cattle, male and female donkeys, menservants and maidservants, and camels" (v. 16; also see 13:2). (Note: Because of the focus of this study, I will not explore the circumstances surrounding Abraham's stay in Egypt. I suggest that you read Genesis 12:10-20 and be prepared to answer any questions, should they arise. Notice that God's command to Abraham in verses 1-8 did not include Abraham traveling to Egypt, and it is significant that his relationship with God is not mentioned during his stay there.)

From Egypt Abraham traveled back toward the land of Canaan (see 12:20—13:4). He left Egypt a wealthier man than he was before. In later years Jacob's sons would leave Egypt with food to sustain their father, themselves and their families (see 42:25,26; 45:21-24). And still 400 years later, the nation of Israel would make their exodus from Egypt with silver and gold given to them by the Egyptians (see Exod. 3:21,22; Ps. 105:37). Abraham had prospered in Egypt. His entourage was so large that it could have been considered a small nation on the move. Abraham had the ability to maintain an army of "318 trained men born in his household" (Gen. 14:14). He also had sufficient influence to make alliances with neighboring kings and compete with hostile forces (see vv. 13-16).

Abraham had the opportunity to use these resources to resolve a situation concerning his nephew Lot. Genesis 13 tells us that in order to resolve bickering among their herdsmen over grazing land, Abraham and Lot parted ways. "Abram lived in the land of Canaan, while Lot lived among the cities of the plain and pitched his tents near Sodom" (v. 12). It is obvious that, despite the fact that the land around Sodom was fertile (see v. 10), Lot had made a bad choice. "The men of Sodom were wicked and were sinning greatly against the Lord" (v. 13). Also, Bera the king of Sodom and the kings of neighboring cities had many enemies. The cities of Sodom, Gomorrah, Admah, Zeboiim and Bela were conquered during a battle in the Valley of Siddim (see 14:8-11). Sodom and Gomorrah were ransacked and Lot and his possessions were carried off among the plunder (see v. 12). When Abraham heard the news, he gathered his trained men and conducted a nighttime raid to rescue Lot. The Bible says that Abraham "brought back his relative Lot and his possessions" (v. 16).

Abraham Is Greeted by Melchizedek

Upon returning from battle, Abraham was greeted by Melchizedek, king of Salem, who brought bread and wine for refreshment (see vv. 17,18). These are the same elements that Jesus appointed centuries later for use as a memorial of His death for humankind (see Mark 14:22-25; 1 Cor. 11:23-26). Melchizedek blessed Abraham and gave praise to "God Most High, who delivered your enemies into your hand" (Gen. 14:20).

Melchizedek, king of Salem, likely was king over the area that is now Jerusalem. Language scholars suggest that the name Salem is a derivative of the Ursalim, which is also the basis of the name Jerusalem. The name "Melchizedek" has significant meaning. Hebrews 7:2 states, "First, his name means 'king of righteousness'; then also, 'king of Salem' means 'king of peace.'" First John 2:1 calls Jesus "the Righteous One." In John 14:27 and 16:33, Jesus speaks as the agent of God's peace. Thus, even the name of Melchizedek testifies that he is a worthy type of Christ.

Melchizedek was king over the region that was to be the center of the Promised Land of Israel. It would become the site of God's Temple and the center of worship in years to come. It would be many years before this promise would be realized, but the story provides us with a glimpse of the kingdom that would be built. Melchizedek was a godly king, ruling where the King of kings was to be crucified (see John 12:12; 19:17-19) and where prophecy is yet to be fulfilled (see Isaiah 40:9-11.)

Melchizedek served as both king and priest, probably presiding over a large family like Abraham's. As king he had authority to set guidelines for his subjects and carry out judgment when needed. He was also responsible for their welfare and spoke on their behalf. Melchizedek's role as king provides us with a picture of Christ that points to Jesus' role as our King, Judge, Lord, Provider and Protector (see Ps. 23; 2 Tim. 4:1).

Although Melchizedek was a Canaanite king, he was a servant of the one true God. As "priest of God Most High" (Gen. 14:18), Melchizedek was able to offer sacrifices and thereby advocate atonement for the sins of his people. It appears that Abraham saw in him the character and nature of the one true God and honored Melchizedek by paying tithes to him (see v. 20).

Jesus and the Order of Melchizedek

This is where the mystery of Melchizedek presents itself. The Jews were aware that the Messiah would come through the tribe of Judah (see Gen. 49:10; Isa.11:1,10). But there was a mystery—a prophecy that the Messiah would be a king/priest (see Zech. 6:13). Because of this prophecy the Jews *might* have expected a redeemer to come through the priestly tribe of Levi, which came from Abraham. Yet Abraham, in paying tithes to Melchizedek, acknowledged him to be of a higher order than Abraham himself. Hebrews 7:4 describes this honor given to Melchizedek: "Just think how great he [Melchizedek] was: Even the patriarch Abraham gave him a tenth of the plunder!" The superiority of the priestly order of Melchizedek over the order of Levi is reemphasized in Hebrews 7:9,10. "One might even say that Levi, who collects the tenth, paid the tenth through Abraham, because when Melchizedek met Abraham, Levi was still in the body of his ancestor."

Why do these two orders exist? What is it about Melchizedek that makes his order of priesthood so important? These questions can only be answered when we look at Melchizedek as a type of Christ. Christ is described as a priest in the order of Melchizedek (see 5:5,6). Priesthood in the order of Levi was inherited by members of the tribe of Levi (see Num. 3:1-13). Jesus' earthly genealogy places Him as a member of the tribe of Judah (see Heb. 7:14). Priesthood in the order of Melchizedek is "not on the basis of a regulation as to his ancestry but on the basis of the power of an indestructible life" (v. 16). Jesus' resurrection gives strong evidence of His fulfillment of this requirement (see Luke 24:1-8).

There are other evidences that point to the necessity of a priesthood that is superior to that of Levi. Hebrews 6:20 and 7:3 describe the order of Melchizedek as an eternal priesthood. There is no record given in the Old Testament of Melchizedek's death. According to the writer of Hebrews, this was to show that Melchizedek is consistent with the eternal Christ whose kingdom has no end. This same verse in Hebrews (see 7:3) describes the divine Christlike attributes of Melchizedek: "Without father or mother, without genealogy, without beginning of days or end of life, like the

Son of God he remains a priest forever." This clarifies that Melchizedek is a clear type of Christ. He is not simply a pawn of chance circumstance, but part of history designed and directed by God. Jesus was without an earthly father (see Luke 2:48-50). He existed before the creation of the world (see John 1:2), He conquered death (see 11:25) and He continues to act as the eternal High Priest. "Because Jesus lives forever, he has a permanent priesthood. Therefore he is able to save completely those who come to God through him, because he always lives to intercede for them" (Heb. 7:24,25).

Because the priesthood of Jesus is eternal and perfect, the sacrifice of Christ is final (see 7:27; 9:12). In contrast to the day-to-day offerings by the Aaronic priests, Christ's giving of Himself was a once-and-for-all accomplishment. He was the sinless one giving Himself once for the sinful, and that was enough. There is no need for anyone else to repeat the atonement, try to improve upon it or add anything to it. The Greek for the phrase "sacrifice of atonement" carries the thought that God's righteous wrath is satisfied by the sacrifice (see Rom. 3:25). Through the Aaronic order the priests had to offer sacrifices for themselves as well as for the people (see Lev. 9:7; Heb. 5:1-3). They suffered the same sins and blemishes as we do. This is not so with Christ; He is the lamb without spot or blemish and the perfect sacrifice that needed no cleansing (see 2 Cor. 5:21; Heb. 7:26; 1 Pet. 1:18,19).

Complete Redemption

This picture of Jesus as our High Priest is one of redemption. Very simply, redemption means to buy back something that is already our own.

When I was a boy, a teacher of mine illustrated this word with a simple story adapted from *Little Boat Twice Owned*. A young lad built a beautiful model boat. He took care to make every part a perfect replication of a well-known sailing vessel. When he had finished it, his friends admired it greatly and were surprised at the great skill he had demonstrated in building the boat. It was as fine a model as they had ever seen. But it did not seem appropriate to have it sit on a shelf in his home. It should be sailed, as boats were meant to do. So he carried it to the nearby brook and set it free to be carried by the winds.

The currents of air and water caught it and since it was so beautifully made and balanced, it rushed out beyond the reach of its maker. The boy chased along the water's edge, trying to find a way to recover his treasure. But he could not. He watched it disappear downstream as it went its unfettered way.

Some weeks later the lad, still sorrowing for his loss, was walking along a street leading to his home. He chanced to pass a hardware store and stopped to look into the window. Something caught his eye. There was his boat! The store was now closed, but early the next morning he rushed down to the shopkeeper and asked to have his boat returned. The shopkeeper could see that he was very determined to get his treasure back, but the man replied, "I paid good money for that boat, and I'll have to get my price for it. It is well made and should attract any number of interested customers."

"But it's mine!" responded the boy.

"I won't sell it for awhile," said the shopkeeper. "I'll save it for you. See if you can get the money."

The boy hurried off and gathered all he had ever saved and quickly brought it to the store. It was just enough, so the shopkeeper handed over the beautiful treasure, the boat. "First I made you, then I bought you, now I'll keep you safe forever!" pledged the lad as he left the store.

In spiritual terms this is a good illustration of redemption. First God made us, then He gave us a free will. We took our own course and lost track of the One who designed and created us. When we became entangled in sin, we were purchased—"bought back"—with all that God could give—His only Son, Jesus Christ (see John 3:16; 1 Cor. 7:23).

The story of the boat fails at one important point. Unlike the boat, which is carried by the wind, we have all set sail upon life under our own will. We chose to get away from our Maker, and we must choose to be returned to our rightful owner. Nevertheless, our redemption has been provided for. God has given us a way to return to Him through the final sacrifice of Jesus Christ, the great High Priest (see John 14:6; Heb. 10:12,19-22). But our way of return to God must be accepted by us. We are His, but our response is vital (see Josh. 24:15; Rom. 10:9). God made us free and does not violate our freedom. As God has given us the gift of His Son, we must make a gift of ourselves to Him to experience His great redemption for us. And what a marvelous redemption it is!

Our redeemer is Jesus Christ, "very God of very God," as one of the great creeds so elegantly states. Abraham knew of Him, in a sense, through Melchizedek who was a type of Christ. Old Testament saints had faith in a coming Christ whom they could know, in a limited sense, through spiritual types God had provided for them. They saw more dimly than we, for in our time we have been privileged to know the person of Jesus, both experientially and historically. The ancients were commended for their faith in what they hoped for and what they knew to be true but could not see (see Heb. 11:1,2).

What Redeemer Do You Seek?

Consider the three following statements (put a True or False by each statement as it expresses your present belief):

1. Every person needs a savior whether he or she knows it or not;
2. Every person seeks redemption, whether he or she understands it or not;
3. Every person worships something, whether he or she realizes it or not.

The response to each of these statements, I believe, is true. People choose interesting saviors as objects of worship. Worship and the choice of a savior is a world-wide personal and cultural activity. That is, everyone, everywhere, in all times, regardless of background chooses a savior and an object of worship. Not only do people do so individually, but they do it corporately or nationally.

Arnold Toynbee, the British historian, says in *A Study of History* that every civilization that has ever existed has grown up, integrated itself, then chosen a savior to prevent its decline. In choosing a savior, Toynbee further states that each civilization has picked one of four possibilities. The first possibility is the savior he calls the *philosopher king*. This savior is a statement of belief and commitment to a high and lofty value that people have derived apart from God. Plato, the ancient philosopher, believed that such a savior was necessary to preserve ancient Greece. He thought that unless all men give themselves seriously to philosophy of a humane sort, the state could not be preserved.

The second savior people seek is the savior of the *sword*. History is full of the terrors of people that have chosen the sword as their means of self-preservation. The Roman Empire, Hitler's Third Reich, Napoleon of France, to name a few, have lived and died by the sword.

The third savior is the savior of the *creative genius*. Nations have believed that by their power of inventiveness they can overcome both nature and their enemies and thus be able to preserve themselves. This is perhaps the savior chosen by highly technological societies, although one might think, with their development of nuclear arms, that the savior of the sword has

been chosen, as well, in such cases.

The fourth savior is a *spiritual savior*. More than 20 civilizations have come and gone in the known history of man. Most of them have chosen one of the first three saviors. Although Toynbee was apparently not sure whether he would prefer Buddhism or Christianity, he recognized the need of nations for a savior and that only a spiritual savior could fill this need.

People, like nations, are constantly driven by their very natures to seek redemption in some form. No person goes merrily through life devoid of the impulse to seek a savior. The question is not whether people will or won't seek saviors, but whether they will choose the only one that can truly save—the eternal High Priest, Jesus Christ.

We all seek a savior. We all seek to be redeemed from our lostness. We will inevitably worship someone or something. We have an innate need to find some organizing center for our lives. We are all keenly aware—unless we have been subjected to so much academic rationalization that we can't see our need—that we need someone or something greater than ourselves to find us, help us with our problem with guilt, give us meaning and justify our existence.

For some years, as a psychologist, I have been a student of personality organization. One of my favorite courses to teach is "Theory of Personality." There is today no formal theory of personality that does not place ego at the center of human existence and experience. Self is king. Self can deal with guilt. Every theory constructs the personality so that the enhancement of self, of ego, is the primary psychological task of man. Self is god, and a poor and diminutive god it is. In the process of making ego god, every form of self-justification, self-gratification and self-enhancement has been tried. But failure is the inevitable result. Human life was made to organize itself around the person of Christ, empowered by the Holy Spirit, with ego as orbital and secondary. This is the reason the Bible describes Jesus by such terms as High Priest, Lord and King. He is primary; only He can save us. Why else do we have the scriptural admonition to "seek first his kingdom and his righteousness, and all these things will be given to you as well" (Matt. 6:33). By choosing Christ as Savior, our needs are met completely.

The human drive for redemption of some sort, for some organizing center to worship is so dominant that it consumes most of the energies of humankind. Current psychology has promoted the idea of the self-fulfilled, self-actualized life as the goal of human effort. This is clearly the god of the humanist who has made self god and discarded any notion of a god outside of human invention. But the fact is that when a person puts God, in Christ, into the center of his or her life and experience, and his or her own ego in a secondary orbital position, that person finds more fulfillment than if fulfillment is sought as an end in itself. Thus it is strange to an unbeliever that "whoever loses his life for my [Christ's] sake will find it" (Matt. 10:39). In contemporary psychological theory and practice in secular society, this makes no sense whatsoever.

Some have tried to make moral uprightness their god and their redemption. Like the efforts of the Levitical and Aaronic priests, their efforts fall short; they do not count for eternity (see Heb. 7:11,23,24). I once studied under a professor who as a youngster confessed Christian belief. But when he had received a generous humanist education, he set out to be as great a moral specimen as any Christian might be, but without the help of God. He discovered that he could be as good as any Christian in moral terms without going through the necessity of surrendering his life to the great High Priest. The result was that this professor was one of the most upstanding and truly caring men I

have ever known. But his effort will fail when he meets the King (see Isa. 64:6; Rom. 3:10,20). He cannot present himself as a worthy substitute for Christ (see John 14:6; Acts 4:12). He has chosen to play god in his own life and his morality has become a form of idolatry. He will have to say to God that he figured out his salvation his own way. But God is sovereign; He will have neither peer nor competitor. My professor will be a lost soul because he would not submit and accept the sacrifice God has provided by which he may be saved.

As you consider this lesson, think about the gods you have sought in the past. Consider how they fell short of the sacrifice of Christ. What gods are your group members being pressured to seek? Is it the god of fun, of fortune, sex, drugs, music, self-importance, Satan? God has gone to great lengths to assure us that only His redemption through Christ is sufficient. Through the ages God has made His redemption known through types and pictures in the Old Testament. Melchizedek was such a type. Redemption has been completed through the sacrifice of God's Son Jesus, our eternal High Priest (see Heb. 7:24,25). We are without rationalizations or excuse.

A B C PLAN FOR THE SESSION

Materials needed:
- Your Session 4 Leader's Guide Sheet;
- One copy of the Session 4 Lesson Outline for each group member;
- Large index cards with questions and Scripture references;
- Chalkboard or overhead projector with transparencies;
- Overhead projector transparency of the Session 4 Lesson Outline (optional).

Advance preparations:
- Read the information under "Advance preparations" for Sessions 5 and 7 in order to make preparations for a special assignment in Session 5 and a Jewish Seder that ties in with the study of the Passover in Session 7;
- On large index cards (one for each small group), write the following question and all three groups of Scripture references: How is Jesus our High Priest in the order of Melchizedek?
  1. Hebrews 7:1,6
     Numbers 3:1,2,5,6; Hebrews 7:11-14
  2. Hebrews 7:3,16
     Luke 2:48-50; 24:1-8; John 1:2; Hebrews 7:24,25
  3. Hebrews 7:4-10
     Hebrews 4:14

A PPROACH (10 minutes)

Write the following statement on the chalkboard or overhead transparency: *Every person seeks redemption whether he or she understands it or not.* Direct

members' attention to the statement and ask, *Do you agree or disagree?* Allow time for the group to think about the statement and decide their opinions and why. Then ask for responses. Learners may stand and move to the sides of the room designated "agree side" and "disagree side." And they may try to convince others of their position. As the discussion takes place, everyone is free to change his or her mind on the issue and move to the other side of the room.

Move to the Bible Exploration by saying something like this, *Your responses have been interesting. Our study today will shed more light on this subject and will prove helpful to us all. And we will consider, from God's Word, how Christ as High Priest in the order of Melchizedek offers to all humankind perfect redemption.*

B | BIBLE EXPLORATION
(40-45 minutes)

Step 1 (10 minutes): Distribute the Lesson Outline to learners. Encourage them to take notes on their outlines as the lesson is presented and discussion takes place. Do the same on the chalkboard or Lesson Outline transparency. Include further lesson material in the discussions from "Insights for the Leader."

Next, announce that the basis for today's study is taken from Genesis 12:1 through 14:20 and portions of chapters 5 and 7 of the book of Hebrews. Invite everyone to open his or her Bible to Genesis, chapter 12. Say *Our study today begins with Abraham, who was called Abram at that time.*

Ask, *What do you know about Abraham's call?* (Allow time for responses.) Next, ask several members to share in reading aloud Genesis 12:1,5 and Acts 7:2-4. Mention God's promise to Abraham (see Gen. 12:2,3) and his journey to Canaan (see v. 5). Also point out that Abraham's nephew Lot made the move to Canaan with Abraham (see v. 4).

Say, *Next we see Abraham traveling to Egypt.* Ask, *What does verse 10 say is the reason for his going to Egypt?* Mention briefly that Abraham experienced some problems while in Egypt that resulted in his return to Canaan. Share Dr. Lloyd Ahlem's comments about Abraham's detour to Egypt in "Insights for the Leader" under the heading "The Setting."

Invite a learner to read aloud Genesis 12:16 and 13:1,2. Say, *We see that Abraham left Egypt wealthier than when he arrived.*

Quickly mention God's blessing upon Abraham as seen in his army of 318 trained men (see Gen. 14:14) and his sufficient influence to make alliances with neighboring kings and compete with hostile forces (see vv. 13-16).

Next, review the events of Genesis 13:1-13 and the circumstances of Lot's capture (see 14:1-12) and subsequent rescue by Abraham (see vv. 13-16).

Invite several persons to share in reading aloud Genesis 14:17-20 and Hebrews 7:1,2. State that there are varying opinions by Bible scholars as to whether Melchizedek was a theophany (a visible manifestation of God) or a man who actually lived. Mention that although time will not allow the presentation of the various arguments, interested Bible students may pursue the subject in independent study during the week.

Ask, *How does Jesus fulfill the meaning of Melchizedek's name, "king of righteousness" and "king of Salem" that means "king of peace"?* (Heb. 7:2). (Allow time for responses.) Include in the discussion the following information:

- Jesus is called "the Righteous One" (1 John 2:1).
- Jesus is the Prince of Peace and the agent of peace (see Isa. 9:6; John 14:27; 16:33).
- Salem, later called Jerusalem, was to be the center of the Promised Land of Israel and their center of worship. It was here, also, that Jesus was crucified (see John 12:12; 19:17,18).
- Jesus, as King, cares for His own and is our Judge (see Ps. 23; 2 Tim. 4:1), even as Melchizedek no doubt cared for and ruled his subjects. Jesus will one day reign as King of kings (see Ezek. 37:24-28; Rev. 19:1-16; 20:4-6; 22:3-5).

Step 2 (15 minutes): Say, *We have discussed how Melchizedek is a type of Christ as a king of peace, a righteous king and a king of Salem. Now let's consider how Jesus is our High Priest in the order of Melchizedek.* Move members into groups of four to six. Assign group leaders and give each leader an index card. Learners are to work together in their respective groups to discover ways Jesus is our High Priest in the order of Melchizedek. Allow about seven minutes for research.

Next, regather everyone into the larger group and ask for feedback from group leaders. Include the following answers in the responses:

1. Hebrews 7:1,6; Numbers 3:1,2,5,6; Hebrews 7:11-14—Jesus was a descendent of Judah and not of Levi; Melchizedek, as well, did not trace his descent from Levi.
2. Hebrews 7:3,16; Luke 2:48-50; 24:1-8; John 1:2; Hebrews 7:24,25—Jesus is eternal and did not have an earthly father; Melchizedek was without father or mother or beginning of days or end of life. Jesus is our High Priest forever; Melchizedek, who had no end of life, was able as priest to offer sacrifices and thereby advocate atonement for the sins of his people.

3. Hebrews 7:4-10; 4:14—Jesus is our Great High Priest and is greater than the Levitical priesthood; Melchizedek, a type of Christ, was a greater priest than the Levitical priesthood by the fact that Abraham honored him by paying tithes to him. In this way, Levi was also honoring the greater one, Melchizedek because Abraham was Levi's ancestor. Therefore, Christ of whom Melchizedek is a type, must be much superior to the Levitical priests.

Follow up the discussion by asking these suggested questions:

- Why was the superior priesthood of Christ needed? (see Lev. 9:7; Heb. 5:1-3).
- Why was Christ able to meet this need? (see 2 Cor. 5:21; Heb. 7:26; 1 Pet. 1:18,19).
- In what way is Christ's sacrifice complete? (see John 19:30; Heb. 7:27; 9:12; 10:4).

Optional Step 3 (5 minutes): Ask, *When you were a child, did you ever hear the story "Little Boat Twice Owned"?* (Those with a church background have possibly heard the story.) If someone is present who remembers the story, ask if they can recall it and then invite him or her to share the story with the group. If no one has heard the story, quickly share it, as well as its application: God created and owned us; humankind sinned and became separated or lost from God; God, through His Son Jesus, paid the price to redeem us—He bought us back.

Step 4 (15 minutes): Draw the group's attention back to the statement used in the Approach to the lesson (Every person seeks redemption whether he or she understands it or not.) Say, *In a moment we will deal with this statement more definitively. First, neighbor-nudge the person next to you and discuss ways, other than Christ, people seek to receive or attain redemption.* Allow several minutes for discussion. Next, regain the attention of the group and ask for feedback. List suggestions on the chalkboard or overhead transparency. They could include: wealth, power, high moral standards, good works, intelligence, secularism, humanism, etc.

Following the group's responses say, *The statement used in the Approach was not meant to be a trick statement. If you were among members who disagreed with the statement, be assured that your arguments were good ones. However, the following information will no doubt convince you that the correct position is to agree:* (Share the information about everyone, everywhere, in all times seeking a savior and an object of worship from "Insights for the Leader"

under the heading "What Redeemer Do You Seek?". Include the four possibilities that every civilization has picked from in choosing a savior, according to Arnold Toynbee, British historian. They are philosopher king, sword, creative genius and spiritual savior.) As you present your lesson, incorporate the suggested questions into your presentation.

- With which of the four saviors would you equate humanism, secularism, materialism, New Age beliefs (include suggestions made by learners in the neighbor-nudge sharing time).
- Explain the deficiencies of each of the mentioned saviors with regard to what we believe to be salvation offered in Christ.
- How would you enlighten people who base their salvation on one of the four saviors?
- What are the reasons an individual would embrace one of the four saviors?

Move to the Conclusion by stating that during our discussion of the savior-substitutes, we have reaffirmed the completeness of redemption offered humankind through the perfect sacrifice of the Lord Jesus Christ, our Priest and King after the order of Melchizedek.

C ONCLUSION (5 minutes)

Say, *We have seen in our study that the Levitical priesthood was inadequate to bring salvation to the world. The necessity to first offer sacrifices for their own sins, the need for repeated sacrifices day after day, and the filling of an office when a priest died, were all abolished when Christ came on the scene. The eternal and sinless One need only offer Himself once to redeem humankind. And like Melchizedek, Christ lives forever to make intercession for us.*

Ask, *Have you received the only One who is able to save and redeem you? Christ is God's gift to the world and is available to everyone. But we must give our lives, as a gift, back to God. We must willingly accept Him.*

Invite learners to compose a paragraph on the reverse side of their outlines in which they state why they personally accepted Christ as their Savior, if they have already done so. If there are those who have not as yet received Him, invite them to list reasons why they have chosen another savior apart from Christ. Allow several minutes for writing.

Next, regain the attention of the group. As this study has shown plainly the claims of Christ as the only Savior of the world, be careful to give an opportunity to anyone who has not received Christ as his or her Savior to do so. Challenge believers to continue to keep Christ central in their lives, seeking Him to be their sufficiency and fulfillment instead of the beggar substitutes of this world.

Close the session in a corporate prayer, thanking God for the gift of His Son Jesus, who alone can offer us complete redemption.

Encourage members to read chapter 4 of the Regal book, *Christ B.C.*, which will assist them in their time of daily devotions. Each day's devotion is based on the theme of *redemption*.

FRIENDS' PRINCIPLES

A Witnessing Friend

The following is an excerpt taken from the Regal book **Won by One** *by Ron Rand:*

What would you say if a friend asked you, "Why are you a Christian? What does it mean to have faith in Jesus Christ?" Could you open the Bible and explain God's method of transforming sinners into children of God?

Could you explain in a simple, understandable way why Jesus died on the cross and how we can be forgiven for all our faults and live continually in a right relationship with God?

If you are terrified at the thought of explaining your Christian faith to someone else, you are not alone. Many people, both lay persons and clergy, do not know how to explain to someone what it means to have a personal relationship with Jesus Christ.

Most Christians have never experienced the joy of bringing their closest friends, their spouse or even their own children into a personal relationship with Christ.

The purpose of Mr. Rand's book, *Won by One,* is to provide a variety of simple, easy-to-learn methods for sharing the Christian faith with those closest to us. These methods are based on seven principles summarized by the acrostic FRIENDS:

F—Find common ground with your friends. Witness through your common interests (see 1 Cor. 9:19-23).

R—Reveal your faith to your friends. Witness through your life-style. Earn the right to speak to your friends (see Jas. 2:14-17).

I—Intercede for your friends. Witness through your prayers. Talk to God about your friends (see Col. 1:9).

E—Express your faith to your friends. Witness through your lips. Talk to your friends about God (see Rom. 10:17).

N—Nurture your friends through teaching, fellowship and prayer. Witness through your caring (see Acts 2:42).

D—Disciple your friends to be followers of Jesus Christ. Witness through your intentional involvement in your friends' spiritual formation and development (see Matt. 28:19,20).

S—Set your friends on a FRIENDS course with their friends. Witness by modeling how to "fish" for friends (see Mark 1:17).

The most effective opportunities for sharing the good news of Jesus Christ occur in personal relationships—Christians honoring and serving Christ where they live. When the FRIENDS principles are followed, seeds of the gospel find fertile soil in which to grow, mature and produce a harvest.

These principles provide a framework that allows friends to deal openly and honestly with the issues of believing in Jesus and becoming His follower.

Abraham and Isaac

SESSION VERSES

"The angel of the Lord called to Abraham from heaven. . .and said, 'I swear by myself, declares the Lord, that because you have done this and have not withheld your son, your only son, I will surely bless you.'" Genesis 22:15—17

"He who did not spare his own Son, but gave him up for us all—how will he not also, along with him, graciously give us all things?" Romans 8:32

SESSION FOCUS

Just as God provided a suitable sacrifice to take Isaac's place on the altar, so God provided His own Son, Jesus, through whom all of our needs, beginning with remission of sins, are met.

SESSION BASIS

Genesis 22:1-18; Hebrews 11:17-19

SESSION GOALS

Discover how the story of Abraham offering Isaac as a sacrifice to God is a type of Christ being offered by God for our sins. Then discuss how our needs are met through the sacrifice of Christ.

INSIGHTS FOR THE LEADER

The Significance of the Improbable

My graduate training contained a lot of study of statistics and probability. Our professors constantly asked us to calculate the chances of the occurrence of any human event or behavior. When we determined that behavior deviated from normal probability, we then had to explain its occurrence. Improbable behavior was seen as significant and therefore meaningful.

One evening a fellow student in a graduate seminar told of a highly improbable student he had taught in an American military academy. My colleague described a young man who was the elite member of his high school class. He could play football with the best of athletes and was eventually presented with the All-American Award for his athletic achievements in college. To be appointed to a military academy meant that he had the recommendations of his mentors who knew him well. They described him as highly gifted in a number of ways. He was an excellent musician. He could play several instruments with sufficient proficiency to qualify for a chair in the symphony orchestra. He was also socially adept. He was elected commandant of the corps—the academy's equivalent to

student body president. After four years of military school, he graduated as the top academic student. He was then selected as a Rhodes scholar and studied in England. A Rhodes scholarship is an honor only conferred upon the highest achievers. While in England he distinguished himself as a rugby player, a game he had not played much previously. Later, while on active military duty in Southeast Asia, he was decorated for valor while in combat. His outstanding record earned him a command post in the Pentagon. A national magazine recorded his story, and he became one of America's heroes.

When the story was finished, we were sitting in amazement at what we had just heard. One of my classmates exclaimed, "Who is this guy? God Himself?!" We were reasonably sure such was not the case. But such an improbable human being had to be regarded as significant. We began calculating the chances that another person with as many aptitudes could emerge in a country the size of the United States. Knowing the approximate rarity of several of the aptitudes this man possessed, we could do some reasonable guessing. We estimated, that only once in about

300 years could a person with this many superior gifts appear in an American university. No wonder his story got our undivided attention!

An Improbable God

When I apply my mathematical mind to the great events of Scripture, I find that God has made Himself known in most improbable ways. No man, however gifted, could duplicate what God has done. His actions, therefore, are significant and noteworthy.

The selection of Abraham to serve as a type of the salvation story is a significant, improbable act of God. In Genesis 12:2-4 we learn that Abraham is 75 years old when God first promised to make him the father of a great nation. What a time to set out to become a great nation!

But the improbabilities continue. Perhaps God had a sense of humor to tell Sarah, who "was past the age of childbearing" (18:11), that she was going to have a child. Furthermore, God allowed 25 years to pass from the time of His first promise in Genesis 12:4 to the birth of Isaac in Genesis 21 (see v. 5; also, Sarah was 90 years old when Isaac was born—see 17:17). Imagine how she felt during all those years. When she first heard the news in Genesis 18:10-12, she was so shocked she could only laugh. How ridiculous it seemed that an old woman was going to have a baby! And then she had to live with the story for so many years before its fulfillment. If they shared the news, people all around her were probably quite sure she was a bit daffy.

I have worked for a number of years in a retirement center, and I can just imagine one of our residents coming to breakfast one morning and announcing that the first baby ever born in our facility was on its way. There wouldn't be a believer in the dining room. Her announcement would be chalked up as a goofy symptom of senility!

But God is improbable. He does the unusual. His work is characterized by serendipity. No one duplicates God. He has no peer and no equal. Abraham in all his improbable experiences is encountering the nature and character of God. And true to that nature and character God provides Abraham with the promised son (see 21:1,2). According to God's command (see 17:19), Abraham named his son Isaac (see 21:3), which means "he laughs"—perhaps a reflection upon the improbability of his very existence.

At this point God's immediate promise of a son had been fulfilled. It seems that now nature could take charge and eventually the promised nation would be procreated. Yet that would be too predictable; it would push the evidence of God's sovereignty into the background. Perhaps that was why God commanded that Abraham's son of promise be sacrificed as a burnt offering on an altar on a particular mountain (see 22:1,2).

This act was to be a test of Abraham's faith (see v. 1). It was not to draw him to sin (God will not test a person in this way; see Jas. 1:13). Its purpose was to discover and prove his spiritual strength (see 1 Pet. 1:6,7). Prior to this testing Abraham had already realized his share of trials (see Gen. 13:5-9; 14:1-16; 16:1-6; 21:8-14). But this fact would not spare him from his most challenging test that was just ahead. In the same way our past testings do not earn us a reprieve. Like Abraham, we, too, can expect our share of trials in this life (see John 16:33; Acts 14:22).

Immediately Abraham responded to God's command. "Early the next morning Abraham got up and saddled his donkey. He took with him two of his servants and his son Isaac. When he had cut enough wood for the burnt offering, he set out for the place God had told him about" (Gen. 22:3). Abraham moved decisively and obediently. In spite of the apparent conflict between God's promise that was to be fulfilled in Isaac (see 17:19) and God's command to sacrifice Isaac, Abraham trusted that God knew what He was doing. Hebrews 11:19 states that "Abraham reasoned that God could raise the dead, and figuratively speaking, he did receive Isaac back from death."

I have two fine sons, both now adults and men of faith in Christ. They are a joy to me as a loving father. But I can scarcely imagine committing such an act as God commanded Abraham to carry out. It is absolutely beyond my comprehension. I am most certain that I could never bring myself to Abraham's position, to the point where he raised his knife over his beloved son of promise.

When my human senses react to the story, I respond in one of two ways: I conclude that either Jehovah is a just God beyond my comprehension, or that He is the most despotic and unfair being I can imagine. There is no middle ground. My lack of comprehension is the obvious answer to this dilemma. Yet Abraham did not rely on a common-sense analysis of God's command. God cannot be understood in this way. Abraham saw God's command to sacrifice Isaac through the eyes of faith, and not knowing the outcome reasoned that God's command would not cancel God's promise that would be fulfilled through Isaac (see Heb. 11:17-19).

Lessons and Types

The element that gives purpose to God's seemingly absurd command to sacrifice Isaac is Christ. When we see these events as typical of God's sacrifice of His only beloved Son (see John 3:16), our understanding of God's ways is enriched. It is my belief that God uses improbable ways such as types to make Himself known so that we will not rationalize that His actions are just another invention of the religious minds of groping people. No mere man could have truthfully claimed to be God in ways Christ has done (see Matt. 9:2—6; 26:63-65). The odds are beyond possibility. The venture into Christian faith is a way unlike any other because it is orchestrated by God, not man. To ultimately believe in Christ is an adventure and a continuing intellectual and spiritual experience different from any other you have had or ever will have.

Abraham's experience is evidence of the remarkable way in which God works. Let's consider how Abraham, an improbable progenitor, is chosen by God who then chooses to work in unsuspecting ways to accomplish an absolutely remarkable purpose. Abraham's experience is presented by God as an Old Testament prototype of a New Testament Christ. Let's enumerate the ways in which Abraham's story is like the Savior, as well as lessons we can learn from it.

1. Abraham was chosen by God (see Gen. 12:1-3; 15:1-5). It was God's move and God's choice. Just as God freely chose to provide His own Son, He freely chose Abraham to model the gift of salvation that would come through Christ (see Gen. 22:1,2; Rom. 5:8). God initiated His covenant with Abraham, and He initiates reconciliation with sinful man through His Son (2 Cor. 5:18,19).

In human relationships, we do just the opposite. If a breach of trust has come between one of us and another, it is assumed that the offending party will initiate the reconciliation. The offended one waits for the other to move. This is also the case with many other religions. Most religions believe that man has morally and spiritually offended their deities. These religions require some move on the part of the offender to initiate reconciliation. Thus we have the motive behind the sacrifices, rituals, prayer wheels, superstitions, self-abasement and atonement efforts. But in Christian faith, God does the unusual. He makes the move toward reconciliation. Romans 5:8 illustrates this by saying, "But God demonstrates his own love for us in this: While we were still sinners, Christ died for us." Many of us have thought of ourselves as hunting for God, only to discover that He has already found us and is waiting for our response of obedience to Him (see Luke 19:10).

2. Abraham received the promise from God, but he had to act upon it to receive the fulfillment of the promise. If Abraham had not willingly obeyed and acted upon God's command to sacrifice Isaac, God's promise to make Abraham's descendants into a great nation would still stand. But by obeying, Abraham was able to participate in and enjoy the fulfillment of that promise. God's personal response to Abraham's trust was, "I will surely bless you. . . .All nations on earth will be blessed, because you have obeyed me" (Gen. 22:17,18). Abraham also had the privilege of seeing Isaac married to Rebekah (see Gen. 24). Through this union, which was also engineered by God, Abraham had the assurance in his final days that God would continue to be faithful to His promise. We, too, have received a promise. It is the promise that God's grace, His sacrifice of Jesus for our sins, is adequate for our need for reconciliation with God (see John 1:12; Heb. 10:4-7,10). If we ignore the promise, God does not withdraw the opportunity to experience His grace, but we cut off ourselves from experiencing the fulfillment of His promise in our lives (see John 3:36).

As believers, God sometimes entreats us to part with an Isaac in our lives. It could be an item dear to our hearts, an interest that is taking too much of our time, or a sin that is depriving us of God's full blessing upon our lives. We must believe, as Abraham, that what God is requiring of us is only for our good.

3. Abraham and Sarah learned that God's agenda cannot be rushed or manipulated by human efforts. When the years began to pass without a son arriving, Sarah tried to help matters along. She arranged for Abraham to father a son by another woman, then—as was the custom—intended to claim that son as her own (see Gen. 16:1-4). But this was not the son of promise (see Gal. 4:22,23); this was the son resulting from human efforts to "build a family" (Gen. 16:2). In the same way, redemption cannot be provided by human effort (see Eph. 2:8,9). We cannot improve on God's sacrifice of Jesus and find salvation by any other means than through Christ (see Acts 4:12). No human effort, no matter how noble, will replace divine action. God is totally responsible for providing for our redemption. We cannot earn it by our efforts; we must accept it by submitting in repentance and faith to Jesus (see Acts 3:19; 16:31). Hebrews 12:2 describes Jesus as "the author and perfecter of our faith."

4. The place God directed Abraham to take Isaac is typical of Calvary—"called the Skull" (Luke 23:33)—

where God's own Son was sacrificed. We know that the mountain in Moriah (see Gen. 22:2) is in the near vicinity of Calvary. More important, Moriah, like Calvary, was a place of promise (see Gen. 22:16-18; John 3:16). And it was located in the heart of the land promised to Abraham's descendants (see 12:1,5-7). As such, the location is an indication that God fulfills His promises to His people. God provided a substitute for Isaac (see 22:13,14), and He provided a Lamb for us on Calvary that can remove all the moral and spiritual blemishes in our lives (see John 1:29). For anyone who accepts God's provision of Jesus, God regards that one as whole and clean, with the status of "son" (see Gal. 3:26). His own provision makes up for our lack of ability to call ourselves members of His family.

5. God's covenant with Abraham is a type of the new covenant He has made with us through Christ (see Heb. 10:15-18). A covenant is not a contract. A covenant is a promise that is valid and exists whether the other party or person keeps the agreement or not. In a contract, the agreement ends when one party does not honor the contract. Christians hopefully live in covenant with one another. Christian marriage is a covenant, not a contract. Church fellowship and membership is a covenant, not a contract. Thus God's covenant with Abraham is a model both for the relationship of Christ to His Church and a model for our relationships with each other.

Abraham and Isaac were living in covenant with each other in carrying out God's will. On the third day of their journey, they saw their destination in the distance (see Gen. 22:4). Leaving their servants behind (see v. 5), Scripture records, "The two of them went on together" (v. 6). Yet, how many Christians resort to contract relationships with each other, rather than living in covenant with each other?

6. We have seen that Abraham's story is a type of Christ in many ways. The type that you will be focusing on with your members describes how God's provision of a substitute for Isaac on the altar is like God's provision of His own Son on the cross. Abraham did not withhold his only son from God (see Gen. 22:10). God willingly gave His only Son for our sake (see John 3:16). God provided a ram as a substitute for Isaac on the altar: "Abraham looked up and there in a thicket he saw a ram caught by its horns. He went over and took the ram and sacrificed it as a burnt offering instead of his son" (Gen. 22:13). This is the first time that a substitutionary sacrifice is mentioned in Scripture. God also provided a substitute for us (see Rom.

8:32). Because of our sins a penalty must be paid. "For the wages of sin is death," states Romans 6:23. We deserve death as a result of our rebellion against God. But God, in His grace, provides a way for us to have our death sentence turned to a sentence of eternal life. Verse 23 also states how God has made this possible for us: "But the gift of God is eternal life in Christ Jesus our Lord." Because of His great love, God gave His Son to die on the cross in our place.

Related to this illustration of God's love is the illustration of how Abraham and Isaac's faith is typical of the person who puts his or her trust in God's promise of salvation through Christ. Faith in Christ trusts before it has full understanding. We trust in advance of understanding. In most western schools we believe only after we have experimented and figured things out. Not so with Abraham and Isaac. Isaac participated in the preparation of the offering of himself without knowing the personal consequences. He willingly carried the wood for the burnt offering (see Gen. 22:6), even as Christ would later carry His own Cross (see John 19:17). Isaac merely asked where the lamb was that was to be sacrificed (see Gen. 22:7). "God himself will provide the lamb for the burnt offering, my son," Abraham responded (v. 8). This answer was enough for Isaac. He trusted without fully understanding. There is much about the nature of God and His will that I don't understand. But to some degree I have learned to let my intellect catch up with my faith. When I am short of answers, I can say with confidence, "God will provide" no matter what my need may be. If I wait until all the evidence is in before I believe, I will never believe. So it was with Abraham and Isaac. They acted ahead of God's provision. When you and I do just that, we stop painting ourselves into intellectual corners limited to our meager mental aptitudes.

As well as providing for the remission of our sins through the sacrifice of His Son Jesus on the cross, God is also anxious to give us all things (see Rom. 8:32). God is for us (see v. 31), and He is ready to meet our needs and bless us beyond our comprehension (see Ps. 34:10; Eph. 3:19,20; Phil. 4:19).

We have seen that Abraham's experience is typical of many aspects of the salvation story fulfilled in the New Testament through Jesus' death. These parallels between the Old and New Testament are amazing. They can serve to strengthen the faith of your Bible students in a God who is actively pursuing a relationship of reconciliation and trust with each one and who is able and desirous of meeting their individual needs.

A B C PLAN FOR THE SESSION

Materials needed:
- Your Session 5 Leader's Guide Sheet;
- One copy of the Session 5 Lesson Outline for each group member;
- Small blank index cards for use in the Approach and large index cards or Post-it Notes, with Scripture references, for use in Step 3 of the Bible Exploration;
- Chalkboard or overhead projector with transparencies;
- Overhead projector transparency of the Session 5 Lesson Outline (optional).

Advance preparations:
- Read the information under "Advance preparations" for Session 6 in order to make a needed advance contact for next week's session;
- Invite a member to prepare a three-minute report on the Theory of Probability. An encyclopedia will supply the enlisted person with information concerning this subject.
- On 10 large index cards or Post-it Notes, list on each card one of the following groups of Scripture references: (A) Genesis 12:1-3; 15:1-5; Romans 5:8; 2 Corinthians 5:18,19; (B) Genesis 22:17,18; John 1:12; 3:36; (C) Genesis 16:1-5; 17:19-21; Galatians 4:22,23; Ephesians 2:8,9; (D) Genesis 22:2,15-18; Luke 23:33; Hebrews 10:9,10,16-18; (E) Genesis 22:2,10,12; John 3:16; (F) Genesis 22:13; Romans 8:32; (G) Genesis 22:6; John 19:17; (H) Genesis 22:9; Mark 15:1; (I) Genesis 22:5,12; Matthew 28:5,6; Hebrews 11:19.

A PPROACH (5 minutes)

Distribute a blank index card to everyone present. Say, *If God were to ask you to give up three things (item, person, activity) in your life, what three things would be the most difficult for you to give up?* Ask learners to write their answers on the index cards. After several moments of thinking and writing, invite several volunteers to share their answers.

Move to the Bible Exploration by saying, *In today's Bible study God called on a patriarch to give up something that was very dear to him. To the average person today, this would be a difficult and confusing request. However, one divine purpose in making such a request of the patriarch was to typify an event that would take place several centuries later and change the history of humankind.*

B IBLE EXPLORATION (45-50 minutes)

Step 1 (5-10 minutes): Distribute the Lesson Outline to learners. Encourage them to take notes on their outlines as the lesson is presented and discussion takes place. Do the same on the chalkboard or Lesson Outline transparency. Include further lesson material in the discussion from "Insights for the Leader" and ask the suggested questions.

Say, *Scripture is filled with improbable things that God has done. The setting for today's study includes*

just such an improbable act. However, before we get into our lesson, a member of the group will present a three-minute report on the Theory of Probability.
- Enlisted member presents report.
- Share the story about the young man who became a national hero from "Insight for the Leader" under the heading "The Significance of the Improbable." Also mention the estimate by Lloyd Alhem and his classmates of the probability of such a person appearing again in an American university.
- What are some improbable events in Scripture that God performed? (Responses could include: Crossing of the Red Sea—see Exod. 14:21,22; manna from heaven—see 16:13-16; water from a rock—see 17:6; the sun standing still—see Josh. 10:12-14; the virgin birth—see Luke 1:30,34-37; 2:5-7.)

Move to the next step by saying, *The setting of our lesson today involves a very improbable act carried out by God.* (If it was mentioned in the responses just given say, *You included this improbable event in your responses. Let's consider it, now, more fully.*)

Step 2 (15 minutes): Invite the group to open their Bibles to Genesis 12:1-4 and ask a learner to read aloud this passage. Point out that this promise was given to Abraham when he was 75 years old (see v. 4).

Share God's promise of a son to Abraham and Sarah by reading aloud Genesis 18:9-12. Say, *Another improbable event. But that promise was fulfilled 25 years after it was given to Abraham* (see 12:4; 21:5).

- Abraham was 100 years old and Sarah was 90 years old when Isaac was born (see 17:17, 21:5).
- Isaac means "he laughs."
- If such an event would happen today, how do you think it would be handled by the media? (Interviews by the major networks; newspaper coverage; offers to buy the story by tabloids and major book publishers; an offer for movie rights, etc.)

Say, *God, who does the unusual and who has no equal, continued to do the improbable by making a very difficult request of Abraham.*

Next, invite a member to read aloud Genesis 22:1,2.
- Explain the meaning of the word "tested" (see v. 1; also see Jas. 1:12,13; 1 Pet. 1:6,7).
- Point out that although Abraham had already experienced many testings (see Gen. 13:5-7; 14:1-16; 16:1-6; 21:8-14), this did not earn him a reprieve from facing the greatest test of his life. Add, *We, too, can expect our share of trials throughout our lifetime* (see John 16:33; Acts 14:22).
- Why does this request by God appear to be a contradiction? (God was asking Abraham to slay the son of promise—see Gen. 12:2; 17:19. Taking a life was not acceptable to God—see 4:8-15. Also, this was a heathen practice that God detested—see Deut. 18:10-13.)
- Say, *In the Approach to our study, you listed three things that would be difficult for you to part with should God request you do so. Had you been Abraham, what would your feelings have been regarding God's request?* After receiving several responses, read aloud Hebrews 11:19.

Next, invite a member to read aloud Genesis 22:3-5.
- What can we learn from verse 3? (Abraham's immediate obedience to God's command; his faith in God's promise—see Heb. 11:8.)
- Why do you think the servants were left behind? (Perhaps in the event they would interfere or intervene.) What can we learn from this?

Step 3 (10 minutes): On the chalkboard or overhead transparency, write the following two questions and Scripture references:

1. The story of Abraham offering Isaac as a sacrifice is a type of what New Testament event? Genesis 22:1,2; John 19:16-18.

2. What other types and lessons do you see in the details of the story?

Next, announce to the group that they will work alone to answer Question 1. Invite everyone to quickly review the listed Scripture passages (Genesis 22:1,2; John 19:16-18) to discover the answer. After several minutes ask for the answer from anyone in the group.

Question 1: The story of Abraham offering Isaac as a sacrifice is a type of God offering His Son, Jesus, on the cross as a sacrifice for our sins.

Follow the individual research by telling the group that Question 2 will be answered in small group research. Move members into groups of four to six. Appoint group leaders and give each leader an index card listing Scripture references. Direct the groups to first research the Scripture references listed on their respective index cards to discover the answers to Question 2 that is listed on the board. (Encourage learners to make notes on their Lesson Outlines.)

Step 4 (15 minutes): Regather into larger group and ask for responses from group leaders. As there are many types and lessons to be seen and learned from the story of Abraham offering Isaac as a sacrifice, be sure to include the following types and lessons in the discussion (see "Insights for the Leader" under the heading "Lessons and Types" for additional information):

Question 2:

A. God initiated His covenant with Abraham (see Gen. 12:1-3; 15:1-5), and He initiated reconciliation with sinful humankind through His Son (see Rom. 5:8; 2 Cor. 5:18,19). God took the first step.

  How do the efforts toward reconciliation that are made in Christianity differ from the efforts made in other religions? How do they differ in our relationships with one another?

B. Abraham had to act upon the promise to receive its fulfillment (see Gen. 22:17,18). We must accept the promise of redemption through Christ in order to be saved (see John 1:12; 3:36).

C. Salvation is a gift of God through His Son, Jesus, and not a result of human effort (see Eph. 2:8,9). God's promise to Abraham was to be fulfilled through Isaac, the son of promise, and not through Ishmael, the result of human effort (see Gen. 16:1-5; 17:19-21; Gal. 4:22,23).

  How have the results of Sarah's human effort continued to be a problem to this day? (Conflict between the Arabs and Israelies in the Middle East.)

D. Moriah (see Gen. 22:2) and Calvary ("called the Skull"—see Luke 23:33) are in the same vicinity, and both are places of promise (see Gen. 22:15-18; Heb. 10:9,10,16-18).

  How does a covenant differ from a contract? Which one should be in effect in a marriage?

Church fellowship and membership? Between Christians?

E. Other Old Testament types include: Abraham gave his only son (see Gen. 22:2,10,12)—God gave His only Son (see John 3:16).

F. God provided a ram as a substitute (see Gen. 22:13)—God provided His Son as a substitute for us (see John 1:29; Rom. 8:32).

G. Isaac carried the wood (see Gen. 22:6)—Christ bore His cross (see John 19:17).

H. Isaac was bound (see Gen. 22:9)—Christ also was bound (see Mark 15:1).

I. Isaac, whose life was spared (see Gen. 22:5,12), was a type not only of the death of Christ, but of Christ's resurrection (see Matt. 28:5,6; Heb. 11:19).

Discuss Isaac's apparent willingness to be offered as a sacrifice.

- Do you believe Isaac allowed himself to be bound without a struggle? Why or why not? What do his actions teach us?

Review the truths of Genesis 22:8,13,14 and Romans 8:32.

- Share that one of God's names in the Old Testament is *Jehovah-jirah*, which means "The Lord will provide." How can this term be applied to all our needs, even though in Genesis 22:8,13,14 it specifically refers to God's provision of His Son as the sacrifice for our sins? (Refer members to Eph. 3:8,19,20; Phil. 4:19.)

Point out that the remission of our sins through Christ's death is only the beginning of God's abundant provision for those who believe on His Son. *Jehovah-jirah* is rightly applied to all things, but we must not forget God's greatest provision—His Son Jesus as a sacrifice for our sins.

Move to the Conclusion by saying, *We have seen many types of God's love and of Christ's death in today's study. The beautiful truth that God took the first step to reconcile sinful humankind to Himself only points up God's immense love for the world.*

C ONCLUSION (5 minutes)

We can never offer a substitute to pay the penalty for our sins outside of Christ. Christ is God's gift to us—God's provision of a substitute in our place. And through Christ all our needs are met; He is our sufficiency! Ask, *Have you been trying, through human effort, to offer your own substitute to God for your salvation? Or have you endeavored to meet the needs in your life through your own schemes or by manipulation, instead of receiving from God's provision through His Son?* Allow time for thinking.

Next, encourage everyone to form a large circle or several small circles for closing prayer. Invite several learners in each circle to pray sentence prayers, thanking God for His gift of Christ and asking His help to receive of His abundant provision made available through His Son. Should there be those in your group who have not accepted Christ as their Savior, always be prepared to give them an opportunity to do so.

Encourage members to read chapter 5 of the Regal book, *Christ B.C.*, which will assist them in their time of daily devotions. Each day's devotion is based on the theme of *provision*.

Joseph

SESSION VERSES

"Joseph said to his brothers. . . .'God sent me ahead of you to preserve for you a remnant on earth and to save your lives by a great deliverance.'" Genesis 45:4,7

"For God so loved the world that he gave his one and only Son, that whoever believes in him shall not perish but have eternal life. For God did not send his Son into the world to condemn the world, but to save the world through him." John 3:16,17

SESSION FOCUS

Joseph, like Jesus, was obedient to God because Joseph trusted that God was using his circumstances to accomplish God's holy purposes. Today we can be obedient to God with the confidence that God will use our daily experiences to fulfill His ultimate goals.

SESSION BASIS

Genesis 37,39—50

SESSION GOAL

Discover lessons that can be learned from Joseph and Christ's examples of obedience.

INSIGHTS FOR THE LEADER

One of the most fascinating stories in the Old Testament is that of Joseph found in Genesis 37,39—50. It is a picture of the grace of God operating in spite of and because of circumstances. Nothing in that day could thwart the will of God in carrying out His purpose in this segment of history.

Joseph and his brothers each had personality traits that would cause trouble for them. Yet God used the conflicts between these personalities to accomplish His will.

You can gain some insight into these traits by reading about Jacob's last hours when he described his sons and gave his last blessing and prophetic declarations concerning their posterity in Genesis chapter 49. This record of Jacob's blessings and prophetic declarations display the diversity of personalities and character traits that existed among his sons.

The story of Joseph illustrates the explosive, unpredictable combination this melting pot of personalities made.

Joseph, the Improbable Survivor

But like the story of Abraham and Isaac, we learn again about the improbability of God who likes to do impossible things. God takes the unstable environment in which Jacob's family members coexisted and gave glory to His name as sovereign Lord. The key in this story that illustrates God's sovereignty over circumstances was Joseph.

In some ways Joseph seems to have been an unlikely candidate to survive all that befell him. Genesis 37:3 says that Jacob "loved Joseph more than any of his other sons, because he had been born to him in his old age." Joseph was the favorite son, with 10 jealous older brothers hating him (see v. 4). He was doted upon by his father and given a "richly ornamented robe" (v. 3) as a sign of his father's favor, a sign that evoked spite from his brothers. He was also the son of Jacob's favorite wife, Rachel (see 29:30; 30:22-24). We see in chapter 37 of Genesis that Joseph had the habit of irritating his brothers and even his father by sharing his dreams with them (see vv. 5-10). In each of the dreams Joseph shared, he was placed in a position of authority over them. As a result of Joseph's tactlessness, his brothers hated him all the more, and he even earned a rebuke by his father (see vv. 8-10). Although Joseph's dreams accurately described his future, his lack of tact in sharing his dreams simply made his home situation more unstable.

One day Joseph was sent by his father to see how the sheep tending was going (see vv. 12-14). Unfortunately he was wearing the special coat given him by his father Jacob (see v. 23). His brothers saw him coming in the distance, and by the time Joseph reached them, they had formulated a plan to get rid of him (see v. 18). They grabbed him, threw him into a cistern and, when a caravan came by, they sold him as a slave (see vv. 24-28). The brothers led Jacob to believe that Joseph had been killed by wild animals, and Jacob mourned Joseph for many days (see vv. 20,31-34).

Now what are the chances that a protected child, beloved by his father and mother, can survive as a slave sold to travelers going to a strange land? Humanly speaking we can doubt that any chance exists at all—at least not without leaving deep emotional scars. Yet we learn through Joseph's many experiences in Egypt that besides surviving, he prospered materially as well as emotionally and spiritually.

Upon reaching Egypt Joseph was sold to Potiphar, one of Pharaoh's officials. Many would be paralyzed by the adjustment to slavery. But, "The Lord was with Joseph and he prospered" (Gen. 39:2). Verse 3 says that Potiphar recognized that the Lord was with Joseph, giving him success. As a result, Potiphar put Joseph "in charge of his household, and he entrusted to his care everything he owned" (v. 4).

While in Potiphar's service, Joseph was repeatedly tempted sexually by Potiphar's wife (see vv. 7,10). Joseph honored God through his actions and words by resisting her and acknowledging her proposition as a sin against God (see v. 9). Joseph's obedience to God finally landed him in the king's prison—a risk he was willing to take to remain faithful to God (see vv. 11-20). At this time Joseph's circumstances seemed grim. But God used—engineered—Joseph's circumstances in several ways. First, by removing Joseph from Potiphar's service, God opened the way for greater responsibility and blessing for Joseph in the service of Pharaoh. Word of Joseph's gift of interpreting dreams, which he exercised in prison, would earn him an audience with Pharaoh (see 41:9-14). After Joseph interpreted a dream of Pharaoh's concerning a coming fam-

ine in the land, Pharaoh installed Joseph as second-in-command over Egypt (see vv. 15-40).

Through Joseph's new position God provided a way for the preservation of the lives of those who came to Egypt for help during the predicted famine (see v. 57). Among these people would be Joseph's brothers (see 42:1-3). God used Joseph's position and the famine to set the scene for reconciliation and reunion between Joseph and his family.

Eventually, Joseph's family would join him in Egypt (see 46:5,6). During these years we see Joseph as the leader of the family. His high level of maturity is evident when we look at the conversation between Joseph and his brothers following Jacob's death. The brothers were still worrying that Joseph would someday take revenge upon them for their past cruelty. They had not matured to a point that they could accept Joseph's forgiveness and see God's working in all of their circumstances. "When Joseph's brothers saw that their father was dead, they said, 'What if Joseph holds a grudge against us and pays us back for all the wrongs we did to him?'" (50:15). The brothers sent word to Joseph, expressing their fear (see v. 16,17). Joseph's response to his brothers illustrates his maturity (see vv. 17, 19-21). Joseph spoke to them as a parent would calm the fears of a child.

What made the difference? Why did Joseph prosper in so many ways instead of perishing? The answer lies in Joseph's faithfulness to God and trust in God's sovereignty. Joseph knew, at each step in his life, that God would use his circumstances to accomplish His divine purposes. We find an illustration of this when Joseph was reunited with his brothers: "God sent me ahead of you to preserve for you a remnant on earth and to save your lives by a great deliverance" (45:7).

Joseph as a Type of Christ

It is in Joseph's obedience to God and God's engineering of Joseph's circumstances that we also see created for us a type of Christ. Joseph is probably the most Christlike of any Old Testament personality. The parallels between the two are too numerous to go into detail on all points, but as you spend time studying Joseph with your group members, encourage them to suggest as many points of comparison that they can.

Let's survey several of these points:

1. Joseph was much loved by his father and lived in fellowship and a position of honor with his father in Hebron (see Gen. 37:3). Jesus was beloved by God the Father and lived in heaven in a position of honor and

fellowship with God before being sent to earth (see Matt. 3:17; John 17:5).

2. Joseph declared openly his brothers' sins, then he shared his dreams declaring his future exalted position over them. In response, he received hate from his brothers (see Gen. 37:2,5-9). Jesus testified against the sins of men and declared His future exaltation. In response, many of His listeners hated Him (see Matt. 24:30,31; Mark 8:31; John 8:31-58; 15:18).

3. Joseph's brothers plotted against him and sold him for 20 pieces of silver (see Gen. 37:19-28). The Jewish leaders plotted against Jesus (see Luke 20:19). Judas betrayed Jesus to them for 30 pieces of silver (see Matt. 26:14-16).

4. While serving in Potiphar's house, Joseph did not yield to the temptation of Potiphar's wife, but was obedient to God (see Gen. 39:7,8). He responded to her by saying, "How then could I do such a wicked thing and sin against God?" (v. 9). Jesus was tempted by Satan in the wilderness. Jesus did not yield to Satan but, rather, used God's Word in resisting him (see Matt. 4:1-11).

5. After Joseph was wrongly accused by Potiphar's wife, he was thrown into a dungeon where he counseled two other prisoners. One prisoner was hung, the other was spared (see Gen. 39:19,20; 40:1-22). Jesus was falsely accused and then nailed to a cross between two criminals. One thief cursed Christ and died, the other gained eternal life through Christ (see Matt. 26:59-65; Luke 23:32,33,39-43).

6. Joseph was raised from the dungeon of death by the king and was given all power in Egypt. Throughout his time in the dungeon, Joseph was helped by God and Joseph prospered (see Gen. 39:20-23; 41:14,41-43). Jesus was raised from the dead by the Lord Almighty, the God of creation. He was then given all power in heaven and earth (see Matt. 28:18; Acts 2:24; Eph. 1:19-23).

7. Joseph was acknowledged as savior and ruler over the Egyptians (see Gen. 47:25). Jesus is acknowledged as Savior and Lord by His followers and will some day be acknowledged as Lord by all people (see Matt. 16:15,16; Luke 24:50-53; Acts 1:10,11; 2:36; Phil. 2:9-11).

8. Joseph sustained the physical lives of the people who came to him for food from all the world (see Gen. 41:55-57). Jesus provides eternal life to all humankind who will come to Him in faith (see John 3:16; Acts 4:12; 1 John 5:11,12).

9. When Joseph's brothers admitted their sin against him and humbled themselves before him, Joseph forgave them and joyfully received them back into brotherly relationship (see Gen. 44:16—45:15). To all who receive Christ and confess their sins to Him, He provides forgiveness. We then become members of His family (see John 20:17; 1 John 1:9).

Such a parallel between Joseph and Christ could only be from God's hand. God took a pampered, immature boy—whose heart was obedient—and through difficult circumstances, prosperity and testings of his faith produced a mature example of Christlikeness. Genesis tells us repeatedly that God was with Joseph (see Gen. 39:2,21,23). Knowing this, Joseph faithfully and obediently trusted God (see Gen. 39:9; 40:8; 41:16,28,32,38,51,52; 43:23; 45:5-8)—even when Joseph's circumstances called for discouragement.

God Uses Our Obedience and Circumstances

We also are called to be like Christ. Jesus said, "I have set you an example that you should do as I have done for you" (John 13:15; also refer to 1 Pet. 2:21). This is an easy task when we clearly sense God's presence with us and when we see prosperity in our circumstances. It is a different thing to obey and submit to God when sacrifice is involved. Consider the anguish of Christ as He prayed in the garden of Gethsemane: "And being in anguish, he prayed more earnestly, and his sweat was like drops of blood falling to the ground" (Luke 22:44). Christ knew the cost of obedience. He willingly endured the pain of crucifixion in order to be obedient to God and fulfill God's purpose for the world. "Let us fix our eyes on Jesus, the author and perfecter of our faith, who for the joy set before him endured the cross, scorning its shame, and sat down at the right hand of the throne of God" (Heb. 12:2). Unlike Christ, we do not often know where God is leading us in bringing about His will in our lives. We, like Joseph during his days in prison, need to realize God is with us and then allow Him to work through us—even when we can't see an end to our difficulties. Joseph didn't sit around waiting for times to get better. He acted, he was productive, and he trusted. His life is a positive model and example to us.

Each of us plays a unique part in God's purposes. If we respond to God with obedience, we will see Him use us as examples to others. The Thessalonian Christians were commended by Paul for such obedience (see 1 Thess. 1:6,7). As Christians we can walk through life blind to God's working around us, or as the Thessalonian Christians, we can, through our obedience, find joy in seeing God use us.

A B C PLAN FOR THE SESSION

Materials needed:
- Your Session 6 Leader's Guide Sheet;
- One copy of the Session 6 Lesson Outline for each group member;
- Chalkboard or overhead projector with transparencies;
- Overhead projector transparency of the Session 6 Lesson Outline (optional).

Advance preparations:
- Enlist two group members to deliver a five-minute presentation each on the life of Joseph. Assign the first person the events in Joseph's life as recorded in Genesis 37,39—41:40 and the second person the events as recorded in Genesis 41:41—50:26. Both persons should allow for the reading aloud of selected key verses of Scripture by group members during their presentations. Scripture references should be written on Post-it Notes and distributed to volunteers at the beginning of the session.
- If Optional Step 5 is used, invite a person in your group or church to share concerning a trial he or she experienced. The experience should be one in which God was able to fulfill His purposes in this person's life and/or plans that affected the lives of others because of this person's obedience to God throughout the trial.

A PPROACH (5 minutes)

Distribute Post-it Notes with references to volunteers who are to be prepared to read aloud key Scriptures during Step 1 of the Bible Exploration.

Write on the chalkboard or overhead transparency the following two categories:

1. A person who refused to obey God's Word and as a result has not enjoyed the fulfillment of God's purposes for his or her life.

2. A person who obeyed God's Word and as a result has realized or is realizing the fulfillment of God's purposes for his or her life.

Invite members present to consider the two categories on the board and to think of a person they know (not necessarily a personal acquaintance) who fits each category. Next, ask them to form clusters of three persons and share briefly how the two people they know, or know of, fit the categories listed.

Move to the Bible Exploration by saying, *Obedience is the key to realizing God's purposes for our lives. Our Bible lesson today will reveal two important examples of persons who were obedient to God and how, as a result, God's purposes were realized in their lives.*

B IBLE EXPLORATION
(40-50 minutes)

Step 1 (10-12 minutes): Say, *Those of us who went to church regularly as children or in later years are probably very familiar with the story concerning the life of the first person we'll study about today who demonstrated obedience to God. The accounts of the beautiful coat given to him by his father, of his dreams and of his being sold into slavery by his brothers are favorite Bible narratives. Since he is such an important and interesting character, entire studies have been done on his life. He was one of Jacob's 12 sons. His name was Joseph, and today we'll focus on how his life and obedience typified or foreshadowed Christ.*

Next say, *To refresh our memories of the major events in Joseph's life, several members will present a brief summary of the life of Joseph. If you are not familiar with Joseph, this summary will serve to give you an overview of his life.* Mention that after the presentations, time will be given for discussion of specific events that underscore Joseph's obedience to God.

Encourage learners to open their Bibles to Genesis, chapter 37 where the story of Joseph begins. Volunteers are to be ready to read aloud assigned Scripture verses.

Two members present summary of Joseph's life from the following chapters:

Genesis 37,39—41:40
    A. Joseph's early years (see 37:1-11).
    B. Joseph sent on an errand (see vv. 12-36).
    C. Joseph as a slave (see 39—41:40).

Genesis 41:41—50:26
    A. Joseph becomes ruler of Egypt (see 41:41-57).

B. Joseph deals with his brothers (see 42—45).

C. Joseph united with his father (see 46:29,30).

D. Joseph's family settles in Egypt (see 47—50).

Step 2 (10 minutes): Ask the following questions regarding key points in Joseph's life that relate to his obedience directly or indirectly to God. (As limited time will make it impossible to include all the suggested questions in the discussion, select those that cover areas most needed by your group members.)

● What special relationship is revealed in Genesis 37:3? (Joseph was loved and favored by his father.)

● What negative attitudes were evidenced in Jacob's home and what do you think caused these attitudes? (See vv. 3-11. The negative attitudes were favoritism, hate and jealousy. The favoritism shown Joseph by his father was probably caused by the fact that Joseph was the son of the wife that Jacob loved most; see Gen. 29:30. The hate and jealousy on the part of Joseph's older brothers probably stemmed from the favoritism shown Joseph, his bad report about them to their father and his dreams that showed him receiving homage from his family.)

● What does Joseph's response to Jacob's command in Genesis 37:13 reveal about Joseph? (He was an obedient son.)

● What did jealousy lead to in the lives of Joseph's brothers? (see vv. 18-28).

● What lessons of obedience can be learned from Genesis 39:1-12? (Joseph refused to sin against God by participating in adultery, and he demonstrated loyalty to his master; see Exod. 20:14; Ps. 51:4. He remained a faithful steward; see 1 Cor. 4:2. Although Joseph had no peer support as he was tested daily, he proved that it is possible to overcome temptation; see Gen. 39:10; 1 Cor. 10:13.)

● What lessons can be learned from Joseph's continued obedience to God as seen in Genesis 39:11-20? (Sometimes obedience is costly; it is not always easy; see Matt. 5:11,12; Luke 9:23,24; John 15:20.)

● After the trauma of being sold as a slave and taken away from his family and homeland, do you think Joseph found his experience of being sent to prison easier or more difficult? Why? Do continued trials tend to strengthen or weaken us? What makes the difference?

● Are Christians today paying a price because they are taking a stand against unrighteousness or are refusing to compromise their beliefs as Joseph did? If so, in what ways?

● How do you react when you are unjustly treated and accused?

● Joseph asked the cupbearer to remember him to Pharaoh when the cupbearer was released from prison (see 40:14). It was two years before the cupbearer remembered Joseph's request (see 40:23; 41:1,9-12). How would the cupbearer's memory lapse have affected you had you been Joseph? Do you think Joseph became bitter? Why or why not? (It appears that he continued to offer faithful service to the prison warden knowing that ultimately he was serving God.)

● What do we learn about Joseph from his reply to Pharaoh in Genesis 41:16?

● Why did Joseph deal with his brothers as he did, instead of lovingly demonstrating love and forgiveness at their first encounter? (He wanted to know if they had repented of their sins against him and their father, Jacob. Joseph was now in a position to cause them to face up to their evil actions.)

● Because Joseph had established a pattern of obedience to God, we can assume that Joseph was acting in obedience to biblical principles when he confronted his brothers regarding their sin (see Gal. 2:11-16). What risks were taken by Joseph in doing this? (The possibility of the death of his father upon receiving the news that Simeon was kept in Egypt in order to guarantee that Benjamin would accompany his brothers on their return trip to Egypt; see Gen. 42:33-36. Mention that there are always risks one must take in obeying God; see Esther 4:15,16).

● Why did Joseph's brothers become fearful upon their father's death as seen in Genesis 50:15? What can we learn from Joseph's response as seen in verses 19-21?

Move to the next step by saying, *God's purposes in allowing Joseph to be sold by his brothers and taken to Egypt were not completely fulfilled when he became ruler over Egypt and his family moved to that land. There was a greater fulfillment in all that Joseph experienced. We will see this greater fulfillment and greater example of obedience in the life of Christ.*

Step 3 (15-20 minutes): Distribute a Lesson Outline to everyone. Next, move members into groups of four to six and appoint group leaders. Direct members' attention to the first point on the outline—"Joseph's Life and Obedience—A Type of Christ." Assign several groups of Scripture references (*A* through *I*) to each group. Tell them that they are to research the references they have been given to discover how Joseph was a type of Christ and how Christ was the fulfillment of the type. Allow eight minutes for research.

When time is up, regather into larger group and ask for responses from each group leader. Joseph as a type of Christ includes the following:

A. Joseph was loved by his father (see Gen. 37:3).
B. Joseph declared his brother's sins and was hated for it. He shared his dreams declaring his future exaltation (see Gen. 37:2,5-9).
C. Joseph's brothers plotted against him and sold him for 20 pieces of silver (see Gen. 37:19-28).
D. Joseph did not yield to temptation (see Gen. 39:7-10).
E. Joseph was wrongly accused by Potiphar's wife and thrown into a prison where he counseled two other prisoners. One prisoner was hung, the other, spared (see Gen. 39:19,20; 40:1-22).
F. Joseph was raised from the dungeon of death by the king and given all power in Egypt (see Gen. 41:14,41-43).
G. Joseph became as "savior" and ruler over his brothers and the Egyptians (see Gen. 42:1,2,6,25; 47:25).
H. Joseph saved the physical lives of those who came to Egypt from all the world for food (see Gen. 41:55-57).
I. Joseph's brothers, admitting their sin and humbling themselves before him, were received back into brotherly fellowship (see Gen. 44:16—45:14).

As the responses are given, ask how Christ's obedience to the Father is evidenced. Say, *While Joseph is probably the most Christlike of any of the Old Testament personalities, Christ is the ultimate example of obedience for us.*

Step 4 (5-8 minutes): Continue by saying, *We have considered how Joseph and Christ were both obedient to God and thus fulfilled God's plans and purposes for their lives.* Direct everyone's attention to the second point on the Lesson Outline—"Results of Obedience." Add, *Team up with a partner and reflect on today's study of the life of Joseph and on your research of Christ's life. Then, working together, determine three results of Joseph's obedience to God and three results of Christ's obedience to the Father.*

List the results on your outlines.

After about four minutes, regain the attention of the group and ask for feedback from members.

Optional Step 5 (5 minutes): Group or church member shares how, because of his or her obedience to God during a time of trial or testing, God was able to fulfill His purposes in this member's life.

C ONCLUSION (5 minutes)

Joseph's obedience to God was demonstrated by his submission to his father and his faithful service to Potiphar, the prison warden and to Pharaoh. As a result, God used Joseph to fulfill His plan to save the lives of people in time of famine and, especially, the lives of Jacob and his family who would become a great nation in the land of Egypt (see Gen. 46:3). A greater example of obedience was Christ who came to do His Father's will (see Heb. 10:7). He demonstrated His determination to fulfill that will when He prayed in the garden of Gethsemane, "Not as I will, but as you will" (Matt. 26:39). Christ completed God's purpose for His life on earth when He cried on the cross, "It is finished" (John 19:30).

Say, *God has a plan and purpose for the testings that we experience in our lives. As we continue to obey His Word and determine to persevere in the face of misunderstanding, God's seeming silence, emotional hurts and possibly physical abuse, we will one day realize God's ultimate goals and plans for our lives. And we will receive the "crown of life" that he has promised to those who persevere under trial and who stand the test* (see Jas. 1:12).

Close the session by encouraging everyone to join with another person for a brief time of prayer. Members may want to share with their prayer partners concerning struggles they are experiencing as they go through a time of testing.

Encourage members to read chapter 6 of the Regal book, *Christ B.C.,* which will assist them in their time of daily devotions. Each day's devotion is based on the theme of *obedience.*

The Passover

SESSION VERSES

"I am the Lord. The blood will be a sign for you on the houses where you are; and when I see the blood, I will pass over you. No destructive plague will touch you when I strike Egypt." Exodus 12:12,13

"For Christ, our Passover lamb, has been sacrificed." 1 Corinthians 5:7

SESSION FOCUS

Just as the Passover reminded the Israelites of how God delivered them from bondage, the shed blood of Jesus reminds us that He can deliver us from the bondage of sin.

SESSION BASIS

Exodus 12,13

SESSION GOAL

Examine from Scripture how Christ is seen in the Passover, and discuss how we may be delivered from the bondage of sin.

INSIGHTS FOR THE LEADER

Exodus 12 and 13 give an account of God instructing Moses and Aaron about how to celebrate the Feast of Passover and its adjoining feast, the Feast of Unleavened Bread. This event was a momentous occasion in Israel's history. It was revolutionary, in a political sense, and defining and prescribing in a spiritual sense. It marked the birth of a special nation and a faith experience.

Nations build their self-identities out of such events. The United States is no exception. It was born in the revolution of 1776 and is remembered on the Fourth of July every year. In 1976 the citizens of the United States celebrated their nation's two hundredth birthday. Every conceivable reminder of its history was brought out. The ringing of bells, orations in hundreds of city parks and fireworks in hundreds of stadiums across America reminded citizens of who they were and how their country came to be. Subsequent events have further defined the identity of the United States. The tragic deaths of presidents and social heroes, the glorious joys of the end of two world wars and the celebration of technological achievements such as landing men on the moon have become epochs that define this nation and create patterns for its future national life. For Israel, Passover was an event of similar character and meaning.

Israel's Bondage in Egypt

Israel entered Egypt as a family of 70 members (see Gen. 46:27) whose descendants lived there 430 years (see Exod. 12:40). When liberation came "six hundred thousand men on foot, besides women and children" (v. 37), plus "many other people" left Egypt (vv. 37,38). During their years in Egypt, the children of Israel went from landowners in the best part of Goshen (Gen. 47:6,11) to slaves under a harsh king. The king said, "Come, we must deal shrewdly with them or they will become even more numerous and, if war breaks out, will join our enemies, fight against us and leave the country" (Exod. 1:10). The king oppressed the Israelites with forced labor (see v. 11), and "the Egyptians used them ruthlessly" (v. 14). In addition, the king decreed that "Every boy that is born you must throw into the Nile, but let every girl live" (v. 22). It is in this context that we read in Exodus, chapter 2 about the birth of Moses. To save his life, Moses' mother placed him in a basket and put the basket in the reeds near the bank of the Nile (see vv. 3,4). Baby Moses was discovered by Pharaoh's daughter, and he became her son and a member of Pharaoh's household (see vv. 5-10). But Moses never forgot his Hebrew heritage. In trying to protect "one of his own people" (v. 11), Moses killed an Egyptian and had to flee to Midian to escape Pharaoh's wrath (see vv. 12,15). In the meantime "the Israelites groaned in their slavery and cried out, and their cry for help because of their slavery went up to God. God heard their groaning and he remembered his covenant with Abraham, with Isaac and with Jacob" (vv. 23,24). God acted on His promise and sent Moses to Egypt to bring His deliverance to the Israelites (see Gen. 15:15,16; Exod. 3:15-17).

The First Passover

The key to the children of Israel's freedom came through the event called the Passover. Exodus 12:1-30 describes in detail what the Passover is and God's instructions to the Israelites. First, God told the Israelites, through Moses and his brother Aaron, to prepare a meal. Specific instructions were given as to what was to be prepared, how it was to be prepared and how it was to be eaten. Then God described what action He would take during the first Passover. "On that same night I will pass through Egypt and strike down every firstborn—both men and animals—and I will bring judgment on all the gods of Egypt. I am the Lord. The blood will be a sign for you on the houses where you are; and when I see the blood, I will pass over you" (vv. 12,13). Thus the term "Passover" gets it meaning. All these symbols and the annual reenactment of the Passover meal would stand as a reminder to the Jewish people that it was God who had delivered them.

Those 430 difficult years in Egypt, culminating in the Passover, served to develop a singular identity among the Israelites. They had preserved in their memory a record of God's covenant with Abraham, Isaac and Jacob, and when in distress they knew to turn to God for help. They also remembered the oath Joseph made his brothers take for that time when God would fulfill His covenant (see Gen. 50:25; Exod. 13:19). In speaking of the covenant Joseph said, "God will surely come to your aid and take you up out of this land to the land he promised on oath to Abraham, Isaac and Jacob" (Gen. 50:24).

Creating an Accurate Memory

Again we see the work of sovereign God doing an impossible thing—from a human point of view. No human effort could have developed and preserved the clear spiritual and cultural identity of Israel while her people were enslaved in a hostile environment. Memories are strange and changeable unless they are actively preserved by deliberate and authentic means. Otherwise they lose their impact upon us, and our abilities to generate life and meaning from them dies. We have a tendency to modify memories to remove pain. As time goes by we prefer to recall the pleasant events and suppress the uncomfortable ones. For what other reason do the good old days seem to be so good? Why is it that the older a man gets the faster he could run as a boy? We modify our own histories to improve our self-images, to protect ourselves from pain or embarrassment. Sins of the past seem so much more innocent. An event as terrible as the Holocaust in Europe in which millions of Jews were exterminated is already being denied by some. Yet we are scarcely a half-century away from the deed. Many Jewish survivors struggle to keep an accurate memory of the horrors of the tragedy alive, saying in essence, "We must never forget. We must remember so that such cruelty is not allowed to happen again." Historians agree that unless we remember difficult days and experiences, we are likely to repeat them.

Israel also had a capacity for memory modification. In the days following the Exodus of Israel from Egypt, the difficulties of desert living came upon them and the people began to grumble, asking to be returned to captivity where at least they would not starve to death (see Exod. 16:2,3). Knowing the tendency of the human heart and mind to "forget," God deliberately provided Israel with a celebration that would accurately preserve the impact of the Passover. Exodus 12:14 says that the Passover "is a day you are to commemorate; for the generations to come you shall celebrate it as a festival to the Lord—a lasting ordinance." God was preserving an accurate memory for the Israelites of how He brought them out of Egypt. This feast would become so special and unique that years later children who had no memory of life in Egypt would ask their parents, "What does this ceremony mean to you?" (v. 26). The parents were instructed to reply, "It is the Passover sacrifice to the Lord, who passed over the houses of the Israelites in Egypt and spared our homes when he struck down the Egyptians" (v. 27; also see 13:14-16).

Seeing Christ in the Passover

As we have seen, the Feasts of Passover and Unleavened Bread have served as a reminder of an historical event. It also stands as a reminder of the coming Redeemer. This historic celebration would make it possible for those faithful Jews who would later meet the Savior to identify Him as the fulfillment of God's promise established long ago. They would be able to say, "Aha! That's what this is all about. I see it now! Christ is indeed the Passover Lamb!" It also serves as a reminder to all Christians of the life and death of Christ. A careful examination of the Passover Feast reveals symbols and meaning that apply to the faith experience of the Christian.

The feast was to be on the tenth day of the month of Abib, which is equivalent to our March or April. This month marked a new beginning in the Israelites' calendar year (see Exod. 12:1-3; 13:3-5). Previously the Jews celebrated the new year in the month of Tishri, which began in what is equivalent to our September or October. The new year would now have a spiritual meaning, indicating the beginning of a new life, free from bondage. This freedom is indicative of the Christian's freedom from the bondage of sin (see Rom. 6:6,7).

Freedom is a wonderful experience. The Israelites had longed for freedom and had cried out to God in their misery (see Exod. 3:7). God gave them a new beginning, asking only that they show their trust in Him through obedience to His commands (see 19:3-8). Through Jesus we also can receive a new beginning (see 2 Cor. 5:17). All Jesus asks is that we submit our lives to Him (see Matt. 16:24). Now these requirements of obedience are not qualifications to be met before freedom can be granted. Rather, they are God's way of helping us avoid our human tendency to enslave ourselves again to that from which He has freed us (see Mark 4:2-20). At first the people of Israel obediently followed Moses out of Egypt. God's deliverance made sense to them because this freedom was what they had prayed for. But when God's actions went beyond their rational understanding, and their new freedom appeared to be a liability rather than a benefit (see Exod. 14:10-12), they were tempted to return to their old life of slavery.

This experience illustrates a principle for us: Freedom is often more anxiety-provoking than slavery. We sometimes see it in the salvation experience of people today. When they are first set free by Christ, they enjoy the headiness of the new experience. But when their faith is challenged and the emotional high has worn off, they are soon tempted to return to their old ways (see Mark 4:16,17). Change is stressful and uncomfortable. Some are not willing to pay the price of change—even to gain the valuable benefits of freedom in Christ. Or instead of enslaving themselves to their old ways, they set up a new realm of enslavement. They make a ritual, a legal system or institution out of their experience, structuring it into predictable, rationally defined compartments. They do this rather than live out the rich meaning and adventure of freedom in Christ. The Pharisees and Sadducees of Jesus' time chose to remain in their religious systems, which embraced both ritualism and legalism, rather than accept the liberty that Christ offered (see Matt. 16:6,12; 23:1-4; Luke 7:29,30). Grace experienced can be an unnerving adventure. It unpins us from the past and forces us into new, unknown areas of faith. But the past, with all its bondages, can provide an unhealthy security that tempts us from time to time.

Exodus 12:3,5 says that a lamb without defect was to be selected from the sheep or goats and prepared for the Passover meal. This is clearly typical of Christ. First Corinthians 5:7 states: "For Christ, our Passover lamb, has been sacrificed." God's insistence that the lamb be perfect—without defect—shows us that we cannot save ourselves from death. We are imperfect and therefore unable to provide for our own salvation (see Rom. 3:10,23). Christ, on the other hand, is perfect and the only one through whom salvation from death is possible (see John 1:29; 2 Cor. 5:15; 1 Peter 1:18,19). Ten thousand times ten thousand angels and the elders in heaven acknowledge the worthiness of Jesus, "the Lamb, who was slain" (Rev. 5:12).

Exodus 12:7 tells us that after the Passover lamb was sacrificed by the Israelites, its blood was to be put on the sides and tops of the doorframes of their homes. The spilling of the blood symbolized the blood of Jesus that was later spilled as the final sacrifice for sin (see Heb. 9:14). During the Last Supper, which was held during the preparation of the Passover (see Matt. 26:17), Jesus "took the cup, gave thanks and offered it to them, saying, 'Drink from it, all of you. This is my blood of the covenant, which is poured out for many for the forgiveness of sins'" (vv. 27,28). The spilling of blood meant death had come. Death is the physical and spiritual consequence for all that is imperfect or sinful in the world (see Gen. 3:17-19; Rom. 3:23; 6:23). Death is the logical conclusion for imperfect people who try to play God in their own lives and reject God's provision for them. Death is the result of humankind's best and noblest efforts to save themselves apart from the righteousness of God.

Deliverance from sin can only come through death. Death is the price God demands for sin (see Rom. 6:23). Since we are unable on our own to be all that God wants us to be—like Himself—only God can make up for our shortfall. On our own that shortfall leads to spiritual death. But God, in mercy, sent His Son to do the dying for us (see John 3:16). Jesus took the consequence for us, sparing us from eternal death (see Rom. 5:8,9). When the Israelites put blood on their doorframes, they experienced firsthand God's grace in sparing their homes from death (see Exod. 12:7-13,29,30). They depended completely on God's provision for their safety. In a greater way, when we apply Jesus' blood to our lives, He saves us from spiritual death (see Heb. 9:14).

We see that the lamb was to be roasted whole, as was the practice of wandering shepherds, and eaten with bitter herbs and unleavened bread (see Exod 12:8,9). The bitter herbs were a reminder to Israel that their experience in Egypt had been bitter (see 1:14). It was important that their memory of the bitterness of Egypt remain accurate and sharp, not softened with the passage of time. Otherwise the impact of the greatness of God's deliverance would become blurred. This was a memory not to be celebrated with cake and ice cream. In like manner, it is important for the Christian to have an accurate picture of the bitterness of life without Christ. Paul referred to his former way of life as a persecutor of Christians in order to show the authenticity of his new life in Christ (see Gal. 1:11-24). Our best witness to others is often the change they see in our lives—both in words and example. Remembering what we were before Christ redeemed us, is also motivation to continue to grow in Him rather than return to our old way of living.

A dominant symbol in the Passover was that of unleavened bread. It illustrated haste because it told of the suddenness with which the Exodus of the children of Israel from Egypt would occur (see Exod. 12:33,34,39). The response of the people of Israel to the command to leave was to be instantaneous. No unnecessary activities were to stand in the way of their escape. This brings to mind Jesus' Parable of the Great Banquet (see Luke 14:15-24). Everything was ready and the servants were sent out to call the guests. Verse 18 says, "They all alike began to make excuses." The master responded to the guests saying, "Go out to the roads and country lanes and make them come in, so that my house will be full. I tell you, not one of those men who were invited will get a taste of my banquet" (vv. 23,24). Jesus was referring to those who would put off committing their lives to Him. One day He will come again to gather the faithful to His wedding feast. For those who are not ready to respond, it will be too late.

The Israelites were told, "Remove the yeast from your houses" (Exod. 12:15). Unleavened bread is a symbol of the body of Christ (see Matt. 26:17,26). It is also a symbol of that from which worldly and evil things have been purged. The New Testament describes why we need to remove evil from our lives: "Don't you know that a little yeast works through the whole batch of dough? Get rid of the old yeast that you may be a new batch without yeast—as you really are. For Christ, our Passover lamb, has been sacrificed. Therefore let us keep the Festival, not with the old yeast, the yeast of malice and wickedness, but with bread without yeast, the bread of sincerity and truth" (1 Cor. 5:6-8). In this passage Paul is telling the Corinthians to remove from their fellowship an immoral man who, if tolerated, will permeate their whole fellowship like yeast permeates a loaf of bread (see vv. 1,5,6).

This passage from 1 Corinthians has a broader application. It tells us that our separation from evil and from a worldly way of life is to be total and complete. The ways of the world and God's spiritual economy are not compatible.

When we separate ourselves *from* evil and a worldly life-style and *into* God's redemptive experience through the blood of Christ, the Passover Lamb, we can then be committed to a lifetime of grace and spiritual development (see 1 Peter 1:13-16; 2:1-3,9-12). And we can then fulfill our call to take the gospel to the world (see Matt. 28:18-20), which will put us in touch with those who are lost in sin and their evil ways. But the most significant and primary areas of our lives need to be kept pure so that we can avoid falling into evil (see 1 Cor. 10:12). This means that our closest friendships need to support our beliefs, our priorities need to provide time for fellowship with the Lord and His people, our work needs to be done with a clear conscience, our homes need to be places where we honor God, and our finances and possessions need to be controlled by God.

Another interesting aspect of the Passover meal is the dress code. "This is how you are to eat it: with your cloak tucked into your belt, your sandals on your feet and your staff in your hand. Eat it in haste; it is the Lord's Passover" (Exod. 12:11). This relates to the point made earlier that, when the Lord calls, we need to be ready to respond instantly (see Gen. 24:52-58; John 4:35). But it also brings to mind another aspect of the Christian life. The life of the believer is a journey, not a territorial occupancy. We are to go through life "riding loose in the saddle" and rejoicing in travel and the places God leads us, knowing that home is yet to come in the presence of God (see Heb. 11:13-16). A look at Jesus' call to His disciples illustrates both an immediate response to His call and a shared ministry (see Matt 4:18-20). When He called Peter and Andrew (two fishermen) to follow Him, "At once they left their nets and followed him" (v. 20). Because of their immediate response, they were able to share in the greatest experience a person could possibly have—being part of God's fulfillment of His promises of old (see Isa. 61:1,2; Luke 4:14-21). Those who are interested in the Christian life but refuse to put Jesus' command to follow Him above other people and responsibilities, will miss the chance to participate in affecting change in the world for Jesus' sake (see Matt. 10:37-39; Luke 9:61,62). Giving Jesus' call priority has a high cost, but the benefits are beyond measure (see Mark 10:29,30).

The Passover is a reminder of God's deliverance of the people of Israel from Egypt. It is also a reminder that only through the shedding of the blood of Jesus is deliverance from sin and spiritual death possible. As Jesus celebrated the Passover with His disciples, He established a reminder for us that is based on the symbols of the Passover. This reminder, the Last Supper, redefines the Passover for us in order to create an accurate memory of what Christ did in order to provide for our freedom. During the Passover meal Jesus "took bread, gave thanks and broke it, and gave it to them, saying, 'This is my body given for you; do this in remembrance of me'" (Luke 22:19). The unleavened bread becomes a symbol of Christ's substitutionary sacrifice on the cross for our sins. It is "given for you," and you are to remember its significance. The cup used in the Passover Feast became Jesus' "blood, which is poured out for you" (v. 20). And of course, Christ Himself represented the Passover lamb about to be sacrificed. Within hours He was on the cross, shedding His blood to make our redemption possible.

[A] [B] [C] PLAN FOR THE SESSION

Materials needed:
- Your Session 7 Leader's Guide Sheet;
- One copy of the Session 7 Lesson Outline for each group member;
- Chalkboard or overhead projector with transparencies;
- Small index cards or Post-it Notes with Scripture references;
- Overhead projector transparency of assignments and Scripture references (optional);
- Overhead projector transparency of the Session 7 Lesson Outline (optional).

Advance preparations:
- Read the information under "Advance preparations" for Session 8 in order to make an advance assignment for next week's session;
- Consider holding a Seder (Jewish ceremonial dinner held on the first evening of the Passover) at a time other than the session hour. The organization Jews for Jesus makes "Christ in the Passover" missionaries available for this purpose. Also, a "Passover Seder Packet" is available from them. Call (415) 555-1212 or write Jews for Jesus at 60 Haight St., San Francisco, CA. 94102.
- Write on the chalkboard or overhead projector transparency the three assignments and Scripture references listed under Step 2 of the Bible Exploration;
- On small index cards or Post-it Notes, write one of the following groups of Scripture references: (1) Romans 6:6,7; 2 Corinthians 5:17; (2) John 1:29; 1 Peter 1:19; (3) Matthew 26:27,28; Hebrews 9:12,22; (4) Romans 5:8,9; 6:23; Hebrews 9:14; (5) Galatians 1:13,14; (6) Matthew 26:26; 1 Corinthians 5:7,8.

[A] PPROACH (5 minutes):

Ask, *In your opinion, what is the most important historical event in the history of our country?* Allow several moments for thinking and then ask for responses. Jot down on the chalkboard or overhead transparency group members' suggestions. Mention that nations build their self-identities out of important events in their histories.

Move to the Bible Exploration by saying, *In today's Bible study we will focus on what was probably the most important event in Israel's Old Testament history. We will then examine how this event was a type of a later event that changed the course of history.*

B IBLE EXPLORATION
(45—50 minutes)

Step 1 (10 minutes): Ask, *What do you remember about the reasons for the move of Jacob and his children to the land of Egypt?* (see Gen. 37,39—47). Allow time for responses. Next say, *This appears to be a nice environment for building a great nation. But God had other plans for His people that did not include their remaining in Egypt. Let's discover what these plans were.*

Move everyone into groups of four to six members. Distribute the Lesson Outline to learners, and encourage them to take notes on their outlines throughout the lesson. (Do the same on the chalkboard or Lesson Outline transparency.) Appoint group leaders and direct learners' attention to the assignments and Scripture references listed on the chalkboard or overhead transparency. Give one of the assignments to each group. Members, working together in their respective groups, research the Scriptures to complete the assignments. Allow groups eight minutes for research and working.

Step 2 (15 minutes): When time is up regather the small groups into the larger group and ask for feedback from each group's leader. Incorporate the following additional information, given under each assignment, into the feedback and discussion. Also include lesson material from "Insights for the Leader."

Assignment 1: Describe the situation in Egypt for the children of Israel, and give the reasons why this situation existed. Also tell how the people responded to these conditions.
Exodus 1; 2:1-8,23,24; Hebrews 11:23-27

● What lessons can we learn from Exodus 2:23,24? (God is mindful of the oppressed and those who suffer. They do not go unnoticed; see Pss. 12:5; 72:14. And He keeps His Word; what He has said He will do, He will surely do.)

● What steps did the parents of Moses take that went beyond crying out in their distress? (refer to Exod. 2:1-3; Heb. 11:23). What can we learn from their actions? (Likewise, we can believe for the impossible regarding our situations and that God is greater than all the powers that may be working against us. We need not fear; see Matt. 19:26; 1 John 4:4. Also, our faith often requires action; see Jas. 2:17.)

● How did Moses demonstrate that he identified with the sufferings of his people? (Refer to Exod. 2:11-15;

Heb. 11:24-27. He was willing to take the risk of going to their rescue. And He chose not to remain in the king's family with its many worldly advantages but, instead, fled to Midian where he embraced desert living; see Exod. 2:10,15. Moses saw the greater picture—the future reign of Christ.) What does his example teach us? (When we put Christ and His purposes first in our lives, it will cost us something and may include times of suffering. But God's plan will prevail; see Matt. 5:11,12.)

Assignment 2: Describe the meal and event of the Passover.
Exodus 12:1-13,21-23,29-50

● What were the three elements of the Passover meal and what were their distinctions? (Refer to vv. 3,5,8,9,46. The lamb was to be without defect—perfect, roasted whole and not a bone broken; the herbs were to be bitter; and the bread was to be made without yeast.)

● In Old Testament times, why was it required that the lamb be perfect? (It was a symbol of the truth that only a perfect sacrifice could pay the debt for sin, required by a holy God, and also bring deliverance from sin's bondage; see Heb. 9:13-15. Mention that the fulfillment of this type will be discussed later in the lesson.)

● Share that the bitter herbs (see Exod. 12:8) represented their bitter life in Egypt (see 1:14).

● Why was the bread unleavened? (Refer to 12:31,33,39. They had to leave Egypt in haste.) What can we learn from their immediate obedience to God's command to leave Egypt? (Share concerning Rebekah's willingness to go immediately with Abraham's servant to Canaan; see Gen. 24. Also mention Peter and Andrew's immediate response to Christ's call to follow Him; see Matt. 4:18-20.)

● Of what does Israel's dress code speak? (Refer to Exod. 12:11. A readiness to respond quickly to God's commands. It suggests, as well, that we are travelers and not permanent residents in this world; see Heb 11:13-16.) What are some of the things in this life that can prove to be obstacles to our readiness to obey God's Word? (Refer to the excuses that were made in the Parable of the Great Banquet; see Luke 14:15-24. Also refer to the reasons that are given in the Parable of the Sower as to why people fail to continue to respond to God's Word; see Mark 4:1-20.)

Assignment 3: What special instructions did God give the people through Moses regarding the day and event of the Passover? What was the purpose of these instructions?

Exodus 12:14-20,24-27; 13:1-16
- The children of Israel had lived in Egypt for 430 years when deliverance came (see 12:40).
- The passover developed a singular identity among the Israelites. Its commemoration would include the Feasts of Passover and Unleavened Bread (see 12:17,26).
- The feast was to be on the tenth day of the month of Abib (our March or April) and was to mark a new beginning in their calendar year (see 12:1-3; 13:4). They previously celebrated the new year in the month of Tishri (our September or October).
- They remembered Joseph's words about God's covenant with Abraham, Isaac and Jacob and their return one day to the land of Canaan (see Gen. 50:24,25; Exod. 12:25; 13:19).
- Discuss the importance of preserving memories by deliberate and authentic means (see "Insights for the Leader" under the heading "Creating an Accurate Memory"). Why is it sometimes easy to forget the painful events in our past and remember only the pleasant ones? Share how quickly the Israelites would forget their suffering in Egypt (see Exod. 16:2,3). Why do you think many Jewish survivors of the Holocaust in Europe struggle to keep an accurate memory of this event alive?

Move to Step 3 by saying, *We have examined Israel's suffering in the land of Egypt and the greatest event, perhaps, in their Old Testament history—the Passover. And we learned that they were to commemorate the Passover yearly so that they would remember its significance.* Add that we will now consider how all these events were a type of the greatest happening in history, as well as the effect it should have in the life of the believer.

Step 3 (20 minutes): Distribute the small index cards or Post-it Notes listing Scripture references to volunteers. Ask them to look up the references in their Bibles and be prepared to read aloud their assigned Scriptures at the requested time. List on the chalkboard or overhead transparency the following headings as they are discussed:

A. Day of the Feast—Tenth Day of Abib
Exodus 12:1-3
This represented a new beginning for the Children of Israel. (Member reads aloud Rom. 6:6,7; 2 Cor. 5:17.) Discuss the principle of freedom as presented in "Insights for the Leader" under the heading "Seeing Christ in the Passover." How is freedom more anxiety-provoking than slavery or bondage? How was this seen in the religious systems of Jesus' day? (see Matt. 16:6; 23:1-4; Luke 7:29,30). How is it seen in the religious systems of today? Can Christians be affected by this principle? How? (Instead of enjoying freedom in Christ, they are controlled by a set of rules and regulations—legalism—as were the Galatians; see Gal. 3:1-5; 5:1.)

B. A Perfect Lamb
Exodus 12:3,5
The animal without defect represented perfection. (Member reads aloud John 1:29; 1 Peter 1:19.)

C. Blood on the Doorframes
Exodus 12:7
The blood symbolized a sacrifice offered as a substitute—a life laid down for another. (Member reads aloud Matt. 26:27,28; Heb. 9:12,22.)

D. Deliverance Through Death
Exodus 12:5,6,12,13
The animal that was slain brought life and deliverance to Israel's firstborn, instead of death. (Member reads aloud Rom. 5:8,9; 6:23; Heb. 9:14.)

E. Bitter Herbs
Exodus 12:8
This was a reminder to the Israelites of the bitter life they experienced in Egypt.
(Member reads aloud Gal. 1:13,14.)
Share more fully concerning Paul's previous life and how he counted his past life as rubbish (see Phil. 3:3-8; Gal. 1:11-14). Even so, we should remember what our life was without Christ and have no desire to return to our former ways.

F. Unleavened Bread
Exodus 12:15,34,39
The Israelites left Egypt in haste so they did not have time to add yeast to the dough. In later years yeast was used as a symbol of sin (see Mark 8:15; Luke 12:1).
(Member reads aloud Matt. 26:26; 1 Cor. 5:7,8.)
The unleavened bread represented Christ's body that was without sin (see 2 Cor. 5:21).

Even as the bread was without leaven, believers, too, need to rid themselves of sin in their lives (see Rom. 6:13; 1 Peter 1:13-16; 2:1-3,9,12). The greatest example a new Christian can be to an unbeliever is for the unbeliever to see a change in the new Christian's life—from a sinful life-style to a godly one. Godliness should be the hallmark of a Christian.

What are some of the areas in a believer's life where godliness should be in evidence? (In relationships with family members and friends, members of the opposite sex, work and/or school relationships, business dealings, etc.)

How may a believer deal with a particular sin or

bondage in his or her life? (see Jas. 4:7; 5:16; 1 John 4:4; also special counseling from the ministerial staff or other qualified personnel may be needed.)

Optional Step 4 (5 minutes): Invite volunteers in the group to give brief testimonies of their conversion experiences. Some may wish to share of specific bondages that they were delivered from and the new freedom they found in Christ.

C ONCLUSION (5 minutes)

As Jesus celebrated the Passover with His disciples, He established a reminder—the Last Supper—for us that is based on the symbols of the Passover (see Luke 22:7-20). The unleavened bread, representing His broken body and substitutionary death for us (see v. 19), and the cup, representing His shed blood (see v. 20), became symbols to us of the ultimate sacrifice He made as the Passover Lamb (see 1 Cor. 5:7). His death on the cross made possible humankind's deliverance from the bondage of sin (see Heb. 9:14).

The children of Israel were delivered from bondage in Egypt so that they could return to Canaan where they would become a great nation and be used by God to fulfill His plans and purposes. Likewise, God has delivered us from sin by the shed blood of His Son Jesus so that we might be free to serve Him and bring praises to His name (see Matt. 5:16; 1 Peter 2:9).

Ask, *Are you still in bondage to sin, or are you free to fulfill God's designs and purposes for your life? If you have not realized His deliverance, you may by believing that Christ's shed blood can cleanse you from all unrighteousness. Confess your sin to Him today and accept His forgiveness* (see Rom. 10:9,10; 1 John 1:9). *Let Him free you to a new life in Him* (see 2 Cor. 5:17). Encourage any believer who is struggling with sin in his or her life to confess the sin to God.

Close the session in small group prayer. Encourage learners, who may be comfortable in doing so, to share their areas of need with one another so that they may agree in prayer concerning these needs. Also invite those who may need special prayer or counseling concerning any bondage of sin in their lives to meet with you following the session. You may want to invite several others in the group to join you in special prayer for any who may respond to your invitation. Also arrange for special counseling with a member of the ministerial staff if it appears this is needed.

Encourage members to read chapter 7 of the Regal book, *Christ B.C.*, which will assist them in their time of daily devotions. Each day's devotion is based on the theme of *remembrance*.

PRAYER DIARY IDEA

Requests and Answers

Make prayer a more meaningful part of your session time together. On a blank sheet of paper, create a prayer diary for use in the early part of your group's study sessions. Title the sheet, "Prayer Diary." Form four columns on the page, titling the first two columns, "Requests" and "Date," respectively. Title the third and fourth columns, "Answers" and "Date," respectively ("Date" columns require less space).

During your group's fellowship time, give members an opportunity to share aloud their ongoing or new prayer requests. Briefly record new requests on the "Prayer Diary" as well as that day's date. Pray as a group each week as requests are received, and make it a point to ask group members to share any answers to prayer they can report on. Look back over your list, and then post the date a prayer request was answered. (Note unmentioned prayers from past weeks and inquire if there was an answer or if the prayer should be continued.) The number of prayer requests that are answered will amaze the members as reports are received back each week. This will result in the strengthening of learners' faith to believe God for some impossible situations that they, perhaps, felt were beyond hope. In addition, your class will be drawn closer together as they share concerns, comfort one another, pray together for each other's needs and rejoice in God's faithfulness.

The Tabernacle Curtain

SESSION VERSES

"The Lord spoke to Moses after the death of the two sons of Aaron who died when they approached the Lord. The Lord said to Moses: 'Tell your brother Aaron not to come whenever he chooses into the Most Holy Place behind the curtain in front of the atonement cover on the ark, or else he will die, because I appear in the cloud over the atonement cover.'" Leviticus 16:1,2

"Therefore, brothers, since we have confidence to enter the Most Holy Place by the blood of Jesus, by a new and living way opened for us through the curtain, that is, his body...let us draw near to God with a sincere heart in full assurance of faith." Hebrews 10:19,20,22

SESSION FOCUS

The Tabernacle curtain separated an unholy people from God's holy presence. Christ's death on the cross caused the curtain to be torn in two, symbolizing that through Christ sinners are made acceptable to God.

SESSION BASIS

Exodus 25—27; Leviticus 16:1-34

SESSION GOAL

Research why and how sinners can be acceptable to God.

INSIGHTS FOR THE LEADER

The Tabernacle and Jewish Life

The Tabernacle was the center of Israel's religious experience. In this most revered place God designed a meeting with His people. The Tabernacle with its holy places, priesthood and sacrifices became the most complete type of Christ in the Old Testament. The structure of the building itself illustrates the condition of the relationship between God and man. The Tabernacle marked the beginning of a defined relationship between God and His people. It was a relationship where God dwelt in the midst of His chosen people, but stood separate and inaccessible, except in limited ways, because of man's sinfulness. Later an event at the Temple in Jerusalem would mark the end of this limited relationship and the establishment of a new order between Christ and His Church (see Matt.

27:50,51). Let's examine some of the facets of the Tabernacle structure and see how the drama of redemption is typed out from Israel and for us.

From the size and structure of the Tabernacle, it is apparent that it was more than a place of worship. It contained a courtyard where large numbers of people could gather (see Exod. 27:9). It was the center of the life of the people. As the Israelites traveled about the Sinai peninsula, they carried the Tabernacle with them. (This was possible since the construction was similar to a tent.) Whenever they stopped to make camp, the tribes of Israel took their assigned places on all four sides of the Tabernacle (see Num. 2:1-34). In Exodus 40:1-3 we see that the Tabernacle is the resting place for the ark, which held the stone tablets upon which were carved the Ten Commandments or "the Testimony" (see 25:21). This indicates that the Tabernacle served a judicial function. The Tabernacle is also called "the Tent of Meeting" (27:21), indicating that it was the place where God communicated with the people (see 29:42,43). It was a place where information and news on a variety of issues was disseminated. When traveling instructions were given to the tribes moving from the Sinai desert, they were delivered at the site of the Tabernacle (see Num. 10:1-7). When a public health issue existed, God delivered instructions to Moses and the Israelites from the Tabernacle as to how to handle the problem (see 5:1-4). From this we learn that all of Israel's life was Tabernacle-related, or rather God-related. There was no distinction or separation between the religious order and the conduct of civic affairs. God was at work in all of Israel's doings, and all issues had spiritual significance.

A Freewill Offering

Exodus 25—27 relates the detailed instructions given by God for the construction of the Tabernacle. The first of the instructions is God's request to take a voluntary offering from the people. "You are to receive the offering for me from each man whose heart prompts him to give" (25:2). These offerings, many of which came from articles taken from the Egyptians (see 12:35,36), would make the Tabernacle a place of value and magnificence. Gold, silver and bronze, three colors of yarn and fine linen, goat hair, animal skins, wood, oil, spices and gems were offered by the people (see 25:3-7).

A principle is illustrated by this giving. We participate in God's divine plans through our willing offerings. Israel did not buy any favor by her gifts because God did not require any payment from His people. It was a gift exchange, illustrating a principle of grace. As Christ gave Himself for us (see John 10:17,18), so we give ourselves freely to Him. As Jesus sent His disciples out to minister, He reminded them, "Freely you have received, freely give" (Matt. 10:8). We serve Christ as our gift of thanks for His free gift of salvation to us (see Eph. 2:8,9). Because our reconciliation experience with God is not a bartered exchange or the result of bargaining, God is indebted to no one, and no human payment can obligate God's favor.

God's instructions for the construction of the Tabernacle were very specific and full of meaning. The Tabernacle consisted of three main sections. The outer court was where the sacrifices were offered. It contained the bronze altar upon which the sacrifices and offerings were made and the bronze basin where the priests would purify their bodies by washing their hands and feet (see Exod. 27:1,2; 30:17-21; 40:6). The outer court measured 150 by 75 feet (45x22.5-m; see 27:18). The inner court, or Tent of Meeting, was divided into two parts: the Holy Place and the Most Holy Place, or Holy of Holies (see 26:33,34). The Holy Place probably measured 30 by 15 feet (9x4.5-m), and the Most Holy Place was a perfect square measuring 15 feet (4.5-m) on each side. Only the high priest could enter the Most Holy Place, and then only once a year in order to offer a sacrifice for the atonement of the people. Special preparation was required by the high priest for this annual venture into the Most Holy Place. If he did not enter properly prepared, his actions were grievous to God and the high priest would die (see Lev. 16:1-34). It is said that the priest wore a rope tied to his ankle as he entered. In case he made an error or was improperly prepared and died, he could be pulled out by the priests in the Holy Place.

The Curtain for the Most Holy Place

Each of the main sections of the Tabernacle—the outer court, the Holy Place and the Most Holy Place—were separated by curtains (see Exod. 26:31-33,36; 38:18). These curtains and the structure of the Tabernacle tell us of the distance that existed between God and His people. The spiritual condition of the people prevented their complete access to God (refer to Gen. 3:8-10,22-24).

All members of the Israelite community could pass through the outer curtain from outside the Tabernacle and into the outer court surrounding the Tent of Meeting. This curtain had an inner lining of "finely twisted linen and blue, purple and scarlet yarn, with cherubim worked into them by a skilled craftsman" (Exod. 26:1). From this lining the people could recognize that they were in the house of the Lord of heaven. The outside was covered by a curtain of goat hair (see v. 7), then a covering of ram skins dyed red, and then by a covering made from the hides of sea cows (see v. 14). This curtain gives us a picture of Jesus' earthly body. The lining, woven with pictures of cherubim, illustrated His divine nature (see Isa. 9:6; John 1:1). The covering of skins reminds us that He was clothed in the flesh of man (see John 1:14).

The second curtain divided the outer court of the Tabernacle from the Holy Place, or the entrance to the Tent of Meeting (see Exod. 26:36). The priests appointed by God entered through this curtain (Heb. 9:6). The curtain was made of "blue, purple and scarlet yarn and finely twisted linen—the work of an embroiderer" (Exod. 26:36). In Jewish tradition, blue is associated with heaven, purple is associated with royalty and scarlet is associated with earthly glory. This curtain gives us a picture of Jesus' character. John 3:13 says, "No one has ever gone into heaven except the one who came from heaven—the Son of Man." This testifies to Jesus' divinity (blue). Revelation 19:12,13,16 describes Jesus' royalty (purple): "His eyes are like blazing fire, and on his head are many crowns. . . .He is dressed in a robe dipped in blood, and his name is the Word of God. . . .On his robe and on his thigh he has this name written: King of kings and Lord of lords." In cruel mockery the Roman soldiers, prior to Jesus' crucifixion, "put a purple robe on him, then twisted together a crown of thorns and set it on him. And they began to call out to him, 'Hail, king of the Jews!'. . . .And when they had mocked him, they took off the purple robe and put his own clothes on him. Then they led him out to crucify him" (Mark 15:17,18,20). The robe was probably the military cloak of one of the soldiers, and it was used to sarcastically mock Jesus' royalty. The symbolism of scarlet as representing Jesus' earthly glory is obvious when we consider His great work of redemption through the shedding of His blood (see Heb. 9:12; 1 Pet. 1:18,19). The finely twined linen tells us of Jesus' purity and righteousness (see 2 Cor. 5:21; Heb. 7:26). In Old Testament times linen was reserved for holy purposes such as the clothing of priests and the Tabernacle curtains (see Exod. 26:1; Lev. 16:4,32). In Revelation we see that fine linen was associated with the righteous or the saints (see Rev. 19:8).

The third and most significant curtain divided the Holy Place from the Most Holy Place (see Exod. 26:31-33). God's presence appeared over the atonement cover of the Ark of the Covenant that was placed behind this curtain (see Exod. 25:22; Lev. 16:2). This curtain was like the curtain at the entrance to the Tent of Meeting or the Holy Place, except that it was embroidered with cherubim. The cherubim indicate the entrance to the throne of God (see Pss. 80:1; 99:1). They symbolize protection of that which is sacred or off-limits (see Gen. 3:24; Ezek. 28:14). The curtain was tightly woven and probably very heavy. It stood as a barrier between God and His people, and access to the Most Holy Place was extremely limited, even to Aaron, the high priest. "The Lord spoke to Moses after the death of the two sons of Aaron who died when they approached the Lord. The Lord said to Moses: 'Tell your brother Aaron not to come whenever he chooses into the Most Holy Place behind the curtain in front of the atonement cover on the ark, or else he will die,

because I appear in the cloud over the atonement cover'" (Lev. 16:1,2; also see Heb. 9:7). Aaron was to follow strict guidelines for cleansing before approaching the Most Holy Place, and he was to approach only on God's terms (see Lev. 16:3-14). The reason for this lies in the fact that a holy and perfect God cannot tolerate the presence of imperfect sinful men. Aaron's cleansing would temporarily make him ceremonially perfect so that he could make a sin offering on the part of the people (see vv. 11-16). This process of cleansing would have to be repeated every year before the annual entrance into God's presence could be made (see v. 34).

Jesus as the Curtain

The New Testament book of Hebrews tells us that cleansing was symbolic of One who would come who was perfect and who could offer a sacrifice once and for all for the sins of the people. "When Christ came as high priest of the good things that are already here, he went through the greater and more perfect tabernacle that is not man-made, that is to say, not a part of this creation. He did not enter by means of the blood of goats and calves; but he entered the Most Holy Place once for all by his own blood, having obtained eternal redemption" (9:11,12).

Imperfect people need a provision of spiritual purity to gain access to God. People today who have not recognized their need try to make their own way to the Divine. But they cannot bridge the distance between themselves and God by their own goodness or the cleverness of their ideas about God (see Isa. 64:6,7).

This is why it was necessary for God to graphically present His separativeness and holiness in the construction of the Tabernacle. It is why the curtain covering the Most Holy Place is such a beautiful type of Christ. It is through Him that access to God is possible. This is symbolized for us in a dramatic historical event. When Jesus, hanging on the cross, breathed His last breath, the Temple curtain "was torn in two from top to bottom" (Mark 15:37,38; also see Luke 23:44-46). By Jesus' day the Tabernacle had been replaced, on God's command, by the Temple in Jerusalem (see 1 Kings 5:3-5; 1 Chron. 22:6-10). The Temple was a permanent structure with outside walls of stone instead of curtains. The design of the Temple followed that of the Tabernacle. However, only the curtain shielding the Most Holy Place remained (see 2 Chron. 3:14). This curtain probably measured 30 to 40 feet (9-12-m) in height[1] and may have been as thick as 42 inches (10-cm).[2] The spontaneous tearing of this large curtain could only have been an act of God. The thickness of the curtain and the fact that it was torn from *top* (30 to 40 feet or 9 to 12 meters above the floor) to bottom indicates a divine act, as does the seemingly coincidental timing of the event to the very moment Jesus died (see Matt. 27:50,51). The sacrifice had been completed; now the way to God was open to all people through Jesus' blood (see Heb. 10:19-22).

Hebrews 10:19-22 describes the curtain as Christ's body: "Therefore, brothers, since we have confidence to enter the Most Holy Place by the blood of Jesus, by a new and living way opened for us through the curtain, that is, his body, and since we have a great priest over the house of God, let us draw near to God with a sincere heart in full assurance of faith, having our hearts sprinkled to cleanse us from a guilty conscience and having our bodies washed with pure water." Jesus lived in human form, His humanity veiling His divine nature, just as the Tabernacle curtain shielded the Most Holy Place from men. From time to time Jesus' divinity shone through and His divine glory was perceived (see Matt. 14:22-33; 17:1-8). When the flesh of Christ expired, His true nature was exposed. Even the centurion standing guard at the cross recognized Jesus for who He is (see Matt. 27:54; Mark 15:39). When Christ gave up His life in the crucifixion (see John 10:17,18), the Most Holy Place was revealed as the curtain was torn apart. Can you imagine the jolt the high priest must have felt when the veil was suddenly rent and the Most Holy Place exposed? It was now open for all eyes to see. The high priest, no doubt, had some difficult explanations to give.

Perfect in God's Sight

From the point of Christ's death and following, the sacrificial system of the Jews was replaced by a new order. The need for continual sacrifices, made by the blood of bulls and goats, was abolished by Jesus. "When this priest had offered for all time one sacrifice for sins, he sat down at the right hand of God. . . .because by one sacrifice he has made perfect forever those who are being made holy" (Heb. 10:12,14). By this sacrifice, Jesus has made those who are cleansed by His blood perfect and acceptable to God. Verse 14 says that these people are seen by God as perfect *forever*. From our point of view, we know that Christians should be striving to become perfect (see Matt. 5:48; Phil. 3:12-14). From God's point of view, Christians have already been made perfect (Heb. 10:14). God has "set his seal of ownership on us, and put his Spirit in our hearts as a deposit, guaranteeing what is to come" (2 Cor. 1:22).

If access to God is now possible, not only once a year but constantly, why are many reluctant to meet Him face to face? Perhaps one reason is that belief is an unveiling process; it requires initial risk in accepting truth before it is completely understood.

God initiated a seemingly strange way for Christians to discover truth. Christians are to believe in what Christ has done and what He claims to be before this truth is personally verified by their experience. This is opposite of all the methods of investigation and comprehension taught in our schools and colleges. In the academic community we are very careful not to draw premature conclusions. The evidence must be weighed very carefully, and when the evidence is confirmed by experimentation or repeated observation, we allow ourselves to believe. The assumption is that truth will yield to investigation if we can discover the research methods necessary to unveil it.

If academic methods were applied to spiritual truth, a moral problem would arise: Only the intelligent, educated person could discover salvation and find understanding. The Christians' position is that understanding comes after belief (see 1 Cor. 2:14-16). They are often criticized for blind faith or regarded as gullible. But the gospel of Christ has been revealed to the simple, and the wise things of God are foolishness to the educated (see Matt. 11:25; 1 Cor. 1:26,27). In fact, intellectuals who deny God's existence are like the Israelites in Moses' day whose minds were veiled from perceiving God's glory and understanding His covenant. This is because the veil that limits their understanding of God's plan "has not been removed, because only in Christ is it taken away" (2 Cor. 3:14; see also Exod. 34:29-35). But the Lord does not depend on faulty human intellect. He is available to all, wise and foolish (see John 6:37). It is by walking in faith that truth is unveiled. Then God can be seen in personal and significant ways. Just as the curtain was the only entrance to the Most Holy Place, so a person must pass *through* Christ before God can be revealed to him or her (2 Cor. 2:14).

A bit of risk accompanies the move to believe before you understand. You are placing your pride on the line, believing that you will be right. You are taking the risk of being wrong. I have known Ph.D.'s who have spent years trying to learn enough so they can figure out God without having to believe Him first. They produce some very interesting ideas but still will be blind, unless they first come to God in repentance and faith. Then the veil that blinds them can be lifted, and they can begin to understand. "Whenever anyone turns to the Lord, the veil is taken away" (2 Cor. 3:16).

Prideful reluctance is not solely the territory of unbelievers. I find myself constantly wanting to resort to human wisdom. So often I want to know more before I take the risk to exercise faith. But faith in Christ alone provides the way through the veil and allows us to know and relate to God as no other means allows us. To add to the personal feeling of risk in believing, we are instructed to not only come by faith, but to charge in boldly with confidence and "full assurance of faith" (Heb. 10:22; see also v. 19, *KJV*)! No inferiority complexes need get in the way. Through Christ, God has esteemed us highly. We are precious to Him and loved as His own children. "How great is the love the Father has lavished on us, that we should be called children of God!" (1 John 3:1). Since we are His children, God gladly opens Himself to our simplest and most absurd questions. He is interested in our least concerns. There is no self-improvement program we can embark upon that will bring us to God's throne. The only way is the way He has provided through Jesus (see John 14:6). And like His own Son who entered the Most Holy Place before you, you can now enter His presence *boldly* and with *confidence*!

Notes

1. *The Bible Visual Resource Book* (Ventura, CA: Regal Books, 1989), p. 185.
2. Charles E. Fuller, *The Tabernacle in the Wilderness* (Westwood, N.J.: Fleming H. Revell Co., 1960), p. 76.

A B C PLAN FOR THE SESSION

Materials needed:
- Your Session 8 Leader's Guide Sheet;
- One copy of the Session 8 Lesson Outline for each group member;
- Blank sheets of paper, three or four felt markers and masking tape;
- Small index cards or Post-it Notes with Scripture references;
- Large index cards with questions and Scripture references;
- Chalkboard or overhead projector with transparencies;
- Overhead projector transparency of the Session 8 Lesson Outline (optional).

Advance preparations:
- Invite a person in the group to prepare a five- to seven-minute presentation on the Tabernacle. It should include a brief listing of the curtains, the other major Tabernacle furnishings and where they were positioned. (Old Testament types should not be included in the presentation.) The member may make an overhead projector transparency of a simple sketch of the Tabernacle. The Regal book, *The Bible Visual Resource Book*, will prove helpful as a resource for his or her preparation. Also, a study Bible or Bible dictionary can be consulted.
- Write one of the following groups of Scripture references on seven small index cards or Post-it Notes—one per card: (1) 2 Corinthians 5:21; Hebrews 7:26; (2) Isaiah 9:6; John 1:1; (3) John 1:14; (4) John 3:13; (5) Revelation 19:12,13,16; (6) Mark 15:17,18,20; (7) Hebrews 9:12; 1 Peter 1:18,19.
- On large index cards (one for each small group), write the following Scripture references and respective questions:
  Exodus 26:31; Leviticus 16:2
  Mark 15:38; Hebrews 9:1,7,11,12,15; 10:11,12,14,19-22.
  1. In what way is the curtain covering in the Most Holy Place a type of Christ?
  2. What did Christ's death accomplish, and what did it abolish?
     John 1:12; 3:16; Romans 10:9,10; Ephesians 2:8,9.
  3. What is required by sinners to be acceptable to God?

PPROACH (5 minutes)

Give each person a blank sheet of paper. Have several felt markers available. Say, *Think of a person who has had an opportunity to accept Christ as his or her Savior but, for one reason or another, has hesitated to do so. Then print one or two words that describe the reason you believe this person will not respond to the claims of Christ.* Allow several minutes for thinking and writing. (Encourage learners to pass the markers along for use by other members.) Next, collect the papers and, using masking tape, quickly post all the responses at the front of the room. Review the reasons listed, especially pointing out those that suggest pride, self-righteousness, good works, unworthiness or intellectualism.

Move to the Bible Exploration by saying, *As we have seen, there are many reasons why a person will not accept Christ as Savior. Many knowingly reject God's way of salvation while others may be unaware that a way has already been made. Our Bible study today will reveal that way, why all may come and how they will be made acceptable to God.*

B **IBLE EXPLORATION** (45-50 minutes)

Step 1 (10-15 minutes): Say, *The most complete type of Christ in the Old Testament is the Tabernacle with its holy places, priesthood and sacrifices.* Add, *We will consider the Tabernacle in our study and especially the curtain or veil before the Most Holy Place that foreshadowed an important New Testament event.*

Distribute the Lesson Outline to learners. Encourage them to take notes on their outlines as the lesson is presented and discussions take place. Do the same on the chalkboard or Lesson Outline transparency. Include in the discussions further lesson material from "Insights for the Leader." Also ask the suggested questions. Announce that as an introduction to the focus of our study—the veil before the Most Holy Place, a member will present an overview of the Tabernacle.

Member makes five- to seven-minute presentation regarding the Tabernacle. If transparency was not made of the Tabernacle, he or she may make a quick sketch on the chalkboard or overhead transparency.

Follow the member's presentation by sharing the following general information about the Tabernacle:

The Tabernacle
Exodus 25—27
- It was the center of life for the children of Israel.
- After the Israelites left the Sinai peninsula, they carried the Tabernacle with them wherever they traveled (see Num 10:1-6).
- It was the resting place for the Ark of the Covenant that contained the stone tablets upon which the Ten Commandments were carved. In this way the Tabernacle served as a judicial function (see Exod. 40:1-3).
- It was the place where God communicated with His people (see Exod. 29:42,43) and where information regarding various issues, such as a public health issue, was given out (see Num. 5:1-4; 10:1-7). The Tabernacle was also called "the Tent of Meeting" (see Exod. 27:21; 29:10-12).
- All of Israel's life was God-related by means of the Tabernacle. This included both religious and civic affairs.

Step 2 (10 minutes): Share the fact that the instructions for building the Tabernacle were given to Moses on Mount Sinai (see 24:15-18; 25:9,40). Invite everyone to open their Bibles to Exodus, chapter 25 and ask a learner to read aloud verses 1-8.

Freewill Offering
Exodus 25:1-8
- Stress that the offering was voluntary, not mandatory (see v. 2).
- Why would a people who made such a quick exodus from Egypt have in their possession the needed metals and precious stones for building the Tabernacle? (refer to 12:35,36).
- Do you think it was difficult for the people to part with these possessions? Why or why not? Point out that these items were actually a gift from God, as it was God who had caused the Egyptians to be favorably disposed to the Israelites (see 12:36; also see Jas. 1:17).
- The people were so generous in their response that Moses had to give an order to restrain their giving (see Exod. 36:6,7). What lessons can we learn from their spirit of giving? Can you think of any Scripture verse or passage that encourages us to give in the same way? (see Luke 6:38; Mark 12:41-44; 2 Cor. 9:7). Share that the Israelites would benefit spiritually and in other ways because the Tabernacle was erected. In the same way, our lives are enriched when we cheerfully give to Him (see Mal. 3:10).

Next, direct everyone's attention to Exodus 26:31-

34 and Leviticus 16:1-34. Read aloud the Exodus passage.

The Curtain for the Most Holy Place
Exodus 26:31-34; Leviticus 16:1-34

- The curtains in the Tabernacle speak of the distance that existed between God and His people. What brought about this distance? (refer to Gen. 3:8-10,22-24).

- Both the outer curtain for the Tabernacle (see Exod. 26:1) and the curtain for the Most Holy Place (v. 31) were embroidered with cherubim. What does this depict? (God's care, protection, entrance to His throne and protection of that which is sacred or off-limits; see Gen. 3:24; Exod. 25:17-21; Ps. 80:1.)

- The curtain in the Most Holy Place was tightly woven and probably very heavy. What does this speak of? (Strong barrier between God and His people, and that access to the Most Holy Place was extremely limited.)

- Who could enter the Most Holy Place? How often and for what purpose? (Refer group to Lev. 16:1-34; also see Heb. 9:7; Allow the group several minutes to examine this passage.) Review the steps and preparations the high priest had to take and make before he could enter into the Most Holy Place. What was the consequence of entering the Most Holy Place carelessly? (see Lev. 16:2). Why was the penalty so severe? (God's presence and glory were there, and a perfect God cannot tolerate the presence of imperfect sinful humanity.) What other Bible characters were struck down or severely dealt with because they did not regard the commandment of the Lord (see 2 Sam. 6:1-7; 2 Chron. 26:16-21). What can we learn from these incidents?

Step 3 (10 minutes): Say, *We have considered the structure of the Tabernacle with its various furnishings. Now let's consider how the curtains are a type of Christ.* Distribute the small index cards or Post-it Notes with Scripture references to volunteers. Ask them to look up the Scriptures in their Bibles and be ready to read them aloud at the requested time.

- The inner lining for the outer curtain that surrounded the Tabernacle and the curtains in the Holy Place and Most Holy Place were all made of linen and yarn (see Exod. 26:1,31,36). Linen was reserved for holy purposes in the Old Testament (see Lev. 16:4). The linen curtains are a type of Christ's holiness and righteousness. (Member reads aloud 2 Cor. 5:21; Heb. 7:26.) What should

the symbolism of the linen curtains speak to in the lives of believers? (see Rom. 12:1; Eph. 1:4).

- The outer curtain that surrounded the Tabernacle was covered by a curtain of goat hair, ram skins dyed red and then hides of sea cows (see Exod. 26:7,14). The inner lining of this curtain, which was made of linen, had cherubim embroidered on it (v. 1). The cherubim speak of Christ's divinity. (Member reads aloud Isaiah 9:6; John 1:1.) The outer curtain of hair and skins depicted Christ's humanity. (Member reads aloud John 1:14.)

- The yarn used in all the curtains was in colors of blue, purple and scarlet yarn (see Exod. 26:36). In Jewish tradition, blue is associated with heaven, purple with royalty and scarlet with earthly glory. This curtain gives a picture of Jesus' character: His divinity is seen in the color blue. (Member reads aloud John 3:13.) His royalty is seen in the color purple. (Member reads aloud Rev. 19:12,13,16.) Add that the soldiers at Jesus' trial mocked His royalty by placing a purple robe on Him. (Member reads aloud Mark 15:17,18,20.) Scarlet, representing Jesus' earthly glory, speaks of His great work of redemption through His shed blood. (Member reads Heb. 9:12; 1 Pet. 1:18,19.)

Step 4 (15 minutes): Say, *There is yet a greater type of Christ that can be seen in this curtain that separated the Holy Place and the Most Holy Place. As you work in small groups and research Scripture together, you will discover what this greater type was.*

Move everyone into groups of four to six members. Appoint group leaders and give each leader a large index card listing Scripture references and questions. Groups are to answer the questions by researching the Scriptures listed on their respective cards. Announce that they will have five minutes for research.

Next, regather into larger group and ask for feedback from the group leaders.

Question 1: In what way is the curtain covering in the Most Holy Place a type of Christ? (As access into the Most Holy Place-where God's presence appeared-was made by passing through the curtain, access to God is possible only through Christ.)

Question 2: What did Christ's death accomplish, and what did it abolish? (Through His shed blood it provided eternal redemption and access to God. It abolished the Old or First Covenant that allowed only the high priest to enter into the Most Holy Place where

God's presence appeared. Also, the sacrifices offered under the Old Covenant did not remove sin; they only covered them.)

Question 3: What is required by sinners to be acceptable to God? (Receive Christ as his or her personal Savior; have faith in the redemptive work of Christ.)

Say, *In the Approach to our study, you suggested reasons why people you know do not accept Christ as their Savior.* Review the suggestions given. Next, point out the risk that is involved in accepting Christ (see "Insights for the Leader" under the heading "Perfect in God's Sight").

Ask, *Why do believers sometimes hesitate to approach God's throne in prayer during times of need?* Responses may include: they don't feel worthy; they are new believers and feel they do not qualify; God is too busy or not concerned about their needs; and lack of knowledge—do not realize they can go to God. Reiterate the truth that because the veil was torn—Christ's body—we may now enter with confidence into the presence of God to make our petitions known-"so that we may receive mercy and find grace to help us in our time of need" (Heb. 4:16).

C ONCLUSION (5 minutes)

Because of humankind's sin, God's people were separated by a curtain or veil from entering into the presence of God in the Most Holy Place. Only the high priest could enter God's presence once a year to make atonement for himself and the people. But when Christ died on the cross, the veil in the Temple was torn from top to bottom and everyone now has access to God through Christ.

Ask, *Are you trying to gain access to God other than through Christ's redemptive work on the cross? Christ said that He is the way and that no man can come to the Father but through Him (see John 14:6). Take a risk and trust Him first, and then you will understand the full benefit of His grace.* Also challenge believers in your group who hesitate to approach the throne of grace with their needs, to begin doing so. Remind them that Scripture has admonished them to enter with *confidence* (see Heb. 4;16).

Give an opportunity to any person in your group who has not received Christ into his or her life to do so. Close the session in prayer, thanking God for His Son Jesus who, by His death on the cross, made possible our access to God's throne anywhere and at anytime.

Encourage members to read chapter 8 of the Regal book, *Christ B.C.*, which will assist them in their time of daily devotions. Each day's devotion is based on the theme of *reconciliation*.

BIBLE STUDY IDEA

In Your Own Words

One of the most effective Bible study methods for making God's Word come alive with meaning is the paraphrase. Essentially, paraphrasing is the activity of writing a Scripture passage in your own words. The purpose is not to change the meaning of the text, but simply to make the meaning more understandable to the group members.

Here are a few variations on the theme of Scripture paraphrase:

Personalized verses. Rewrite verses using names and personal pronouns in appropriate places. For example, "If anyone is in Christ, he is a new creation" becomes "Since I, Bill Forbes, am in Christ, I am a new creation" (2 Cor. 5:17, *NIV*).

Abridged edition. Take a large segment of Scripture such as a complete chapter and reduce it to 1-3 sentences which capture its meaning.

Contemporary story. Rewrite a biblical narrative or parable in a contemporary setting. For example, the Good Samaritan parable might become the story of a current ethnic minority helping a disabled motorist who has been ignored by others.

The Ark of the Covenant

SESSION VERSES

"Make an atonement cover of pure gold. . . .And make two cherubim out of hammered gold at the ends of the cover. . . .The cherubim are to face each other, looking toward the cover. Place the cover on top of the ark and put in the ark the Testimony, which I will give you." Exodus 25:17,18,20,21

"For all have sinned and fall short of the glory of God, and are justified freely by his grace through the redemption that came by Christ Jesus. God presented him as a sacrifice of atonement, through faith in his blood." Romans 3:23-25

SESSION FOCUS

The Ark of the Covenant is a picture of Christ dwelling in our midst, providing atonement and mercy to all who come to Him in faith.

SESSION BASIS

Exodus 25:10-22

SESSION GOAL

Examine New Testament examples of mercy being extended to individuals. Then consider and discuss ways mercy may be extended in similar situations today.

INSIGHTS FOR THE LEADER

The Ark

The Ark of the Covenant was a simple box whose size gives no clue to its significance. It measured only 3¾ feet long (112.5-cm), 2¼ feet wide (67.5-cm) and 2¼ feet in height (67.5-cm); (see Exod. 25:10). The meaning of the word *ark*, in this instance, means chest or box. God had given special instructions for its making (see vv. 10-16) because He intended to symbolize in its construction His relationship to His people. It was made of acacia wood (see v. 10)—a strong, enduring material common in the desert in which Israel traveled while on route to the Promised Land. The wood was overlaid with pure gold (see v. 11)—no doubt part of the treasure plundered from Egypt (see 12:35,36).

These materials, wood and gold, are generally believed to symbolize the humanity and divinity of Jesus Christ. Gold is repeatedly used as a symbol for the enduring character of the Kingdom of God. The New Jerusalem, or heavenly city, as described in the New Testament is made of gold (see Rev. 21:18). Gold was the most decay-proof material known to man at that time and therefore represents permanence—Christ's eternal, heavenly character (see 1 Tim. 1:17; Rev. 15:3). The wood, an impermanent substance, represents Jesus' human body (see Luke 2:7,52; John 1:14; 4:6), and our human condition: perishable (see Heb. 9:27).

It is interesting to note that God had the ark built out of a common wood which was readily available in the desert, rather than out of cedar from Lebanon or oak from Palestine. A long difficult journey would have been required to obtain these fancier woods. In the same way God sent His Son to earth as a man, with common flesh like ours (see John 1:14), rather than sending an angel or other being. Like the wood growing in their midst, Jesus is readily available to us (see Rev. 3:20).

The Atonement Cover

After giving instructions for making the ark, God said, "Make an atonement cover of pure gold" (Exod. 25:17). No wood was to be used on the cover because this was where God's holy presence would rest and where His work of atonement for the Israelites' sins would be carried out. In the same way, it is through Jesus' divinity, His triumph over death, that our sins can be forgiven (see 1 Cor. 15:55-57; 2 Tim. 1:10).

Next, God instructed that two cherubim be hammered out of gold and made to stand facing each other on top of the atonement cover (see Exod. 25:18,20; the atonement cover was also called the mercy seat). Their wings were "spread upward, overshadowing the cover" (v. 20), and their faces were looking down, focused on the cover. God told Moses, "There, above the cover between the two cherubim that are over the ark of the Testimony, I will meet with you and give you all my commands for the Israelites" (v. 22). It is also on the cover, as well as before it, that Aaron was directed to sprinkle the sacrificial blood that was spilled in atonement for the sins of the people (see Lev. 16:15). The cherubim represented God looking upon the blood as satisfying the people's need for forgiveness. Even as God's judgment passed by the homes in Egypt where blood had been painted on the doorframes (see Exod. 12:23), so the cherubim looked upon the offering of blood as sufficient to restore people's broken relationships with God. Yet, unlike Christ's sacrifice, this atonement sacrifice by Aaron had to be repeated each year (see Lev. 16:34). The sacrificial system God initiated in Moses' day was insufficient in terms of effectively removing our sin; it only covered it. Yet the old system served as an introduction or picture of the perfect sacrifice that was to come through Jesus. Jesus' sacrifice would perfectly replace this imperfect covering for sin by providing instead its removal and cleansing, with our sin never to be remembered against us (see Gal. 3:23-25; Heb. 10:8-12,17).

God in Our Midst

The ark was the holiest of all the furnishings in the Tabernacle. On this box, settled into the innermost part of the Tabernacle, appeared the glory of God (see Lev. 16:2). The curtain that hung before the ark is called the "shielding curtain" in Numbers 4:5 (also see Exod. 26:31,33). This name infers that the curtain was used to shield the radiance of the presence of God that appeared on the ark. When the Tabernacle was moved, the ark was covered by this "shielding curtain" or veil and by heavy cloths (see Num. 4:5,6). This radiance is called the Shekinah Glory of God (God's manifested glory. Shekinah Glory is a rabbinic term derived from an Old Testament Hebrew word for dwelt or tabernacled; see Exod. 25); it is of a magnificence so powerful that anyone who stood in its presence would die, unless perfectly atoned for by blood sacrifice (see Lev. 10:1,2; 16:1,2). Even then God's glory had to be shielded from view. When Aaron had made the atonement sacrifice for his own sins, as well as the sins of the people, he then prepared to enter the Most Holy Place where the ark stood. In so doing he was instructed by God to "take a censer full of burning coals from the altar before the Lord and two handfuls of finely ground fragrant incense and take them behind the curtain. He is to put the incense on the fire before the Lord, and the smoke of the incense will conceal the atonement cover above the Testimony, so that he will not die" (Lev. 16:12,13). The awesomeness of God's glory is obvious. In the Old Testament the people were limited in their approach to God. Today, through Christ's sacrifice, we have free access to God (see Heb. 10:19-22). Charles E. Fuller stated: "This Shekinah Glory was a local manifestation of the very presence of God, and since this presence was located between the Cherubim over the place where the shed blood was applied, we see once again the fact that it is impossible to come into the presence of God unless one comes to the Cross of Christ, humbly admitting his sin, his inability to save himself, and trusting completely in the finished work of Christ."[1] It is through atonement—initiated and designed by God—that entrance into His presence and mercy through His grace are possible (see Rom. 3:25; Eph. 2:13; Col. 1:19,20). In this sense the ark is a symbol of God's gift of atonement through Christ.

What if God had let man design the ark? What would it have looked like? Most likely it would have been some magnificent cathedral. It has been my privilege to visit some of the great cathedrals of the world: St. Paul's in London, Notre Dame in Paris and St. Isaac's in Leningrad. Each is a grand structure, far beyond my ability to describe. Each is rich in symbolism and creative form with stained glass windows artistically and superbly crafted. Many of these cathedrals were designed to reproduce the awesomeness of entering God's presence, of being in heaven. The efforts of the designers and builders are to be praised, but the buildings do not represent how God chooses to relate to man. We do not have to enter heaven to meet with God, God has come to us first, in His presence over the mercy seat (see Exod. 25:22) and then through His Son Jesus who would be called "'Immanuel'—which means, 'God with us'" (Matt. 1:23). God chose to meet with the Israelites by means of a little box, housed in a temporary movable structure. He dwelt in their midst, traveled with them and communicated with them. And as He did so, His glory was evident to the people. "So the cloud of the Lord was over the tabernacle by day, and fire was in the cloud by night, in the sight of all the house of Israel during all their travels" (Exod. 40:38).

King Solomon built a Temple that emulated his impression of God (see 2 Chron. 3,4). Although it was based on the design of the Tabernacle, which was directed by God, Solomon played a part in its design. The Temple was so magnificent that those who visited it were awestruck (see 1 Kings 10:4,5; 2 Chron. 9:10,11). But it was like all our imaginations of God—it was an imperfect, one—sided picture. We create great structures, great ideas and theologies about God, yet miss the point.

By building up a picture showing only God's greatness, we put Him at a distance—completely out of reach. We also do the opposite. We dwell on Jesus' human character, His goodness and His wise teachings. We call Him our "friend," yet we do not always remember to call Him "Lord." God's presence and glory came to Israel in a simple box, the ark. He came again in a simple manger in Bethlehem (see Luke 2:12,16). Even so, He finds His way into our midst, the insignificant places of our lives, without losing one particle of His awesomeness and power. God's glory and greatness cannot be separated from His accessibility and presence in our midst.

Mercy and Wrath

God dwelling in the midst of the Israelites is certainly a picture of Christ and His mercy and grace. Christ humbly left His exalted position in heaven to take on the flesh of a man. "The Word became flesh and made his dwelling among us. We have seen his glory, the glory of the One and Only, who came from the Father, full of grace and truth" (John 1:14). Christ did this to fulfill God's plan to provide complete and perfect atonement for humankind's sin. Through Christ, undeserving people can receive mercy and escape the wrath of God that they have dully earned. "God presented him as a sacrifice of atonement, through faith in his blood. He did this to demonstrate his justice, because in his forbearance he had left the sins committed beforehand unpunished—he did it to demonstrate his justice at the present time, so as to be just and the one who justifies those who have faith in Jesus" (Rom. 3:25,26).

Ignoring God or trifling with God brings His wrath, as Israel was to learn bitterly in the days to come. Placed in the ark were three special objects that stood as reminders to the people of God's involvement in their lives. These objects and their meanings were to help the people remain in God's will and thereby stave off His wrath. They included the Ten Commandments carved on stone tablets (see Exod. 31:18), the rod of Aaron that budded, bloomed and bore almonds (see Num. 17:8) and a pot of manna that was Israel's food during the sojourn through the desert (see Exod. 16:4,5; Heb. 9:4). These are symbolic of the fact that God's truth, God's direction and God's sustenance are available to His people and are the means by which His people should make their way through life. To do otherwise would result in experiencing God's wrath.

The wrath of God is the natural result of not living in obedience or conformity to the spiritual principles of God (see Gal. 6:7,8). It is not that God reacts in anger, as humans do, toward some individual who displeases Him as much as it is the result of breaking His imitable spiritual law. God's wrath is a permanent and consistent attitude of a holy and just God who is confronted by sin and evil. This is not to say that God's wrath is a process of cause and effect that operates in the world at large. It is, rather, a personal trait of God expressed in response to humankind's sin.[2] For example, if I choose to organize my life around my own self-pleasure, I'm going to run into trouble. I was created to organize my life with God at the center (see Matt. 22:37,38). If I place ego in the central position, I have replaced God with myself. If I go against God's guidelines for faith and conduct, I will suffer spiritual, and sometimes physical, and emotional consequences. And in many instances I will cause others to suffer, also. By myself, and under my own direction, I am terribly shortsighted, selfish and vain. There is neither pleasure nor spiritual health in vanity. My own desires are unfulfillable, and my ambitions are empty. The evidence of the wrath of God may be a miserable, lonely existence of trying to play God for myself and failing. What amazes me most is that I persist, even though I know better. But I am truly grateful for forgiveness and mercy and the opportunity for a new start. I may still suffer physical and emotional consequences of my actions and may need to repair broken relationships. However, in the light of eternity I have, through confession and repentance, been cleansed from all unrighteousness (see 1 John 1:9) and have been saved from

God's wrath. "God's wrath is always tempered with mercy,"[3] especially for the redeemed. First Thessalonians 1:10 describes Jesus as the one "who rescues us from the coming wrath." And Romans 5:9 states, "Since we have now been justified by his blood, how much more shall we be saved from God's wrath through him!" In these verses the wrath referred to is that which will come on the "day of God's wrath" (2:5). The unrepentant are storing up wrath that will be expressed against them in the future.

Israel experienced wrath by refusing to believe the promise that God would lead, sustain and provide for them. They grumbled and became fearful. This is illustrated in their response to the men who scouted out the Promised Land and found it full of intimidating enemies (see Num. 13:1,2,26—14:2). As Israel measured herself against these impossible foes, many cried to return to Egypt (see 14:1,3). The mistake was classic—they measured themselves against their problems when they should have measured their problems against God's resources. Israel refused to enter God's Promised Land and spent 40 years experiencing the wrath of God in the desert (see vv. 22,23,28-35).

Yet even in their disobedience, the people experienced God's mercy (see vv. 4-35). God could have turned His anger on them and destroyed them, but, instead, He extended His mercy and forgiveness to them. God held back His anger and allowed the Israelites to experience the discipline required for their rebellion. This experience is also true of many Christians who rebel against God. They may experience pain as a direct result of their actions, as well as creating a spiritual chasm between themselves and God. They also inflict pain on others—especially other Christians with whom they are close. Many times these people, like the Israelites, repent and turn back to God only to find that He has, in His mercy, never left them. They receive spiritual healing and relief and the strength to deal with any unresolved consequences of their sin. Some who rebel may not feel God's wrath immediately. Rather, God, in His mercy, will withhold punishment in order to create an opportunity for repentance (see Rom. 2:4). This withholding of punishment is not because God wants us to think of Him as a "nice guy." It is only to promote repentance. If repentance doesn't come then God in His holiness and justice must eventually express His wrath (see vv. 8,9). If repentance does come, then God has just grounds to withhold His wrath and give mercy and peace to the repentant one (see v. 10).

In Numbers 14:40-45 we read of an event where the people of Israel endeavored on their own to do what God had originally wanted them to do—possess the land He had promised to give them (see 13:1,2). After the Israelites had refused to enter the land and they were told that they must wander in the desert for 40 years for their disobedience and unbelief, the people regretted their bad choice—not because they wanted to do the Lord's will, but because they wanted to escape the consequences of their rebellion (see 14:36-39). Moses saw through their wrong motives and warned them that by going into the land without the Lord's approval would only increase their suffering (see vv. 41-43). "Nevertheless, in their presumption they went up toward the high hill country, though neither Moses nor the ark of the Lord's covenant moved from the camp. Then the Amalekites and Canaanites who lived in that hill country came down and attacked them and beat them down all the way to Hormah" (vv. 44,45). Again they had left God out of the picture, and because of their lack of wisdom, they suffered severe consequences.

There are many people who try to bring God along in their lives for a little comfort or security, but they do not regard God as central to their purposes or decision-making. They hatch plans, perhaps muttering a prayer over their schemes. God is treated as a talisman, taken along for good luck. The fact is that God will not be extra baggage. He will only take the central position in our lives, being fully in charge rather than following our lead. It is not His nature to be the servant of a human ego.

I remember a radio program that aired on Sunday afternoons when I was a boy. The show opened with a rich baritone voice uttering in sonorous tones, "There is a power for good in the universe, and *you* can use it!" How contrary to all that we know about the nature of God. God is not a power to be turned on at the whim of our egos or selfish desires, as inferred in the introduction to the radio show.

The principle of placing God at the center of life and allowing Him to lead us is one of the immutable spiritual laws of life. Yet we stubbornly cling to serving ourselves and placing ourselves in the middle of our little worlds. This human tendency is so pervasive that it has become endemic in all our thinking. But as we seek first to do God's will and place our egos in orbit around the centrality and leadership of God, we find mercy and grace instead of wrath. When God is in charge, we find healing in our values, priorities become well ordered and our needs are satisfied (see Ps. 37:4; Matt. 6:33).

Israel struggled hard to learn these lessons and never fully succeeded (see Acts 7:51-53). We also struggle to rely on God to direct and sustain our lives. It is encouraging to know that whenever we turn to God through faith in Christ Jesus, He is with us in our midst and ready to guide us in obedience. We deserve to be cast out of His presence, but in His mercy He allows us to come to Him through the blood sacrifice of His Son, Jesus Christ (see Rom. 3:23-25).

Notes
1. Charles E. Fuller, *The Tabernacle in the Wilderness* (Westwood, N.J.: Fleming H. Revell Co., 1960), p. 82.
2. *New Bible Dictionary* (Leicester, England: Universities and Colleges Christian Fellowship, 1982), p. 1262,1263.
3. *New Bible Dictionary*, p. 1263.

A B C PLAN FOR THE SESSION

Materials needed:
- Your Session 9 Leader's Guide Sheet;
- One copy of the Session 9 Lesson Outline for each group member;
- Large index cards with Scripture passages and question/assignments;
- Chalkboard or overhead projector with transparencies;
- Overhead projector transparency of the Session 9 Lesson Outline (optional).

Advance preparations:
- Read the information under "Advance preparations" for Session 10 in order to make a needed advance assignment for next week's session;
- On large index cards, one for each small group, write one of the following groups of Scripture references and all three question/assignments:
    Leviticus 6:4,5; Luke 19:1-10; Ephesians 4:32
    Luke 23:32,33,39-43; Ephesians 4:32
    1 Corinthians 5:1-5,11; 2 Corinthians 2:5-11; Ephesians 4:32
    1. In what way was mercy extended in this situation?
    2. Think of a situation today where similar mercy may be extended.
    3. How should a Christian respond to the offender?

A PPROACH (5 minutes)

Make two columns on the chalkboard or overhead transparency. At the top of one column, write the word *wrath* and at the top of the other column, write the word *mercy*. Invite members to suggest synonyms for both words. Jot down their suggestions under the corresponding words on the board as they are given. Next, ask learners to think of an incident in their lives when they felt God dealt with them in His wrath or in disciplinary action and an incident when they realized God's mercy. Invite volunteers to share with the group concerning these incidents.

Move to the Bible Exploration by stating that in today's study we will consider how God's mercy was demonstrated to the children of Israel, as well as reasons why His wrath was invoked. Add, *And we will see how His extension of mercy to the Israelites was a type of the mercy that is extended to everyone who, in faith, accepts the atoning work of Christ.*

Alternate Approach (5 minutes)

Sing together the well-known hymn, *Redeemed*, by Fanny J. Crosby. Especially emphasize verse 1 that mentions Christ's blood and His mercy. (If this is not a familiar hymn, use one familiar to your group that bears a similar message.)

Move to the Bible Exploration by saying, *In our Bible study today, we will see how God's mercy is demonstrated to the children of Israel and how His presence is displayed among them. We will also see how both of these acts are a type of the mercy that is extended to everyone through the atoning work of Christ.*

B IBLE EXPLORATION
(45-50 minutes)

Step 1 (20-25 minutes): Distribute the Lesson Outline to learners and encourage them to take notes on their outlines throughout the lesson. Jot down notes, yourself, on the chalkboard or Lesson Outline transparency. Include in the discussions the listed lesson material and suggested questions. Also incorporate further information from "Insights for the Leader."

Say, *It was in the Tabernacle that God designed a meeting place with His people* (see Exod. 25:8,9; 29:42,43). Ask, *Do you recall the three divisions in the Tabernacle?* (Outer courtyard—see 27:9; Holy Place and the Most Holy Place—see 26:33,34.) Add, *God gave instructions regarding the furnishings that would go in the Tabernacle, and His instructions began with the most important piece—the Ark of the Covenant.*

The Ark of the Covenant
Exodus 25:10-16
- Invite a volunteer to read aloud Exodus 25:10-16.
- The ark was 3¾ feet long (112.5-cm), 2¼ feet wide (67.5-cm), and 2¼ feet deep (67.5-cm). It was the size of a fairly large chest.
- The word *ark*, in this instance, means chest or box.
- The materials—wood and gold—are generally believed to symbolize the humanity and divinity of Christ, respectively (wood, refer to Luke 2:7,52; John 1:14; 4:6; gold, refer to 1 Tim. 1:17; Rev. 15:3).
- Acacia wood was a common material and readily available in the deserts of Palestine. God sent His Son to earth as a man, with common flesh like ours (see John 1:14). In what way is Christ readily available to us? (see Rev. 3:20).
- Can you think of an incident when the children of Israel did not carry the ark as instructed in Exodus 25:14? (see 1 Chron. 13:1-10; also see 15:1,2,11-15). What can we learn from this incident? (see 1 Sam. 15:22).

The Atonement Cover
Exodus 25:17-22
- Invite a member to read aloud Exodus 25:17-22.
- The atonement cover is also called the mercy seat.
- Why do you think gold was used in the cover and not wood? (Refer to the information in "Insights for the Leader" under the heading "The Atonement Cover".)
- The cherubim symbolized the throne of God (see 1 Sam. 4:4).
- The cherubim also represented God looking down

upon the blood as satisfying the people's need for forgiveness and sufficient to restore people's broken relationships with God. In what other event in Israel's prior history did God see the blood and withhold His judgment? (refer to Exod. 12:23).
- The blood from the atonement sacrifice that Aaron sprinkled both on and before the atonement cover and that the cherubim looked down upon, had to be offered yearly (see Lev. 16:34; Heb. 9:25). Christ died once for all, and His blood not only covered sin, but removed it (see Heb. 10:10,12,14).

God in Our Midst
- The ark was the holiest of all the furnishings in the Tabernacle. On this box, placed in the innermost part of the Tabernacle—the Most Holy Place—appeared the glory of God.
- Invite a learner to read aloud Leviticus 16:2. The cloud is also referred to as the Shekinah Glory—God's manifested glory. Do you recall what the consequence would be of one entering God's presence in the Most Holy Place without making the proper preparations and/or in an improper manner? (refer to Lev. 10:1,2; 16:1,2).
- After sharing the inference in Scripture that God's glory on the ark had to be shielded from view (see Exod. 26:31,33; Num. 4:5,6), invite a learner to read aloud Leviticus 16:12,13.
- What do the aforementioned rules and regulations, as well as the precautions, tell us about the presence of God? (It is awesome and no one can stand in His presence.)
- Invite a learner to read aloud John 1:14. What does this Scripture reveal to us about the man Jesus? (The Shekinah Glory took its abode in Him as the Son of man.)
- Share the statement by Charles E. Fuller from "Insights for the Leader" under the heading "God in Our Midst." In this sense the ark is a symbol of God's gift of atonement through Christ (see Rom. 3:25; Eph. 2:13; Col. 1:19,20; 1 Peter 1:18,19).
- Invite members to neighbor-nudge the person next to them and tell this person if they agree or disagree with Dr. Fuller's statement and why or why not.
- What have people constructed over the centuries to represent the awesomeness of entering God's presence? (Magnificent cathedrals.) Allow persons in the group who have visited such cathedrals to share of their beauty and design. Do you think these magnificant structures represent how God chooses to relate to humankind? Why or why not?

• Point out that Solomon's Temple was so magnificent that its visitors were awestruck by its magnificence (see 1 Kings 9:8; 10:1-7; 2 Chron. 9:10,11). Yet, when God came to Israel "in the flesh," He did not come to the Temple in Jerusalem but, instead, to a simple manger in Bethlehem (see Luke 2:12,16).

• What does the place of Christ's birth tell us about God coming to us? (His glory and greatness cannot be separated from His accessibility and presence in our midst.)

• What can this truth tell us personally? (That God in all His glory and greatness is anxious to enter and become involved in the seemingly small and insignificant areas of our individual lives.)

God's Mercy and Wrath

• How was God dwelling in the midst of the Israelites a picture of Christ and His mercy and grace? (Christ left His exalted position in heaven to become a man in order to fulfill God's plan to provide complete and perfect atonement for humankind's sin; see John 1:14; Phil. 2:6-8).

• Invite a volunteer to read aloud Romans 3:25,26. What is the key to being justified? (Faith; see v. 26.)

• How were God's people recipients of God's mercy instead of His wrath in Old Testament times? (By the atoning blood sprinkled on and before the atonement cover or mercy seat; see Lev. 16:11,14-17.)

• Point out that when the Israelites ignored God or did not do things His way, it brought on His wrath. Briefly relate the incident of the children of Israel refusing to enter the Promised Land as a result of choosing to believe the negative report of the 10 spies instead of Caleb and Joshua's positive reports. Also share the consequence of their disobedience when they tried to possess the land without the Lord's presence being with them (see Num. 13:1,2,26—14:45).

• Mention that the Israelites' disobedience was without excuse because God put in the ark three objects whose meanings should have helped them obey His commands and thus stave off His wrath. They included: (1) The Ten Commandments carved on stone tablets—truth; (see Exod. 31:18); (2) Aaron's rod that budded and bloomed—direction (see Num. 17:8); and a pot of manna that sustained the Israelites in their wilderness journeys—sustenance (see Exod. 16:4,5; Heb. 9:4).

• As believers, can you think of at least three things God has given us in order to help us obey Him? (Responses may include the following: The Word—see Ps. 119:105; the Holy Spirit—John 16:13;

church leadership—Eph. 4:11-13; power of the Holy Spirit—Acts 1:8.)

Move to Step 2 by saying, *Anyone who accepts Christ as his or her Savior is a recipient of God's mercy because of the atoning work of Christ on the cross. And this person continues to receive of God's grace in countless ways from day to day. In order that we might extend mercy to people who have sinned and are hurting around us, let's examine several New Testament examples where mercy was extended to people who sinned.*

Step 2 (10 minutes): Move everyone into small groups of four to six members. Appoint group leaders and give each leader a large index card. Each group is to research the Scripture passages listed on their index card to answer or complete the three question/assignments. Announce that groups will have about nine minutes for research and writing.

Step 3 (15 minutes): Regain everyone's attention and move smaller groups back into the larger group. Ask for reports from the group leaders regarding their respective group's responses to the three question/assignments and jot down the responses on the chalkboard or overhead transparency. As time permits incorporate into the discussion the following information and additional suggested questions:

Zacchaeus

Leviticus 6:4,5; Luke 19:1-10; Ephesians 4:32

• Why do you think Zacchaeus was considered a "sinner" by the people? (Luke 19:7. Publicans were tax collectors for the Roman government who were often guilty of extortion and of overcharging in taxes due. They became wealthy through their fraudulent practices and were regarded as traitors and apostates by the Jewish people; refer to 3:2,12,13; 19:8).

• Is it always possible to make restitution? Why or why not? What should our attitude be toward the offender if total restitution is not possible?

• What can we learn from Jesus' immediate acceptance of Zacchaeus?

Thief on the Cross

Luke 23:32,33,39-43; Ephesians 4:32

• How does this incident demonstrate that salvation is by faith in Christ and not by good works? (Other than crying out to the Lord for His mercy, the thief did not have an opportunity to perform any good works in order to earn his salvation; refer to Eph. 2:8,9. Point out that this again demonstrates the complete atonement that Christ's death on the cross would provide.)

• Read aloud Mark 15:32. Next, draw members' attention to Luke 23:39-41. What change has taken place between these two passages of Scripture? (One of the criminals repented and asked to be included in Jesus' Kingdom.) What admirable trait is demonstrated in Luke 23:41 by the penitent thief? (He admitted that he had sinned and was receiving a just punishment for his sins.)

● Point out that this incident demonstrates that God's mercy extends to what is known today as "deathbed conversions." Ask learners to share of such conversions that they may know of.

Immoral Brother

1 Corinthians 5:1-5,11; 2 Corinthians 2:5-11; Ephesians 4:32

● In the two previous incidents, both offenders were unconverted when they sinned. In this situation the apostle Paul is dealing with immorality in a Christian brother. What preceded the extension of mercy in this instance? (Christian discipline.) What can we learn from this? (God's mercy is extended to us through the forgiveness of our sins when we repent of them, but we can expect to be disciplined as His children; refer to Heb. 12:5-11.)

● What must be kept in mind when disciplining a Christian brother? (When godly sorrow and repentance are demonstrated, the offender should be restored to fellowship.) Does this always happen in the Church? Why or why not?

C ONCLUSION (5 minutes)

We have reviewed how a loving God desired to dwell among a people who were unworthy of His presence because of their sin. But God's plan for a Tabernacle where the Ark of the Covenant would rest would allow His glory and presence to abide over the atonement cover upon which the blood was sprinkled. Instead of judgment, God extended mercy to His people as the high priest made atonement once a year for the sins of the people.

The Ark of the Covenant and all it represented to the children of Israel was only a type of the greater grace and mercy that would be extended to all humankind through the blood of Christ shed on the cross (see Matt. 26:28). Christ's blood so completely satisfied a holy God that anyone who puts his or her faith in Christ may now experience His abiding presence and realize complete forgiveness for sin (see John 15:4; Rom. 3:23-25; Heb. 10:12—14,22). And God's glory and presence that appeared above the cherubim and that was entered into by a selected few, may now be enjoyed and realized by all who come to Him through faith in His Son Jesus (see Heb. 4:14,16).

Ask, *Have you put your faith in Christ's finished work on the cross and, as a result, are a recipient of God's mercy and the forgiveness of your sins? If you have not taken this important step, you may by asking God to forgive you of your sins and by believing that Christ's blood will cleanse you from all unrighteousness* (see Acts 16:31; 1 John 1:9). Always take time to lead a group member to Christ who may desire to receive Christ as his or her personal Savior.

Continue by asking, *As a believer, are you allowing God to use you as a channel of His mercy to sinning and/or hurting people in your world? Think of ways God may want to use you in this way.* Allow several moments for thinking.

Next, refer to the list of synonyms on the board that were given in the Approach to the lesson for the word *mercy.* Say, *All that mercy embraces is available to those in your world who are without Christ, as they put their trust in the atoning work of Christ on the cross. And it is available to you as you enjoy His presence in your life.*

Close the session by inviting persons to give brief sentence prayers, thanking God for His mercy and abiding presence and asking for His help to extend His mercy to those around them.

Encourage members to read chapter 9 of the Regal book, *Christ B.C.,* which will assist them in their time of daily devotions. Each day's devotion is based on the theme of *mercy.*

The Bronze Snake

SESSION VERSES

"The Lord said to Moses, 'Make a snake and put it up on a pole; anyone who is bitten can look at it and live.' So Moses made a bronze snake and put it up on a pole. Then when anyone was bitten by a snake and looked at the bronze snake, he lived." Numbers 21:8,9

"Just as Moses lifted up the snake in the desert, so the Son of Man must be lifted up, that everyone who believes in him may have eternal life." John 3:14,15

SESSION FOCUS

As the bronze snake lifted up by Moses saved all who looked upon it from death, so Jesus offers salvation to all who look to Him.

SESSION BASIS

Numbers 21:4-9; 2 Kings 18:1-4

SESSION GOAL

Discover how Christ's death on the cross fulfilled the foreshadowing of the bronze snake lifted up in the wilderness and discuss why God alone is worthy of our worship.

INSIGHTS FOR THE LEADER

Grumbling Israelites

The Lord spoke to Moses and told him to "Make a snake and put it up on a pole; anyone who is bitten can look at it and live" (Num. 21:8). The background to this event is important. Israel had struggled in their meanderings in the desert. They had encountered Edom, and the Edomites had refused passage through their land (see Num. 20:14-21). As a result they had to follow a circuitous route around Edom. When they reached Arad in the Negev desert, they were attacked by the local king's forces (see 21:1). Although the Lord gave the Israelites complete victory (see vv. 2,3), the business of being aliens was taking its toll. The people grew impatient, began to gripe and "spoke against God and against Moses, and said, 'Why have you brought us up out of Egypt to die in the desert? There is no bread! There is no water! And we detest this miserable food!'" (v. 5). In response, God sent poisonous snakes through their area (see v. 6). This experience was God's way of chastising them for defaming His character and all He had done to provide for their needs. It was also God's way of establishing a symbol that would point to Christ, as we will soon see.

Among the Israelites, multitudes were bitten (see v. 6). The snakes infiltrated the encampment and a great cry went up to Moses for relief from the plague. "We sinned when we spoke against the Lord and against you. Pray that the Lord will take the snakes away from us," the people pleaded (v. 7). Many had died and the survival of Israel may have been at stake. When Moses prayed for the people, God responded by commanding Moses to fashion a snake and put it up on a pole so that it might be clearly seen (see v. 8). Then whoever "was bitten by a snake and looked at the bronze snake" would live (v. 9).

Because the worship of snakes was common in that part of the world, this practice apparently influenced the children of Israel to worship Moses' bronze snake instead of God centuries later (see 2 Kings 18:4). God's snake was never intended to be an object of worship. Worship of the bronze snake would have gone directly against God's commandment, "You shall not make for yourself an idol in the form of anything in heaven above or on the earth beneath or in the waters below" (Exod. 20:4). The purpose of the bronze snake was to point the people toward God, the One who could heal their affliction and the One deserving of their worship. When Hezekiah became king of Judah approximately 700 years later, he destroyed the bronze snake because the Israelites had been worshiping it (see 2 King 18:4).

Lessons for Life

Several lessons emerge from Israel's experiences relating to the bronze snake. First, it is God who is to be adored, not the symbols of Him. Symbols are to remind us of Him but are not to be the focus of our worship. The reason for this is obvious: The symbol has no power; God is the source of power represented by the symbol. John 3:14,15 tells us that the symbol of the snake lifted up by Moses is also a symbol or type of Christ lifted up on the cross. "Just as Moses lifted up the snake in the desert, so the Son of Man must be lifted up, that everyone who believes in him may have eternal life." For the Israelites, the result of looking to the serpent was restored health and continuing life on earth (see Num. 21:9). For those who look to or put their faith in Jesus, the result is cleansing from sin and eternal life (see John 3:15; Heb. 9:14; 10:22; 1 John 1:7). Therefore we worship Christ: we do not worship the cross and repeat Israel's error when they worshiped the bronze snake. The cross is a symbol pointing us to Christ, the deserving object of our awe, praise and devotion. I remember the story of a missionary to India who was challenged by an Indian intellectual. The Indian said, "Why do you bring all your theology with you? Why don't you just do the good works missionaries are known to do and leave the religious stuff alone?" The Indian was making an argument for the integrity of local religions and found Christian teaching upsetting to him. The missionary was clear in his reply, "By themselves these good things we do call attention only to themselves. We must point you to Christ who is the author and source of the good works."

And in relation to salvation in Christ, we must remember that the means by which we obtain our knowledge of salvation is not to become an idol that we substitute for the God of our salvation. We must not adore the experience or the person who led us to the Lord more than the Lord (see 1 Cor. 1:10-17). The Lord is eternal and a righteously jealous God; He will not take a back seat to anything or anyone (see Exod. 20:4,5; Deut. 4:15-19; Isa. 42:8).

I heard a preacher once say that people are incurably worshipful and that they become like that which they worship. People also have the nasty habit of inventing diminutive gods out of their own experi-

ences, as Israel has illustrated. If this is so, then it is incumbent upon us to be careful of what and who we worship. I have come to believe that each of us will worship something. It is not a matter of worshiping or not worshiping; it is a matter of our choice of where we will direct our worship. This is not an entirely religious idea. Non-religious people worship as well. Their object of worship might be money, intellectual pursuits, their spouses, Elvis or some other late or current superstar. They may not identify their adorations and devotions as worship, but indeed they worship.

God who is the Creator of all is the legitimate object of our worship. In the Israelites' situation He was also the source of healing from the plague.

The second lesson that can be learned is derived from the point that the look cast toward the serpent was to be an individual view. It was a requirement of "anyone who is bitten" (Num. 21:8). It would not do for the head of a household to take a look and report to his family that he had seen the serpent image and then expect the ill in his family to be made well. Nor would it do for Israel to cast a vote to affirm the validity of the healing process and then expect, as a result, that all Israel would be saved. Unless each individual took advantage of healing by viewing, the result was death from the sting of the viper. The requirement, "looking," was so simple that every individual had the opportunity to receive healing—from the small child to the elderly grandmother. The fact that the snake was raised up on a pole where it could be seen easily, even by the desperately ill, reinforces this fact (see v. 8). So it is with us in relation to Christ. We must come to Him individually. It will not do to belong to a church that affirms Christ; we must individually acknowledge Christ as our Savior and Lord before He cleanses us of our sin. No one can experience His saving grace on our behalf. Coming to Christ is not a group phenomenon or cultural tendency. It is personal.

Third, all Israel was affected. The Scripture does not say that each and every person was bitten by a serpent, but many had been poisoned; perhaps the very survival of the nation was in question (see v. 6). Humanly speaking, the demise of Israel was possible and with it the representation of God to humankind. Because of this possibility, the need for salvation from the snake plague became a universal concern. The plague typifies sin. This tells us that the notion that some people are exempt from the need for redemption is inconsistent with clear Bible teaching. Romans 3:23 tells us that "all have sinned."

People who conclude that they are exempt from the

need for God's transformation and forgiveness, do interesting things. Often their primary goal is to make themselves the center of their religious and psychological experience and find ways to worship their humanity. Such is the case with present-day humanism. Humanists believe that people are basically good and are to be affirmed as such. They admit that people have made some awful mistakes, but they have within them the intelligence and capacity to right their wrongs and create a better world. The humanist manifestos that have been written make this abundantly clear. Some of the great people of our time—some of our most learned scholars and a number of religious people—have signed the humanist manifesto. These people clearly declare that no outside force, such as a concept of God who is external to human experience, is necessary and all that people need is built into their natures. Of course they don't know where this "built-in" nature came from, but they vouch for its existence.

Fourth, we see that the means for healing is singular. Either look upon the serpent or no healing will take place. Ada R. Habershon's comment is apt: "It would have been no use for the bitten Israelites to bathe their wounds, or to put ointments or plasters on them, or to bandage them up; but there are many who try to get rid of their sins in this way. They bathe their wounds with tears of repentance; they put on the ointment of good works, or plasters of good resolutions, and bandage themselves with doing their best; but the bites of sin get no better with this sort of treatment; a look at the Crucified One is what they need, and all they need."[1] Moses did not go from tent to tent prescribing one kind of medicine for one person and another kind for others. He did not send some to the local psychiatrist for release of emotional tensions and another to the herbal medicine man for an exotic cure. Nor did he form small groups to discuss the matter so they could report their findings to the whole congregation. Healing came by a singular means. To be healed, one had to face the *one* who was lifted up (see Num. 21:9; John 3:14,15; 14:6; Acts 4:12). The term for "lifted up," *hupsosen* (John 3:14), is from the same term Jesus used to describe Himself being lifted up on the cross (see John 8:28; 12:32). This term is also used in Acts 2:33 and 5:31 in reference to His ascension to heaven. In these verses it can be translated as "exalted." Paul used this same term in Philippians 2:9. Crucifixion and ascension are tied together with the same language. One cannot look to the Crucifixion without looking to the Resurrection and Ascension. As Paul clearly says in 1 Corinthians 15:17, "If Christ has

not been raised, your faith is futile; you are still in your sins." It is by Jesus' death *and* resurrection that we are saved from our sins (see Rom. 5:9-11; 6:5-10; 10:9).

Fifth, the serpents that bit the people of Israel are symbolic of Satan. The serpent as a symbol of Satan is used several times in Scripture (see Rev. 12:9; 20:2). Not only have we all been infected with the poison of sin (see Rom. 5:12), but control of our natures is being battled for by an evil being, a fallen angel called Satan (see 1 Chron. 21:1; Job 1:6-9; Isa. 14:12; 1 Thess. 3:5; 1 Pet. 5:8). There is a tendency among some Christians to regard God as personal and the virtue of goodness as godly, and at the same time regard sin as impersonal and not under anyone's control in particular. Believers who view sin in this manner need to clearly understand that evil is personally dominated by Satan (see John 12:31; 2 Cor. 4:4; Eph. 2:2; 6:11,12) and that he must be dealt with personally by God (see Gen. 3:15). We are in the middle of a battle and must fight with God's direction (see Eph. 6:10,11,13-18). Even though we continue to battle with Satan and sin, we do know that God has already won this war with Satan. He did this, of course, through the sacrifice of His Son, Jesus Christ (see John 3:16; Gal. 4:4; Col. 2:13-15). In doing so, "God made him who had no sin to be sin for us, so that in him we might become the righteousness of God" (2 Cor. 5:21). Christ took upon Himself that which afflicts us all and has made it possible for us to stand as righteous in the midst of Satan's scheming (see 1 Tim. 3:7). All we need to do is look to Christ (see John 10:7-10; Acts 2:21; 16:31; Rom. 4:23—5:1; 10:9). This picture of Christ becoming sin for us explains why God directed Moses to make an image of a snake, rather than some other object. What was afflicting the people became a symbol of healing from their affliction. Christ became sin for us and bore our sins in order that we might find healing and forgiveness (see 2 Cor. 5:21; 1 Pet. 2:24).

An Illustration of Grace

The spiritual warfare that we are engaged in against Satan and his cohorts and the tendency in human beings to create false gods reemphasize for us the role of the bronze snake and the cross in our experience. Their purpose is to point us to God and to illustrate for us His grace. It is by the means of Christ lifted on the cross and Christ exalted in heaven as Lord that we can be reconciled to God. It is purely by God's grace that this means is made available to us (see Eph. 2:8,9). Like the Israelites who were afflicted and dying, we are unable to save ourselves from the disease of sin (see Rom. 7:21-24). We are only able to call out to God for healing. "You see, at just the right time, when we were still powerless, Christ died for the ungodly-.…God demonstrates his own love for us in this: While we were still sinners, Christ died for us" (5:6,8). This is grace in a nutshell. With this picture in mind, how offensive to God and ridiculous our misplaced worship and false gods are. Also, like the Israelites, after receiving salvation we need to fight our tendency to demote the Lord. Thankfully, grace again reigns, and we can turn back to God and with His help resubmit ourselves to Him as Lord (see 1 John 1:9; 2:1,2).

To evaluate my life in terms of false worship there are several questions I can ask. If, as a result, I am able to turn my focus back upon the Lord, I will find grace and peace. These questions include the following:

1. What dominates my thought life—my fantasy life? (see 2 Cor. 10:5; Phil. 4:8). That dominating theme is a good clue to what is most important and most adored in my personal purposes. I may be in love with increasing my financial status (for God's viewpoint on wealth, see Matt. 6:19-21; 1 Tim. 6:10). I may be captivated by my physical image or seek to improve it by dressing it to the point of irreality (for biblical comments on vanity, see 1 Sam. 16:7; 1 Tim. 2:9; 4:8). Any of these things may be competing for my worship.

2. What consumes my emotional and physical energy? How am I expending myself in this world? Am I fighting for the preservation of the environment, for the acquisition of possessions and cash, for the security of my family, for the defense of the nation or for the preservation of a particular religious dogma? My object of worship may be that which consumes my emotions and activities.

3. What or who commands most of my behavior? To be sure, I'm stuck with certain accommodations in life. But can I identify who calls the shots in my life?

4. What is my primary reason for living? Do I feel that I am merely a biological accident of my parents, or have I assumed responsibility for the life God has given me and submitted its management to God and His service?

The need to worship is so dominating a force in psychological and spiritual life that it will be met, even if it is not met in completely rational ways. That is why we see educated people latch onto spellbinding political and religious leaders and follow them to their demise. Remember that coming to Christ in humble worship and submission brings healing to both mind and soul (see 2 Tim. 1:7, *KJV*; Heb. 10:19-22). Growing in your knowledge of Christ will correct faulty perceptions and shatter false gods in your life. Experiencing Christ will bring peace to a troubled emotional experience (see John 14:27). Believing in Christ places the outcome of our earthly lives in divine hands and assures us of eternal life with God the Father in His place prepared for us (see Jude 24). Because of His grace we are able to receive healing and salvation. "In him we have redemption through his blood, the forgiveness of sins, in accordance with the riches of God's grace that he lavished on us with all wisdom and understanding" (Eph. 1:7,8).

Note

1. Ada R. Habershon, *Hidden Pictures in the Old Testament* (Grand Rapids: Kregel Publications, 1916, public domain), pp. 90,91.

A B C PLAN FOR THE SESSION

Materials needed:
- Your Leader's Guide;
- Your Session 10 Leader's Guide Sheet;
- One copy of the Session 10 Lesson Outline for each group member;
- Four large index cards with questions and Scripture references;
- Chalkboard or overhead projector with transparencies;
- Overhead projector transparency of the Session 10 Lesson Outline (optional).

Advance preparations:
- Invite a group member to prepare a five-minute report on the role serpents played in the cultures of various nations in biblical times. Refer this person to a Bible dictionary for research;
- On four large index cards, write the four groups (*A-D*) of questions and respective Scripture references listed under Step 4 of the Bible Exploration—one group on each card.

A PPROACH (5 minutes)

Print horizontally on the chalkboard or overhead transparency *God's.* Using the *G* from the word *God's,* print vertically the word *grace.* Invite members to create an acrostic by suggesting words or phrases related to God's grace. The acrostic would be formed by using each letter of the word *grace.* Mention that the letters in grace do not necessarily have to be the first letters in the suggested words or phrases. They may be a letter in any part of the suggested words. An example would be the word *mercy.* It could intersect grace horizontally at the letter *r.* When the acrostic is complete, spend a few minutes discussing the suggested words or phrases.

Move to the Bible Exploration by stating that in today's session we will examine a particular incident in the history of the children of Israel when they desperately needed God's grace to be extended to them. Add, *We will discover the means God used to extend His grace to them and how it was a type of a greater grace that would be extended to all humankind.*

B IBLE EXPLORATION (45-50 minutes)

Step 1 (10 minutes): Say, *The setting for today's study finds the children of Israel continuing their wanderings through the desert wilderness. As they approached Edom, a land southeast of Canaan, they were refused passage through this land by the Edomites (see Num. 20:14-21). Forced to bypass Edom, the Israelites were attacked by the forces of the king of Arad when they reached the Negev desert*

(see 21:1). Add, *Although God gave the Israelites victory over these forces* (see 21:1-3), *we will see how their low morale caused them to sin.*

Distribute the Lesson Outlines to the group and encourage members to take notes on their outlines throughout the lesson. Do the same on the chalkboard or Lesson Outline transparency. Include in the discussions to follow the listed lesson material and suggested questions. Also include further lesson information from "Insights for the Leader."

Invite learners to open their Bibles to Numbers, chapter 21. Ask several volunteers to share in reading aloud verses 4-9.

Grumbling Israelites
Numbers 21:4-9
- What do you think caused the people to become impatient? (Perhaps weariness, living as nomads without permanent dwellings. While these may have been contributing factors, it appears that the underlying cause was rebellion, which seemed to be a recurring problem with the Israelites; see Exod. 16:2,3; 17:1-3; 32:1-6; Num. 14:1-3; 16:1-3,41; 20:2-5.) How can we deal with circumstances that try our patience? (refer to Rom. 15:1-4; Gal. 6:2; Phil. 4:5-7,13).
- Invite a volunteer to read 1 Samuel 15:23 and Proverbs 17:11. What can be learned about rebellion from these Scriptures?
- Is there ever any justification for grumbling and complaining? Why or why not? How does one's attitude enter into the picture?
- Share concerning God's daily provision of manna to the children of Israel throughout their desert wanderings (see Exod. 16) and His provision of water

(see 17:1-7; Num. 20:2-11). How did the Israelites demonstrate a lack of gratitude for God's provisions? (see Num 21:5).

● What lessons can we learn from Israel's lack of gratitude? (It can lead to the sins of rebellion, blasphemy, etc. and eventually result in God's discipline or judgment.)

Say, *From God's severe dealings with the children of Israel in this and other instances* (see Num. 12:1-14; 16:1-35), *one would think that they would live lives of extreme dedication to God. However, this was seldom the case in their history. This bronze serpent that Moses lifted up was to reappear in the record of Israel's history about seven centuries later.*

Step 2 (10 minutes): Say, *Before we consider the reappearance of the bronze snake in Israel's history, let's hear about the role that serpents played in the culture of different nations in Bible times.*

Member presents a five-minute report on serpents.

Following the report, point out that the practice of serpent worship by these nations eventually had an influence on the children of Israel. Say, *Let's see what happened about 700 years later when Hezekiah became king of Judah.*

Invite a learner to read aloud 2 Kings 18:1-4. Share that it is not known for sure when the Israelites began worshiping the bronze snake. Add, *Some commentators believe it could have begun during the reign of Hezekiah's father Ahaz* (see 2 Kings 16). *In any event, the Israelites were worshiping the bronze snake instead of God who was the source of the healing that their forebears received from the plague.*

Step 3 (10-12 minutes): Announce that we will now work together in small groups to discover lessons that we can learn from Israel's earlier and later experiences with the bronze serpent.

Move members into small groups of four to six and appoint group leaders. Give one index card (*A-D*) to each group. Tell the groups that they are to first research the Scripture references listed on their index cards and then answer the respective questions. Announce that they will have 10 minutes for research. (You may want to move among the groups to offer your assistance if needed.)

Step 4 (15-18 minutes): When time is up regather into larger group and ask for feedback from each group leader. As time permits incorporate the additional lesson material and suggested questions into the discussion.

Group A

1. How was the lifting up of the bronze snake a type of

an important event in Christ's life? Numbers 21:8,9; John 3:14,15; 12:32,33; Hebrews 9:14.

2. How did the Israelites sin in worshiping the bronze snake? Exodus 20:4,5; 2 Kings 18:4; Isaiah 42:8; Romans 1:22,23,25.

3. What forms of idolatry exist in our society today?

Discussion:

● How are idols that we have today often disguised? (They do not appear as an idol in a pagan sense of the word, but may be a form of recreation, an inordinate love for material things or activities that consume our time, energies, loyalties, etc.)

● How can we know that something in our lives is an idol? (When it precludes a lively relationship with Christ and inhibits our Christian service.)

● How can the person who helped lead us to Christ become an idol or center of our worship? (refer to 1 Cor. 1:10-17).

● Why is God alone worthy of our worship? (see Exod. 15:11; Deut. 4:31; 6:4,5; 32:4; Job 42:2; Ps. 24:10; John 3:16; 17:3; 1 John 1:8,9). Point out the fact that people will worship something—either good or bad. They must choose who or what they will worship.

Group B

1. The view of the serpent was an individual look ("anyone"; see Num. 21:8). What does this tell us about our acceptance of and relationship with Christ? John 3:16-18; 2 Corinthians 5:17; Revelation 3:21.

2. Had the plague not been arrested, the entire nation would no doubt have been afflicted. In what way can sin be compared to the serpent's bite? Isaiah 53:6; Romans 3:23; 6:23.

3. What are some philosophies and teachings people embrace when they refuse to accept the biblical truth that they are sinners and need a Savior?

Discussion:

● Does church membership or being raised in a Christian family insure salvation? Why or why not? (Remind the group of the well-known saying that God has no grandchildren.)

● People accept philosophies and teachings such as humanism, New Age beliefs, metaphysics, etc. in an effort to work out their own salvation apart from Christ.

Group C

1. The means for healing from the serpent's bite was singular; one merely looked at the serpent. What is the similarity in salvation in Christ? Numbers 21:9; John 3:14,15; 14:6; Acts 4:12.

2. How do people today complicate the gospel message or endeavor to add to it?

3. What do you believe is the bottom line for saving faith? (see John 1:12; 3:16; 5:24; Acts 16:31).

Discussion:

● Read what Ada R. Habershon has written regarding healing being singular that appears in "Insights for the Leader" under the heading "Lessons for Life" (fourth point).

● People complicate the gospel message today by endeavoring to add certain rules and regulations to it (see Gal. 1:6; 3:1-11).

Group D

1. How were the serpents that bit the Israelites a type of Satan? Genesis 3:14,15; Numbers 21:6; John 10:10; Romans 5:12; Revelation 12:9; 20:2.

2. How do we know evil is personally dominated by Satan? 2 Corinthians 4:4; Ephesians 2:2; 6:11,12.

3. What did Christ become for us on the cross, and how is this related to the bronze snake? Numbers 21:8,9; 2 Corinthians 5:21.

Discussion:

● The venomous snakes were a type of Satan in that Satan's purpose is to destroy humankind (see John 10:10; 1 Peter 5:8).

● Evil is personally dominated by Satan by the fact that he rules and influences the governments of this world (see John 12:31; 14:30; Eph. 6:12), as well as the spiritual forces of evil in the heavenly realms (see Eph. 6:12). When Christ was tempted by the devil, the devil offered Him all the kingdoms of the world (see Matt. 4:8,9). However, Satan is never called "King" of this world only "prince" (see John 12:31). As such, he is still under the dominion of God who reigns supreme.

● How was Satan defeated by God? (see John 3:16; Gal. 4:3-5; Col. 2:13-15; 1 John 3:8).

● When Christ became sin for us on the cross, He became the fulfillment of the serpent (representing sin) who was lifted up on the pole and through whom healing was provided to the Israelites. Christ, taking our sins upon Himself and becoming sin for us, provided healing and eternal life through His death and resurrection (see Rom. 5:9-11; 6:5-10; 10:9; 1 Pet. 2:24).

Move to the Conclusion by stating that we have seen how the bronze snake that was lifted up in the wilderness by Moses is a type of the Lord Jesus Christ who was lifted up on the cross for our redemption. While the bronze snake offered only physical healing, Christ's death offers forgiveness of sins and eternal life to all who will put their trust in Him (see John 3:16; Eph. 1:7,8).

C ONCLUSION (5 minutes)

Say, *Today's society offers many options for the healing of troubled souls or the fulfillment of empty lives. Many are pursuing these avenues and by doing so are believing Satan's lies that a savior may be found in materialism, pleasure, wealth, power, false religions, etc. If you have been looking to a false savior, look to Jesus Christ who alone is able to forgive your sins and grant you eternal life.*

Challenge believers to evaluate the object of their worship. Ask, *Are you giving God the worship that is due Him, or have idols crept into your life, unawares, and become the focus of your worship? Where do you need to put God first in your life? Or what areas need to be brought into line?*

Close the session by first providing an opportunity for persons who do not know Christ as their personal Savior to receive Him into their lives. Next, encourage everyone to pray with another member in the group and agree together for God's help to keep the Lord central in their lives. Some who are having struggles may want to share with their partner concerning specific areas that need to be brought into line so that God may be the sole object of their worship.

Encourage members to read chapter 10 of the Regal book, *Christ B.C.*, which will assist them in their time of daily devotions. Each day's devotion is based on the theme of *grace*.

Prophecies of the Messiah

SESSION VERSES

"But you, Bethlehem Ephrathah, though you are small among the clans of Judah, out of you will come for me one who will be ruler over Israel, whose origins are from of old, from ancient times." Micah 5:2

"So Joseph also went up from the town of Nazareth in Galilee to Judea, to Bethlehem the town of David, because he belonged to the house and line of David. He went there to register with Mary, who was pledged to be married to him and was expecting a child. While they were there, the time came for the baby to be born, and she gave birth to her firstborn, a son." Luke 2:4-7

SESSION FOCUS

The amazing accuracy of prophecies foretelling Jesus' birth, ministry, death and resurrection prove that the Bible is trustworthy. The Bible is not just history or literature, it is truth.

SESSION BASIS

Isaiah 53

SESSION GOAL

Examine major prophecies and their fulfillments regarding Christ's birth, ministry, death and resurrection. Then discuss how those fulfilled prophecies strengthen one's faith in the Word of God.

INSIGHTS FOR THE LEADER

Some people over the past two centuries have struggled with the validity of God's Word and with Christ's deity. And they have asked, If Jesus is the Christ, is He the only way to God? The Old Testament prophecies concerning Jesus' birth, ministry, death and resurrection will be examined in this session and will serve to resolve these struggles and answer many questions concerning Christ.

Prophecy and Faith

As a young high schooler, I entered a speaking contest that set me on a course that eventually shaped a good part of my life. In the contest, which was sponsored by the churches of my denomination, I was privileged to reach the state finals and win second place. But for me the most important aspect of the entire tournament was reading a book that had been recommended to me. It has long since gone out of print, but

it had a marked effect upon my thinking as a young Christian.

The book was titled *The Credentials of Jesus* and was written by an old Swedish pastor named Hjalmar Sundquist. He clarified answers to a number of questions that I had pondered a good deal. The questions were, How do I know that the Bible is true? and How do I know that Jesus Christ is the only way to know God?

Pastor Sundquist developed a line of reasoning that has, to this day, satisfied these questions for me and also helped me a great deal in taking the leap of faith in Jesus Christ and in God's Word. Sundquist states, "The Christo-centric approach. . .is in full accord with the words of the Master himself who said, 'I am the way, the truth, and the life: no man cometh unto the Father, but by me' [John 14:6, *KJV*]. As Christ himself is the center of our faith—its 'author and perfecter'

[Heb. 12:2],—so he is also the center of the Bible.

"Throughout the Old Testament we are constantly being led forward to him, who came in 'the fulness of time,' [Gal. 4:4, *KJV*] and the New Testament is brimfull of him from beginning to end. As he, in his own person and in what he was [has] wrought, has amply authenticated himself as the Son of God, so he has also authenticated the Scriptures, wherein he has made himself known to us, as the word of God. If we take Jesus at his word and accept him as the one he claims to be, we need have no difficulty in accepting and believing any of the details of his life and work. Why should we have any difficulty in accepting the miracles if we have already accepted the greatest miracle of them all, Jesus Christ himself with all his claims of one-ness with God."[1]

So as you study the messianic prophecies, ask yourself whether you believe in Jesus Christ because He was prophesied accurately or whether you believe in the prophesies because of the nature and character of Christ. There are people who withhold belief in Jesus as the Son of God because they have doubts about Scripture. I suspect that such withholding is a dodge, a means of avoiding the leap of faith. Their understanding of Scripture is limited to the rational and devoid of the spiritual. So often they claim that Jesus was a great man, but don't dare trust their lives and eternal destinies to Him. They would like to measure Christ by their own intellects and create doubts about Scripture to keep from surrendering in faith. I remember a missionary who stated that he believed in Jesus Christ, not because of the fact of the virgin birth of Christ, but he believed in the virgin birth because of the fact of his personal relationship with Christ.

Christ and Scripture are validating of each other. Christ affirms the Scripture and the Scripture affirms Him. Jesus was the Word of God incarnate: "The Word became flesh and made his dwelling among us. We have seen his glory, the glory of the One and Only, who came from the Father, full of grace and truth" (John 1:14). Scripture is the active, life-changing Word of God in written form (see 2 Thess. 2:15; 2 Tim. 3:16,17; Heb. 4:12). Both Christ and His Word are essential to our fully developed faith. I have suggested the previous ideas to get you to consider whether or not you have erected some intellectual barrier to a full understanding of and commitment to Jesus.

Jesus Fulfills God's Plan

One important aspect in removing intellectual barriers is prophecy, which in most cases is history written beforehand. It has been suggested that a history of Jesus Christ and His purchase of our salvation could have been written entirely from the prophecies concerning Him. First Corinthians 15:3,4 illustrates this: "For what I received I passed on to you as of first importance: that Christ died for our sins according to the Scriptures, that he was buried, that he was raised on the third day according to the Scriptures." The Old Testament is laced with prophetic material, from early in the book of Genesis to its very last books that declare God's plan, which was fulfilled by Jesus. Had the gospel—Christ's ministry and redemptive work—not been the fulfillment of prophecy, and had it not been consistent with God's plan proclaimed throughout Old Testament history, it would have been a false gospel. Many religious movements such as Mormonism and Jehovah's Witnesses have been established on some "new revelation" that is not consistent with the message of Scripture. These religions are false and their adherents are eternally lost unless they turn to Christ and believe the truth of the gospel.

Prophecies not only declare God's plan, but Jesus often referred to Old Testament prophecies in order to give evidence of His divinity and His authenticity as the promised Messiah (see Matt. 21:13-16,42-46; 22:41-46; 26:51-54; 9:11-13). Yet despite their exposure to Christ and His teachings, most of the religious leaders of Jesus' day missed the Messiahship of Jesus and sought to destroy His influence on the Jewish community (see Mark 11:18; 14:55,56).

Isaiah 53: An Illustration of Christ

The greatest sweep of prophecy concerning Jesus may be found in the book of Isaiah. Isaiah was a man, inspired by God, who spoke boldly to the problems of his day as well as to future events. This great prophet lived more than 600 years before the birth of Christ, at a time when the kingdom of Israel had been divided into two nations and the northern kingdom had been swallowed by Assyrian hordes (see 2 Kings 17:7-23). At the beginning of Isaiah's ministry, King Ahaz came to power in the southern kingdom and openly sacrificed to idols (see 2 Kings 16:1-4). During this time Isaiah predicted the Assyrian invasion of Israel, which included both the southern and northern kingdoms (see Isa. 8:6-8). At the same time the prophet saw an end to Israel's troubles in the coming of the Messiah (see 7:14; 8:13-15; 11:1-5,10-12).

Later on in Isaiah's ministry, after Ahaz had died, Isaiah recorded what is now considered the largest concentration of messianic prophecy in the Bible.

These prophecies are found in Isaiah, chapters 40-66. These chapters tell us of both the restoration of Israel (see 49:8-26) and the coming of the Messiah.

The focus on the Messiah becomes sharpest in Isaiah 53. With Bible in hand, let's "walk" through Isaiah 53 and compare each verse to New Testament verses about Christ.

Isaiah 53:1: "Who has believed our message and to whom has the arm of the Lord been revealed?" This verse is quoted in Romans 10:16 and refers to the fact that many of the Jews rejected Jesus' message of good news.

Isaiah 53:2: "He grew up before him like a tender shoot, and like a root out of dry ground. He had no beauty or majesty to attract us to him." This reference to "a tender shoot" refers to the fact that Jesus would be born of the house and lineage of David, a shoot "from the stump of Jesse" (11:1). Jesus' genealogy is listed in Matthew 1. It includes King David, the son of Jesse (see v. 6). Romans 15:8,12 confirms that Jesus is the Promised One: "For I tell you that Christ has become a servant of the Jews on behalf of God's truth, to confirm the promises made to the patriarchs so that the Gentiles may glorify God for his mercy. . . .Isaiah says, 'The root of Jesse will spring up, one who will arise to rule over the nations; the Gentiles will hope in him.'" The "root out of dry ground" (Isa. 53:2) is believed by scholars to be a reference to Jesus' humble beginnings (see Lev. 12:1-8; Luke 2:6,7,21,24). The lack of beauty and majesty in Jesus' appearance is thought to be a reference to Jesus' final days of suffering when He was beaten, humiliated and mocked (see Luke 18:31,32; 22:63,65). Isaiah describes His appearance at this time as "so disfigured beyond that of any man" (Isa. 52:14).

Isaiah 53:3: "He was despised and rejected by men, a man of sorrows, and familiar with suffering." The beginning of this verse describes the event in Luke 4:16-29 where Jesus was rejected by the people in whose midst He grew to manhood. The references to His suffering and rejection in Isaiah 53:3 (also see 52:14) also bring to mind the description of Jesus being beaten and mocked by the soldiers before being led away to be crucified (see Matt. 27:27-31).

Isaiah 53:4-6: "Surely he took up our infirmities and carried our sorrows, yet we considered him stricken by God, smitten by him, and afflicted. But he was pierced for our transgressions, he was crushed for our iniquities; the punishment that brought us peace was upon him, and by his wounds we are healed. We all, like sheep, have gone astray, each of us has turned to his own way; and the Lord has laid on him the iniquity of us all." These verses graphically describe the reason for Jesus' suffering and the purpose behind His death on the cross. Christ died for us, a sinful people who had turned our backs on Him. Count the number of times you see the words "our," "we" and "us" repeated in these verses. Jesus' purpose in dying was clearly for our sake and we are certainly undeserving of such a sacrifice. (For further study read Matthew 8:16,17; John 19:33-37; Romans 4:25; and 1 Peter 2:24,25.)

Isaiah 53:7-9: "He was oppressed and afflicted, yet he did not open his mouth; he was led like a lamb to the slaughter, and as a sheep before her shearers is silent, so he did not open his mouth. By oppression and judgment he was taken away. And who can speak of his descendants? For he was cut off from the land of the living; for the transgression of my people he was stricken. He was assigned a grave with the wicked, and with the rich in his death, though he had done no violence, nor was any deceit in his mouth." These verses are direct references to Jesus' trial, death and burial. First, Jesus is referred to as a lamb, willingly giving His life (see v. 7). This is supported by the words of John the Baptist, "Look, the Lamb of God" (John 1:29,35); the words of Revelation 5:6; and by Phillip as he explained these verses from Isaiah and their reference to Christ to the Ethiopian eunuch (see Acts 8:26-35). Isaiah 53:7 also describes Christ as silent before His oppressors. Matthew 27:12 says, "When he was accused by the chief priests and the elders, he gave no answer" (also see Mark 14:60,61; 15:4,5; Luke 23:8,9; and John 19:8,9). Isaiah 53:8, "who can speak of his descendants?" points to the fact that Jesus had no physical children. Verse 9 also indicates that Christ was given an unfair trial. This is supported by the accounts of false witnesses in Jesus' trial before the chief priests and in Pilate's inability to find fault with Him (see Mark 14:55,56; Luke 23:4). Verse 9 of Isaiah 53 also describes Jesus' crucifixion between two deserving criminals (see Matt. 27:38). Isaiah 53:9 continues, "and with the rich in his death." Jesus was buried in the tomb of Joseph of Arimathea, a prominent member of the Jewish Council and a wealthy man as declared in Scripture and as evidenced by the sort of tomb He had prepared for himself (see Matt. 27:57-60; Mark 15:43-46). Finally, Isaiah 53:9 suggests Jesus' sinlessness when it declares that there was no "deceit in his mouth." First Peter 2:22, in speaking of Jesus, quotes this verse, "He committed no sin, and no deceit was found in his mouth."

Isaiah 53:10-12: "Yet it was the Lord's will to crush him and cause him to suffer, and though the Lord makes his life a guilt offering, he will see his offspring and prolong his days, and the will of the Lord will prosper in his hand. After the suffering of his soul, he will see the light of life and be satisfied; by his knowledge my righteous servant will justify many, and he will bear their iniquities. Therefore I will give him a portion among the great, and he will divide the spoils with the strong, because he poured out his life unto death, and was numbered with the transgressors. For he bore the sin of many, and made intercession for the transgressors." The most obvious theme of these verses is that Jesus died for our sins as a part of God's plan to redeem us from our fallen state. The phrases "cause him to suffer," "makes his life a guilt offering," "will bear their iniquities," "poured out his life unto death" and "bore the sin of many" all testify to Jesus' saving sacrifice on the cross. First Peter 2:23-25 supports this in saying, "When they hurled their insults at him, he did not retaliate; when he suffered, he made no threats. Instead, he entrusted himself to him who judges justly. He himself bore our sins in his body on the tree, so that we might die to sins and live for righteousness; by his wounds you have been healed. For you were like sheep going astray, but now you have returned to the Shepherd and Overseer of your souls." Isaiah 53:11, "he will see the light of life," is a reference to Jesus' resurrection. In Luke 22:37, Jesus quotes Isaiah 53:12, "And he was numbered with the transgressors," in reference to Jesus' arrest as a criminal and His crucifixion with criminals as a fulfillment of prophecy.

Lastly, Isaiah 53 makes reference to the fact that Jesus makes "intercession for the transgressors" (v. 12). Hebrews 7:25 repeats this role of Christ in saying, "Therefore he is able to save completely those who come to God through him, because he always lives to intercede for them."

Other Prophecies of the Messiah

In Isaiah 53 we have it. The whole of the gospel enveloped in a single chapter of Old Testament Scripture. What assurance this presents that the Bible is truth and the claims of Christ are trustworthy! But this is only a small slice of Old Testament prophecy concerning Jesus Christ. To supplement what is written in Isaiah 53, you may want to read the following Old Testament prophecies concerning Jesus' birth, ministry, death and resurrection as well as their corresponding New Testament fulfillments.

The Event:	The Prophecy:	The Fulfillment:
The way prepared	Isaiah 40:3-5	Luke 3:3-6
Preceded by John	Malachi 3:1	Luke 7:24-27
Born in Bethlehem	Micah 5:2	Luke 2:4-7
Born of a virgin	Isaiah 7:14	Luke 1:26-34
Flight to Egypt	Hosea 11:1	Matthew 2:13-15
Slaughter of children by Herod	Jeremiah 31:15	Matthew 2:16-18
Taught in parables	Psalm 78:2	Matthew 13:34,35
Betrayal by a friend	Psalm 41:9	Luke 22:47,48
Forsaken by the Father	Psalm 22:1	Matthew 27:46
Resurrection from death	Psalm 16:9-11	Mark 16:6,7; Acts 2:22-28
Ascension into heaven	Psalm 68:18	Ephesians 4:7-9

The Truth about Jesus:

Old Testament prophecies cover a full sweep of Jesus Christ's birth, life, death, resurrection and ascension. Each significant event is set forth in the Old Testament and confirmed in the New. The apostle Peter describes the important role prophecy plays in undergirding and reinforcing our faith in Christ: "Concerning this salvation, the prophets, who spoke of the grace that was to come to you, searched intently and with the greatest care, trying to find out the time and circumstances to which the Spirit of Christ in them was pointing when he predicted the sufferings of Christ and the glories that would follow. It was revealed to them that they were not serving themselves but you, when they spoke of the things that have now been told you by those who have preached the gospel to you by the Holy Spirit sent from heaven. Even angels long to look into these things" (1 Pet. 1:10-12).

The words of prophecy are holy and grounded in the Spirit of Christ. They are not empty sounds, belching out catechisms and creeds. We can repeat these great mysteries to the point that they become like meaningless monosyllables, or we can find in them strength for our faith and a renewed awe of God and what He has done in Christ.

Malcolm Muggeridge in his book *Jesus Rediscovered* describes his life-changing encounter with God. Muggeridge says, "What can be said with certainty is that, once the confrontation has been experienced— the rocky summit climbed, the interminable desert crossed—an unimaginably delectable vista presents itself, so vast, so luminous, so enchanting, that the small ecstasies of human love, and the small satisfactions of human achievement, by comparison pale into insignificance."[2]

The testimony of faith of Muggeridge is humble and gentle while C.S. Lewis makes a similar point but more sharply. Having encountered the claims of Jesus and the validity of the prophecies about Him, Lewis says, "I am trying here to prevent anyone saying the really foolish thing that people often say about Him: 'I'm ready to accept Jesus as a great moral teacher, but I don't accept His claim to be God.' This is the one thing we must not say. A man who was merely a man and said the sort of things Jesus said would not be a great moral teacher. He would either be a lunatic—on a level with the man who says he is a poached egg—or else he would be the Devil of Hell. You must make your choice. Either this man was, and is, the son of God: or else a madman or something worse. You can shut Him up for a fool, you can spit at Him and kill Him as a demon; or can fall at His feet and call Him Lord and God. But let us not come with any patronising nonsense about His being a great human teacher. He has not left that open to us. He did not intend to. . . .He was neither a lunatic nor a fiend: and. . .unlikely it may seem, I have to accept the view that He was and is God. God has

landed on this enemy-occupied world in human form."[3]

The testimony of the Bible, especially the prophets, confirms that Jesus Christ is the Son of God. Belief in Him still requires a step of faith, but that step can be taken on solid ground.

Notes

1. Hjalmar Sundquist, *The Credentials of Jesus* (Chicago: The Covenant Book Concern, 1930), pp. 95,96.
2. Malcolm Muggeridge, *Jesus Rediscovered* (Wheaton: Tyndale House Publishers, 1974), p.49.
3. C.S. Lewis, *Mere Christianity* (New York: The Macmillan Publishing Co., Inc., 1943,1945,1952), pp. 55,56.

A B C PLAN FOR THE SESSION

Materials needed:
- Your Leader's Guide;
- Your Session 11 Leader's Guide Sheet;
- One copy of the Session 11 Lesson Outline for each group member;
- Sixteen small index cards or Post-it Notes with Scripture references;
- Chalkboard or overhead projector with transparencies;
- Overhead projector transparency of the Session 11 Lesson Outline (optional).

Advance preparation:
- Write the following Roman numerals, letters and Scripture reference(s) on 16 index cards or Post-it Notes (one for each card):

  I. A. Matthew 1:1,6; Romans 15:8,12;

  I. B. Luke 1:26-34;

  I. C. Luke 2:4-7;

  II. A. Matthew 2:13-15;

  II. B. Matthew 2:16-18;

  III. A. Luke 3:2-6;

  III. B. Luke 7:24-27;

  IV. A. Romans 10:16;

  IV. B. Matthew 13:53-58; Luke 4:16-29;

  V. A. Matthew 27:27-31; Luke 18:31,32;

  V. B. Matthew 27:12; Revelation 5:6;

  V. C. Matthew 27:38,57-60; Mark 14:55,56; 1 Peter 2:22;

  V. D. Matthew 8:16,17; John 19:33,34; Romans 4:25; 1 Peter 2:24;

  V. E. Luke 22:37; Hebrews 7:25; 1 Peter 2:23-25;

  VI. A. Mark 16:6,7; Acts 2:22-28;

  VI. B. Acts 1:10,11; Ephesians 4:7-9.

 PPROACH (5-8 minutes)

Before the session begins write on the chalkboard or overhead transparency the suggested steps that are used by scientists to test if a theory or hypothesis is true. (Keep these steps out of view until you are ready to share them.)

Ask, *What criteria do scientists use to prove if*

something is true or not? Allow several moments for thinking and then receive responses from the group. Next share the following steps used in the scientific world to test a theory or hypothesis (a tentative formula or explanation for a principle operating in nature).

1. A scientist begins with a preliminary observation as to what he or she thinks may be true.
2. The scientist then decides what information is needed in order to prove if his or her preliminary observation is true.
3. Next, an experiment must be devised by which the scientist's preliminary observation can be tested.
4. The experiment is then conducted several times and the results are weighed against the preliminary observation. If necessary, the observation is revised to reflect the results of the experiment.
5. The experiment must be repeated several times with the same results supporting the observation in order for the observation to be considered true.

Move to the Bible Exploration by saying, *Today we are going to look at Old Testament prophecies of Christ's birth, life on earth, death and resurrection. These prophecies were written long before Jesus was born, and they predicted certain events that would take place in His life. Let's examine these prophecies to see if they were accurately fulfilled, if they prove the trustworthiness of the Bible, and what effect they may have on our faith in the Word of God.*

B IBLE EXPLORATION
(40-45 minutes)

Step 1 (15 minutes): Distribute the Lesson Outline to everyone. Next, move members into small groups of four to six and appoint group leaders. Distribute equally among the groups the index cards or Post-it Notes you prepared in advance. Point out that the Scripture reference(s) on each card corresponds with a Roman numeral and letter on the Lesson Outline. Announce that group members are to research the Scriptures listed on their outlines and the corresponding Scriptures on their cards to discover the accuracy of the prophecies concerning Jesus. Encourage learners to list on their outlines the content of the prophecies and their fulfillments researched by their respective group. Tell members that they will have 15 minutes for research and working.

Step 2 (15 minutes): When time is up regather into larger group and receive feedback from group leaders in the order of the points on the Lesson Outline. Discuss the various points and encourage learners to take notes on their outlines regarding areas that were not researched by their respective group. Use the following as a basis for completing and discussing the points of the outline (also refer to the "Isaiah 53: An Illustration of Christ" section of "Insights for the Leader" for additional information):

- Isaiah 11:1; 53:2/Matthew 1:1,6; Romans 15:8,12—Jesus Christ was from the lineage of Jesse, King David's father.
- Isaiah 7:14/Luke 1:26-34—A virgin gave birth to Jesus.
- Micah 5:2/Luke 2:4-7—Jesus was born in Bethlehem.
- Hosea 11:1/Matthew 2:13-15—Joseph and Mary fled for a time to Egypt with Jesus.
- Jeremiah 31:15/Matthew 2:16-18—Herod had all baby boys slaughtered in Bethlehem and its vicinity from ages two and under. (Ramah was about 10 miles from Bethlehem.)
- Isaiah 40:3-5/Luke 3:2-6—The way was prepared for Christ's ministry.
- Malachi 3:1/Luke 7:24-27—Christ was preceded by a messenger, John the Baptist.
- Isaiah 53:1/Romans 10:16—Many Jews rejected Jesus' message.
- Isaiah 53:3a/Matthew 13:53-58; Luke 4:16-29—Jesus was rejected by His own people.
- Isaiah 52:14; 53:3/Matthew 27:27-31; Luke 18:31,32—Jesus suffered greatly especially during the time between His trial and death on the cross. He was beaten, flogged, mocked, insulted and then crucified. (Optional: If time permits, read the account of Jesus' crucifixion from Luke 23:32-49.)
- Isaiah 53:7,8/Matthew 27:12; Revelation 5:6 (also see Acts 8:26-35)—Jesus is the Lamb of God who was slain for our sins; He was silent before His accusers.
- Isaiah 53:9/Matthew 27:38,57-60; Mark 14:55,56; 1 Peter 2:22—Jesus was falsely accused but was found faultless; He was crucified between two criminals and buried in the tomb of a wealthy man. He committed no sin.
- Isaiah 53:4-6/Matthew 8:16,17; John 19:33,34; Romans 4:25; 1 Peter 2:24—He healed the sick and possessed; after He had died on the cross, Jesus was pierced in the side by a soldier's sword; Jesus died for our sins; He bore our sins so that we can be healed of sin.

● Isaiah 53:10-12/Luke 22:37; Hebrews 7:25; 1 Peter 2:23-25—Jesus was arrested and crucified as a criminal; But He rose from the dead to intercede for (speaks to God on the behalf of) those who come to Him in faith; Jesus died for our sins as part of God's plan of salvation for the world.

● Psalm 16:9-11/Mark 16:6,7; Acts 2:22-28—God raised Jesus from the dead. (If time permits, read the account of the empty tomb from John 20:1-18.)

● Psalm 68:18/Acts 1:10,11; Ephesians 4:7-9—Jesus ascended into heaven.

Move to Step 3 by saying, *We have discussed the various prophecies concerning Jesus' birth, life, death, resurrection and ascension to heaven.* Add, *The accuracy of these prophecies are quite obvious. Now let's discuss how these facts and faith work together.*

Step 3 (10-15 minutes): As outlined in the Approach, refer to the criteria by which scientists establish something to be true. Then ask the following questions and discuss possible answers with your learners:

● In evaluating spiritual matters to see if they are true, what problems do you see in applying only a scientific approach to your study?

● In what ways can a scientific approach to studying Scripture help you in understanding some facts about the Bible? What areas of Scripture cannot be understood scientifically?

● What are some ways you can evaluate if your understanding of something in the Bible is correct?

● At what point do you think a person needs to place his or her faith in Christ in order to understand what the Bible says?

● In what ways does faith in Christ help a person understand what God is saying in His Word?

After several minutes of discussion, share Lloyd Ahlem's comments in "Insights for the Leader" under the heading "Prophecy and Faith" concerning the Christo-center approach to Scripture. Do this by reading the paragraph that begins with the words, "So as you study the messianic prophecies. . . ." Then move to the Conclusion.

C ONCLUSION (5-7 minutes)

Say, *If you have not received Christ as your personal Savior, could you be one who because of a lack of understanding of **all** Scripture refuses to accept any part of it as truth, especially that which deals with the claims of Christ? Could you be using these intellectual doubts to avoid taking the leap of faith?* Encourage and give any person in the group who may fit into this category an opportunity to receive Christ as his or her personal Savior.

Next ask, *As believers, how may the fulfillment of Old Testament prophecies that we have considered strengthen our faith in the Word of God today?* Allow several minutes for responses. Point out that God's trustworthiness in fulfilling these prophecies only reassures of His faithfulness to one day bring to pass prophecies concerning future events that are yet unfulfilled. Add, *And His promises concerning our spiritual growth and details of our personal lives can surely be realized as we obey His Word and meet the requisites of these promises.*

Close the session in prayer, thanking God that He has given us so much evidence that proves that Jesus Christ is the Savior promised to us in the Old Testament. Ask God to help learners put their faith in the truth given in His Word.

Encourage members to read chapter 11 of the Regal book, *Christ B.C.*, which will assist them in their time of daily devotions. Each day's devotion is based on the theme of *truth*.

The Suffering Servant

SESSION VERSES

"Surely he took up our infirmities and carried our sorrows." Isaiah 53:4

"The next day John saw Jesus coming toward him and said, 'Look, the Lamb of God, who takes away the sin of the world!'" John 1:29

SESSION FOCUS

The prophet Isaiah foretold the suffering that Christ would experience. Because Christ understands pain and suffering, He understands our needs and our suffering.

SESSION BASIS

Isaiah 42:2,3,6,7; 49:1; 50:6; 52:14; 53:1,2,9; Hebrews 2:18; 4:15

SESSION GOAL

Examine Jesus' qualifications for the role of Savior of the world and then list reasons why Jesus, as the Savior, is able to understand people's sufferings.

INSIGHTS FOR THE LEADER

In this session you will be looking at the prophecies of Isaiah that are commonly called the "Servant Songs." Through an examination of these prophecies and their New Testament fulfillments, you and your Bible students will clearly see why Jesus is completely qualified to serve as the Savior of the world.

Qualifications for Leadership

Often political campaigns are circuses—theater and politics all wrapped into one brazen show of human ostentation. Candidates announce themselves as the answer to all the problems of the world. The difficult issues associated with international and domestic affairs will be corrected if only the current candidates are elected to office. In the candidates' brazen declarations, they sometimes forget that their war, college and medical records are all open to public scrutiny.

But apparently all the hype and baloney of political campaigns have become a necessary part of getting one's favorite candidates elected. This is the means by which leaders are sometimes promoted as qualified for serving in a public office in our world today.

What a contrast to Christ's qualifications for His

leadership role and to His methods of service as outlined in the Old Testament. They are listed in Isaiah in four passages called the "Servant Songs." These passages are little vignettes illustrating the character of the One whom God appointed as our Savior and Lord (see Isa. 42:1-7; 49:1-7; 50:4-11; and 52:13—53:12).

The Unacceptable Image

The obedient, suffering servant described by Isaiah would never have fulfilled our concept of a leader in our world. So also Christ, the King-on-a-donkey, did not fulfill the Jews' concept of who the Messiah would be. Isaiah 53:1 says, "Who has believed our message and to whom has the arm of the Lord been revealed?" John 12:38 repeats this verse in reference to many of the Jews who, after witnessing many miraculous signs done by Jesus, still refused to believe in Him (see v. 37). Jesus' image was unacceptable to them; it didn't fit their misconceptions.

Another area in which Jesus would probably be considered lacking, in human terms, was His outward appearance. In Isaiah He is described as one who "had no beauty or majesty to attract us to him, nothing in his appearance that we should desire him" (53:2). During the time before His death, after He had been flogged and tormented (see Isa. 50:6; Matt. 27:26,29,30), His outward image must have been hideous. Isaiah 52:14 says that "there were many who were appalled at him—his appearance was so disfigured beyond that of any man and his form marred beyond human likeness." To the nonbeliever His image was that of a criminal.

Isaiah 42:2 describes another aspect of Jesus' image. He would "not shout or cry out, or raise his voice in the streets." Often in the Gospels, Jesus makes a point not to draw attention to His deeds. After healing a deaf and mute man, Jesus commanded those who witnessed the miracle "not to tell anyone" (Mark 7:36).

Christ works quietly and unobtrusively. He accomplishes His task without a public relations consultant, political advisor or without flashy diplomacy. This is a definite contrast to the TV splashes leaders make today. Modern candidates' acceptability often depends upon their media images. If God were to operate according to the guidelines set by Madison Avenue professional campaigns, His Son Jesus would be out of the running for any position of leadership.

God's Concept of the Messiah

Obviously God's standards for leadership are different from worldly standards. It is not His method to launch some great political campaign to deal with the problems of suffering in society. It is His way to work from the inside out, to initiate change within people, one person at a time (see Phil. 2:12,13). Then change and help for the suffering will come to our society (see Matt. 25:34-40). For this task, Jesus is uniquely qualified (see John 3:3; 2 Cor. 5:17).

The servant of Isaiah illustrates Jesus' unique qualifications as the Messiah. He is one who will reach out to people where they hurt and encourage them where they are weak. Isaiah 42:3 says, "A bruised reed he will not break, and a smoldering wick he will not snuff out. In faithfulness he will bring forth justice" (also see Matt. 12:15-21). God's appointed Messiah is gentle, mending broken lives, and He will not put out the struggling fires of faith that burn in us. He has put ministering to our needs for healing in a position of importance. Bringing healing from our sin is the *primary* purpose of His presence.

Isaiah 42:6,7 tells us that Jesus came to be "a covenant for the people and a light for the Gentiles, to open eyes that are blind, to free captives from prison and to release from the dungeon those who sit in darkness."

Isaiah 53:4 says, "Surely he took up our infirmities and carried our sorrows." These prophecies were fulfilled both in the miracles of physical healing that Jesus wrought as well as in the spiritual light He has brought to searching souls. Matthew 8:16,17 reveals that both the spiritually oppressed—the demon possessed—and the physically sick were healed by Jesus. Jesus did all this to "fulfill what was spoken through the prophet Isaiah: 'He took up our infirmities and carried our diseases'" (v. 17). Again a contrast can be drawn between the sacrificial, servant leadership of Christ and the privileged existence that worldly leaders may expect. Whereas political leaders are often so far removed from the hurting and oppressed that they have to take special tours and talk to consultants to find out how the "other half" lives, Jesus is personally acquainted with grief and suffering and therefore perfectly empathizes with our hurt.

Another characteristic of the Messiah is that He was chosen by God. Isaiah 49:1 says, "Before I was born the Lord called me." God's identification of Jesus as His chosen One is repeated on the Mount of Transfiguration. In the presence of Peter, John and James, God proclaimed of Jesus: "This is my Son, whom I have chosen; listen to him" (Luke 9:35). Jesus does not beg, coerce, campaign or request our acceptance of Him as Savior. He is Savior despite any acknowledgement on our part. He has no competition, because He is the only authentic means of salvation for us. Jesus said, "I am the way and the truth and the life. No one comes to the Father except through me" (John 14:6). Jesus can never be demoted, voted out of office or replaced by any means. He stands forever as the only Savior of the world.

From time to time elected officials break the law or rules for ethical conduct. In a democratic society special prosecutors may be appointed and committees named to hold hearings on such conduct. Usually, elaborately constructed defenses exalting the virtues of the accused are presented. Opposing witnesses may parade before the panels presenting contradictory views. Efforts to get media exposure for each one's biases are strongly made. When the proceedings are concluded, no one has admitted guilt and questions of truth and falsehood linger unresolved.

What a contrast to the servant of Isaiah who "had done no violence, nor was any deceit in his mouth" (Isa. 53:9). He required no defense, because all accusations against Him were false. In Matthew 27:13,14 we read, "Then Pilate asked him, 'Don't you hear the testimony they are bringing against you?' But Jesus made no reply, not even to a single charge—to the great amazement of the governor."

We also may be falsely accused at times. It is a comfort to know that Christ can empathize intimately with such suffering. Sometimes we will see God's vindication for the wrong done to us, but often we will not. In either situation we are to be examples, providing justice and mercy to our world and never forgetting that vengeance is not our affair (see Mic. 6:8; Rom. 12:19). Only God can repay such wrong. Such examples—extending justice and mercy—are a rarity in our self-oriented world and may, like Jesus' example, result in amazement in others.

In being falsely accused, Jesus was labeled as a felon and died a felon's death—crucifixion. Crucifixion was a common way for Romans to execute their prisoners. Isaiah says, "He was assigned a grave with the wicked" (53:9), and so Jesus died painfully, hanging on a cross between two thieves (see Matt. 27:38). Jesus' disciples were afraid of being associated with their crucified leader. Such an association might not only endanger them, it would also taint them with the reputation of a despised felon.

Jewish believer Moishe Rosen in his book Y'Shua, tells of the days after his conversion to Christ. He was enthusiastic about his faith and determined to tell every one of his fellow Jews about his experience. But in his culture he soon realized that by committing his life to Christ, he had likewise been tainted by association with a despised person. His people, once his friends, now dug up every real and imagined fault of his past and made it common lore concerning him. With Jesus, Rosen had been assigned to the ranks of those held in contempt.

As a result of his loyalty to Jesus, Rosen had one particularly challenging and eventually rewarding encounter with a man to whom Rosen had shared his faith. This man was so elated at defeating the arguments and testimony of Rosen that he sought out a rabbi to direct him in further study of Isaiah 53. The rabbi felt that the passage was not regarded by Jews as a messianic passage. But the man did further research and saw the messianic message. Eventually he had to conclude that Jesus was the subject of Isaiah 53 and surrendered to Him as the Messiah. The man was happy to tell Rosen of his pilgrimage 11 years later when Rosen was addressing the church where the man was now a deacon.[1]

Jesus' experience of death adds the final qualification to His job description as Savior of the world. Raised up on the cross as a felon, Jesus took the sins of the world, our sins, upon Himself and experienced the pain of separation from God. In darkness and aloneness Jesus cried out, "My God, my God, why have you forsaken me?" (Matt. 27:46; also refer to 2 Cor. 5:21). Jesus identified with us when we were separated from God, crushed by the burden of our sins. Jesus also identifies with our physical pain because He experienced the ultimate in physical suffering: a painful torturous death.

Unlike Any Human Idea

Our concept of what we need in order to solve the problems of the world can be colored by many influences. We may think that we need a highly visible savior, with the political clout and material resources to relieve suffering and combat sin in society. We may think we need programs that will reach the masses and lift them out of their misery and into a better life. We may look for a defense attorney to fight for justice on our behalf. Often people cling to political or social leaders who seem to have answers or whose charismatic personalities capture the world's attention for awhile. Or people may become cynical and apathetic, feeling that the solutions to this old world's problems are too tall of an order for anyone to fill.

The inadequacy of humans to resolve the problems of the world points to the fact that our real needs are deeper and have a spiritual source. The world needs the Savior, Jesus Christ, who chose to change the world one person at a time. Christ could have wielded His power in its fullness and destroyed evil with a blink of the eye. But He did not. He came personally and, by changing human hearts, has and is changing the world in powerful ways.

Our ideas about what is needed to deal with sin, pain and suffering are limited compared to God's insight. An illustration of this comes from the difficulty many Jews had in accepting Jesus as the promised Messiah. They had expected the Messiah to come as a political figure who would break the yoke of Roman oppression. Because of this misconception they did not recognize Jesus. Human ideas such as these have a number of predictable characteristics that, without the guidance of God's insight, will lead people to fail in recognizing Jesus' Lordship. These characteristics include the following:

1. Human ideas are colored by human preconceptions. We bring our limitations and biases to all we think.
2. Human ideas are inevitably limited to human

comprehension and logic. God is above logic; logic is a human invention to help us think clearly within human limitations.

3. Human ideas measure attributes and abilities in terms of our own needs for those attributes and abilities. What is desirable reflects what we want to see in our own lives. What is weak is like that which we do not want to be. What is beautiful is that which appeals to our limited senses and that which we are persuaded to think of as attractive.

4. Human ideas, without divine light, are inevitably self-centered. We value that which seems good to us in our very shortsighted vision.

5. Human ideas about God inevitably diminish God to mere human character and size. Thus a God who could be a man, a God who could suffer, a God who could die, a God who was of unattractive appearance was not desired or recognized by anyone who had a human vision of grandeur in mind.

Many people today feel that, as a point of freedom of religion in a pluralistic society, no one should be able to tell them if their concepts about Jesus are wrong. To them, it becomes a matter of "open-mindedness" to be able to form a personal belief system. The problem is, Jesus isn't an elected official and God's Kingdom isn't a democracy. Jesus is the Savior and He does not work according to personal agendas. If we cannot recognize Him as Lord, then we are lost.

Prophecy gives us a basis by which we can identify Jesus as the Christ because it is by God's authority and with His insight that the prophets spoke. Second Peter 1:20,21 declares, "Above all, you must understand that no prophecy of Scripture came about by the prophet's own interpretation. For prophecy never had its origin in the will of man, but men spoke from God as they were carried along by the Holy Spirit."

All of the prophecies foretelling the coming of the Messiah to earth have been fulfilled in Jesus. In reading them we have learned that the Messiah is one who has suffered for the sake of our sins, and through whose suffering we can find healing for our souls. Because of His suffering, we have a Savior that can care for us and meet our needs for redemption from sin, compassion in times of pain and assurance of ultimate triumph over death (see Heb. 2:14-18). (NOTE: If your church or denomination's tenets of faith include physical healing through Christ's sufferings, be sure to incorporate this belief into this study.)

The Question of Suffering

It is difficult to describe Jesus as a suffering servant without raising the question asked by people who challenge the fact that God is loving. The question is this: If God is loving why does He allow suffering? The world is filled to the brim with the suffering, and to some there doesn't seem to be a God to abate it. If this question comes up during your group's discussion, the following points may help them:

1. It is important to establish that it is in God's nature to love. If this were not so, Christ would never have come into the world. In loving us, God set us free so that we can choose to love Him in return. God loves us willingly and wants us, of our free will, to return His love (see Matt. 22:37; John 3:16; 1 John 4:7-10).

2. In freedom we have the right to refuse God's love, to disobey His Word and to follow our own designs. Adam and Eve illustrate this point for us. They chose to play God for themselves and to serve themselves (see Gen. 3:1-24). Given their limited human aptitudes and visions, they made some bad choices. Pain and death resulted. At this point the reality of physical and spiritual death entered the world, and with it all its trappings: separation from God, disease, enmity between people (see 2:17; 4:8). Death has a ripple effect, touching lives indiscriminately. We experience pain oftentimes because we live in a fallen world (see Rom. 5:12).

3. As people, it is our tendency to put ourselves first, to play God. In doing so we discover that others are trying to do the same. Because we cannot play God and have our wishes thwarted, we will experience conflict with others—who are seeking their own ends—and will probably inflict pain to preserve our wills. In the same way our pain sometimes finds its source in the selfish will of others—whether we deserve it or not (see Jas. 3:16; 1 Pet. 2:19).

4. In order to deal with the problem of pain, God became one of us and suffered with us. No god invented by man could do such a thing. God, out of the depths of His love, has responded to the pain that exists in our fallen world because of sin. He has personally identified with all that we suffer through Christ's experience on earth. Hebrews 4:15 says, "For we do not have a high priest who is unable to sympathize with our weaknesses, but we have one who has been tempted in every way, just as we are—yet was

without sin" (also see 2:18). Only a suffering servant could bring salvation to our broken hearts and identify with our human needs.

5. As Christians, our question should not be so much, Why do we suffer? as it should be, How can my suffering be used to God's glory? Hopefully one of the greatest differences between godly people and the ungodly is how they suffer. Like the apostle Paul we can regard our suffering as not worthy of comparison to the wonderful things we will experience in eternity (see Rom. 8:18). It has been said that pagans waste their pain because they see no meaning in their suffering. When we understand the truth of Romans 8:18 (in the light of eternity our suffering is inconsequential), then we will stand as witnesses to nonbelievers. When we see our suffering as a means of identifying ourselves with Christ's suffering for our sake, then we become part of the great drama of salvation (see Luke 21:12-18; 2 Cor. 1:3-11; 12:7-10; 1 Pet. 5:1).

Only a loving God would both love us and suffer for us as one of us. And He did both by sending His only Son to suffer and die for our sins—and not for ours alone, but for the sins of all humanity. Only God could have conceived of such a magnificent plan!

Note

1. Moishe, Rosen *Y'Shua* (Chicago: Moody Press, 1982), pp. 67,68.

If your members are interested in reading further on the subject of suffering, you may want to refer them to the following resources:

Lewis, C.S. 1962. *The Problem of Pain*. New York: The Macmillan Co.
Yancy, Phillip. 1977. *Where Is God When It Hurts?* Grand Rapids: Zondervan Publishing House.

A B C PLAN FOR THE SESSION

Materials needed:
- Your Leader's Guide;
- Your Session 12 Leader's Guide Sheet;
- One copy of the Session 12 Lesson Outline for each group member;
- Large poster, felt pens and masking tape;
- Chalkboard or overhead projector with transparencies;
- Overhead projector transparency of the Session 12 Lesson Outline (optional).

Advance preparations:
- Read the information under "Advance preparations" for Session 13 in order to make a needed advance assignment for next week's session;
- Prepare a poster by printing the title "Qualifications for a Great Political Leader" across the top of a large sheet of newsprint or shelf paper. Tape the poster to a wall in the room easily accessible to members.

A PPROACH (5 minutes)

As members arrive encourage them to write on the poster attributes the world identifies as important for a person to have who is in a position of great influence over others. After everyone has had an opportunity to write his or her ideas say, *In today's study we will consider God's qualifications for the One He appointed to fill the position of Savior and Lord of all people: Jesus Christ, God's only Son. We will do this by looking at several Old Testament passages of Scripture that foretold Jesus' character and the suffering He would experience as God's chosen Messiah.*

B IBLE EXPLORATION (40-50 minutes)

Step 1 (15-20 minutes): Introduce this study by saying that the Old Testament prophecies of Jesus that we are going to look at are commonly called the "Servant Songs." Add, *They foretold events that would happen during the Messiah or Savior's life on earth. They also give us a clear picture of the character and suffering of Jesus.*

Next, distribute the Lesson Outline to everyone. Ask volunteers to share in reading aloud the verses listed under the section titled "His Qualifications" (A-

F) of their outlines. As the verses are read, lead a discussion of the Scriptures using the following guideline and questions as well as additional information from "Insights for the Leader": (Encourage learners to take notes on their outlines as the discussion progresses and do the same, yourself, on the chalkboard or Lesson Outline transparency. Continue to use the outlines in this manner throughout the session.)

A. Isaiah 50:6; 52:14; 53:1,2/Matthew 27:27-30; John 12:37,38

- Mention that Isaiah 53:2 describes Jesus' everyday outward appearance. The other verses describe the Jews' rejection of Jesus and His ministry and the time before His death when He was badly beaten.
- How is this picture of Jesus' appearance and circumstances different from what the world looks for in a person of authority? Reread Isaiah 53:1 and John 12:37,38. Point out that the Jews refused to believe in Jesus because He was not like what they expected the Messiah to be; they didn't recognize Him for who He is, God's promised Savior. In the eyes of these unbelievers, Jesus was a criminal.

B. Isaiah 42:2/Mark 7:31-36

- Often Jesus made a point of not drawing attention to His deeds. He was not a seeker of attention. Many believe He did this in order to prevent His rising popularity from heightening tension with the religious leaders before He had fulfilled His purpose for coming to earth.
- How is Jesus' attitude of shunning untimely attention different from the attitude commonly held by a person seeking a position of power today? Share Lloyd Ahlem's comments at the end of "The Unacceptable Image" section of "Insights for the Leader." Begin with the words "Christ works quietly and unobtrusively. . ." and continue to the end of the paragraph.

C. Isaiah 42:3/Matthew 12:15-21

- What aspects do these verses say are part of Jesus' purpose as the Messiah?
- What kinds of people do you think the words "bruised reed" and "smoldering wick" are describing? (Those with damaged lives or flickering, fragile faith.) What types of people today would fit into these categories?

D. Isaiah 42:6,7; 53:4/Matthew 8:16,17

- What needs did Jesus minister to in these verses? (Spiritual and physical oppression and disease.)
- In what way and by what means does Christ minister to these same needs today?

E. Isaiah 49:1/Luke 9:34,35

- What do these verses tell you about Jesus?
- By what authority has Jesus been appointed as the Messiah or Savior? (He is chosen by God and has the authority to speak for God. Although both Jesus and the prophets spoke with God's authority, Jesus alone is God incarnate.)
- What do these verses tell you about those who try to compete with Christ for the role of Messiah or Savior? Refer to false religions such as Mormonism and the Jehovah's Witnesses who have redefined Jesus' character to the point that they do not ascribe to Him divinity and the authority of God. Share Lloyd Ahlem's comments concerning Jesus as the only authentic means of salvation that are found in the fourth paragraph of the "God's Concept of the Messiah" section of "Insights for the Leader."

F. Isaiah 53:9/Matthew 26:59-61; 27:13,14

- What do these verses tell us about Jesus' character? (He is without fault or corruption; He maintained His integrity in the face of false accusations and oppression.)
- Why do you think integrity is a crucial attribute for the Messiah to have?

Step 2 (5-8 minutes): Summarize the study concerning God's qualifications for the One He appointed to be Savior and Lord by asking the following questions:

- How are God's qualifications for Jesus as Savior and Lord different from what people might think are necessary qualifications?
- Share Lloyd Ahlem's five characteristics of human ideas as outlined in the "Unlike Any Human Idea" section of "Insights for the Leader."

Move to Step 3 by saying, *We have looked at how God's qualifications for the Savior may be different from what we see as important qualifications. We have also seen through the book of Isaiah how Jesus, God's Son, fulfilled what God had planned for the Savior to do and be while living on earth. Now let's look at how Jesus' experience of suffering while He lived on earth has qualified Him to understand our suffering and help us in times of painful need.*

Step 3 (10-12 minutes): Move members into pairs or trios. Next, direct them to "His Experience of Suffering" section on their outlines. Say, *The passages in Isaiah you have been studying portray Jesus as One who suffered greatly. Because of the content of these verses, Jesus is often referred to as the "Suffering Servant of Isaiah."* Ask pairs or trios to review the New Testament passages they have considered in this study and then list on their outlines (A-C) several ways Jesus suffered. Allow about four minutes for working. When time is up regather into the larger group and ask volunteers to share several ways Jesus suffered.

Next, invite several learners to each read aloud one of the following two verses: Hebrews 2:18 and 4:15. Ask, *In the light of these verses and other passages of Scripture you have studied today, what are several reasons why Jesus is able to understand people's suffering.* Allow time for responses. Move to the next step by saying, *What a blessing it is to know that because Jesus suffered for us while He lived on this earth, He is able to understand our sufferings today. But this truth raises an important question in the minds of many people. Let's consider this question at this time.*

Step 4 (10 minutes): Say, *Many ask, If God is loving, why does He allow suffering? How would you respond to a person who asked you this question?* Allow learners several moments to share their thoughts. Mention that this is a complex question that every generation of people has probably asked and one that has no easy answers.

Next, share Lloyd Ahlem's five points addressing this question from "Insights for the Leader" under the heading "The Question of Suffering." Be sure to share the principle Scriptures used with each point. Also suggest resources that deal with this topic that you feel will benefit those who wish to study further.

C ONCLUSION (5 minutes)

Say, *We have examined in our study how Christ met God's qualifications to be the Savior of the world and reasons why as the Savior He is able to understand our sufferings.*

Next ask, *What painful experience have you realized that yet needs Jesus' healing touch? Will you accept the truth that he identifies with your suffering and that He wants to bring healing to your situation? Or perhaps you are struggling with the "big" question of why a God of love allows suffering.* Challenge members to allow the truths of this study to minister to their needs, whatever they may be.

Encourage learners to form small prayer groups and to share, if they feel comfortable in doing so, their areas of need relating to suffering and pain.

After several minutes of prayer, close the session by offering a corporate prayer thanking God that we are not alone in our pain because He has provided One who understands our difficulties and the pain we experience.

Before everyone leaves, tell them that in your next session you'll be exploring a very different side of Jesus' character—His role as mighty *victorious King.* Encourage members to read chapter 12 of the Regal book, *Christ B.C.,* which will assist them in their time of daily devotions. Each day's devotion is based on the theme of *compassion.*

The Victorious King

SESSION VERSES

"The Lord will be king over the whole earth. On that day there will be one Lord, and his name the only name." Zechariah 14:9

"The kingdom of the world has become the kingdom of our Lord and of his Christ, and he will reign for ever and ever." Revelation 11:15

SESSION FOCUS

For God's people, the end of history is the beginning of a glorious eternity with Christ as their victorious King.

SESSION BASIS

Genesis 2:8,9; Isaiah 63:1,3; Jeremiah 29:8,9,11; Daniel 10:5,6,14; Matthew 10:29; 24:24,36,42-51; 28:16-20; Luke 21:25-28; Romans 8:1; 1 Corinthians 1:8,9; 2:9,10; 15:24,25; Philippians 2:10,11; 1 Peter 5:9; 2 Peter 2:1-6; Revelation 1:12-18; 11:5; 19:13-19; 21:1-8; 22:1-6

SESSION GOAL

Examine prophecies about Christ that deal with end-time events and discuss why believers may face the future with hope.

INSIGHTS FOR THE LEADER

This session is more than a discussion of the complete fulfillment of God's plan as presented in Old and New Testament apocalyptic Scripture. As the point of this study is to get a picture of the whole forest, not to examine the tree, a discussion of the chronology of events or the interpretation of specific details and symbols will not be undertaken. Instead, a basis for hope in the future where the end of history will be the beginning of a glorious eternity for God's people and where Christ will reign as the victorious, eternal King will be presented.

History: A Divine Drama

In my sophomore year in high school, we were required to take a course in world history. World War II was plunging ahead, and our teacher did not know if he would be drafted into military service. He was obviously asking questions about his own life's meaning as well as the meaning of the events of war and their part in the flow of history. His concern lent a lot of spirit to his teaching. From time to time he writhed in anguish over the horrors of war and his possible involvement in combat. But occasionally he looked hopefully ahead to an end to despotism from Nazi rule and Japanese militarism. He was a mixture of fear and hope. I can't say

that I learned a great deal from the history book that semester, but I have one vivid memory from the class and it is the following conclusion my teacher drew from the events of the time: "History is up for grabs and will be made by whomever seizes its making."

The teacher was from a religious background, but that did not figure strongly in his thinking. He had been educated in a university that was obviously Christian, but no concept of God's involvement in history was evident in his perception of events. He had come to see Christianity as an addendum to his life, not a structure of personal faith upon which to build a reason for living or a basis for reasoning. Faith was peripheral and impersonal, not central and vital. As a result, his conclusion that history is up for grabs reflected his lack of faith.

This illustrates one of the essential differences between Christian and humanist thought in regard to the outcome of history. Christians face the future with the certainty that a divine drama is being played out. Humanists on the other hand regard history as something to be created. Positive humanists live with a hope that what they create will be wholesome and helpful. Negative humanists structure their lives around avoidance—seeking to prevent the worst that people can do. Negative humanists would support the position that the best we can hope for is to build on the firm ground of despair in the hope that we won't repeat destructive behavior.

Hope for the Future

Jeremiah 29:11 gives God's point of view on the issue of history. In writing to the Jews exiled from Jerusalem to Babylon, Jeremiah's message from God was, "'For I know the plans I have for you,' declares the Lord, 'plans to prosper you and not to harm you, plans to give you hope and a future.'" Jesus also gave a message of hope concerning the future to His followers. It is recorded in John 14:3,4. He said, "And if I go and prepare a place for you, I will come back and take you to be with me that you also may be where I am. You know the way to the place where I am going." These passages from both the Old and New Testaments apply to us as well because they express truth concerning God's view of history and the future. This concept of history is quite different from the one propounded by my high school teacher. To be a Christian is to take a radical view of history—that is, history is in the hands of God and the future is both certain and of His making.

In Jeremiah's declaration to the exiles, there are several principles that we should keep in mind as we look through God's eyes to the future and the end of history. The first principle is a warning against false prophets.

There was a false prophet named Hananiah, who was spreading the lie among the exiles that their captivity would be short and that an early relief from Babylonian oppression was coming (see Jer. 28:10-17). However, God told Jeremiah that the actual time of captivity would last 70 years (see 29:5-7,10). Through Jeremiah the Lord said to the captives, "Do not let the prophets and diviners among you deceive you. Do not listen to the dreams you encourage them to have. They are prophesying lies to you in my name. I have not sent them." (vv. 8,9).

Today, we also need to be on guard against false prophets. In describing the signs of the end of the age Jesus said, "At that time if anyone says to you, 'Look, here is the Christ!' or, 'There he is!' do not believe it. For false Christs and false prophets will appear and perform great signs and miracles to deceive even the elect—if that were possible" (Matt. 24:23,24; also refer to 2 Thess. 2:1-4).

The second principle from Jeremiah that we should adhere to when looking at prophecies of the future is:

Because the future is in God's hands, His faithful children can live in hope, not despair. Although the Lord warned through Jeremiah that the Jews' exile would not be over quickly and that difficulty would come to those who did not listen to the Lord, He also spoke words of hope to those whose hearts were faithful. The Lord said, "'Then you will call upon me and come and pray to me, and I will listen to you. You will seek me and find me when you seek me with all your heart. I will be found by you,' declares the Lord, 'and will bring you back from captivity. I will gather you from all the nations and places where I have banished you'" (Jer. 29:12-14). In the difficult days of estrangement from their homeland, God would be close at hand ministering to them. Ultimately God fulfilled His promise and delivered the Jews from captivity (see Ezra 1,2).

In the same way, Jesus discussed at length the extreme difficulties and fearful upheaval that will occur at the end of the age (see Matt. 24:1—25:46; Mark 13:1-37; Luke 21:5-36). Yet for the faithful, upon recognizing the signs of these difficult times, there is hope. Jesus said, "Do not be frightened" (Luke 21:9), "Make up your mind not to worry beforehand" (v. 14) and "By standing firm you will gain life" (v. 19). Jesus also said, "When these things begin to take place, stand up and lift up your heads, because your redemption is drawing near" (v. 28). As we watch and wait for evidence of the fulfillment of God's plans for the end of history, we have the assurance that we will not be abandoned. In leaving the world, Jesus reassured His disciples saying, "I am with you always, to the very end of the age" (Matt. 28:20). Throughout history God has been faithful to His promises; in the future He will continue to be faithful.

Promises for the Future

The prophecies that we will focus on for this session are those depicting Christ as victorious King. In these passages we will see the complete fulfillment of God's plan for the world and the source of our hope for the future.

There are several Old Testament passages that picture Christ as King and the final victor over Satan and evil. A phrase often used in the New Testament in conjunction with this picture is "the day of the Lord" (see Acts 2:20; 1 Cor. 1:8; 1 Thess. 5:2). This speaks of the time when Christ will return and all things will be put into submission to Him. The Old Testament prophet Zechariah said, "The Lord will be king over the whole earth. On that day there will be one Lord, and his name the only name" (14:9). This prophecy is consistent with the words of Philippians 2:10,11, "That at the name of Jesus every knee should bow, in heaven and on earth and under the earth, and every tongue confess that Jesus Christ is Lord, to the glory of God the Father" and the words of 1 Corinthians 15:24,25, "The end will come, when he hands over the kingdom to God the Father after he has destroyed all dominion, authority and power. For he must reign until he has put all his enemies under his feet."

The confirmation of these declarations is found in the book of Revelation. It describes seven trumpets sounded by seven angels (see 8:2,6—9:21; 11:15-19). The sounding of the first six trumpets results in various disasters reminiscent of those described by Jesus as signs of the end of the age (see Rev. 8:6—9:21; also see Matt. 24:1-51; Mark 13:1-37; Luke 21:5-36). The sounding of the seventh trumpet points to the establishment of Christ as victorious, eternal King (see Rev. 11:15-19). When this trumpet is sounded, voices will declare, "The kingdom of the world has become the kingdom of our Lord and of his Christ, and he will reign for ever and ever" (v. 15).

There are many Old Testament prophecies that describe Christ's coming as victorious King. The most obvious is in Daniel 10:5,6. In these verses Daniel describes a vision of a man "dressed in linen, with a belt of the finest gold around his waist. His body was like chrysolite, his face like lightning, his eyes like flaming torches, his arms and legs like the gleam of burnished bronze, and his voice like the sound of a multitude." This man, who Daniel refers to as "my lord" and in whose presence Daniel is overwhelmed (v. 17), strengthened Daniel (see v. 18) and told him "what will happen to your people in the future, for the vision concerns a time yet to come" (v. 14). Daniel's response to this man expresses submission as to a powerful king (see v. 15). The description of events the man in Daniel's vision gave includes the destruction and establishment of many earthly kingdoms (see chapter 11). These earthly conflicts are accompanied by spiritual battles between the divine and the demonic (see 10:12,13). The book of Daniel concludes by describing the end times when deliverance will come to the righteous (see chapter 12).

Revelation 1:12-16 gives us a vision similar to Daniel's. This vision is seen by John, the writer of Revelation, and consists of someone "like a son of man" (v. 13). Like Daniel, John was also overwhelmed and then encouraged by the Son of man (see v. 17). This is obviously a vision of Jesus. His description of Himself as the "First and the Last" (v. 17), identifies Him as equal

with the Lord God who proclaimed, "I am the Alpha and the Omega. . .who is, and who was, and who is to come, the Almighty" (v. 8). Like the book of Daniel, Revelation also describes the rise and destruction of many kingdoms (see chapters 17,18). Revelation concludes with a description of the final judgment and the establishment of the "Holy City, the New Jerusalem" (21:2) where man and God will dwell together perfectly. In our day we see evidence of the political upheaval described in Revelation—especially in the Mideast and Eastern Europe. Although tragedy usually accompanies such experiences, we can be reassured that the time of peace in God's presence is that much closer.

In Revelation 19:16 Jesus is called by the title "King of Kings and Lord of Lords." As such, He is "dressed in a robe dipped in blood" (v. 13) and "He treads the winepress of the fury of the wrath of God Almighty" (v. 15; also see 14:19). This description was also given long ago by Isaiah, "His garments stained crimson. . . .'I have trodden the winepress alone; from the nations no one was with me. I trampled them in my anger and. . .their blood spattered my garments'" (63:1,3). These vivid verses describe Jesus as King, dispensing judgment.

We must live knowing that God's final judgment is coming and thankful that if we are Christians we will be spared and vindicated (see Rom. 5:9; 1 Thess. 1:9,10). We must also respond to the need of our neighbors who do not know the Lord. We should share Jesus' desire that all people submit to Him. "He is patient with you, not wanting anyone to perish, but everyone to come to repentance. But the day of the Lord will come like a thief. The heavens will disappear with a roar; the elements will be destroyed by fire, and the earth and everything in it will be laid bare" (2 Pet. 3:9,10). The non-Christian's opportunities to turn to the Lord are quickly diminishing. Time will someday, unexpectedly run out.

Knowing that God will establish Jesus as eternal, victorious King is cause for joy among God's faithful. With Jesus as reigning King, Satan will be bound, the problem of sin will be obliterated and life as God intended it will be restored. Revelation 22:2 describes the tree of life as standing in the New Jerusalem, bearing 12 kinds of fruit. The symbolism here is of the reestablishment of a perfect relationship between God and His servants. "Now the dwelling of God is with men, and he will live with them. They will be his people, and God himself will be with them and be their God. He will wipe every tear from their eyes. There will be no more death or mourning or crying or pain, for the old order of things has passed away" (Rev. 21:3,4). What a reason for joy and hope among those who belong to God!

Today's Situation

Despite the hopeful message of Bible prophecy, many today struggle with putting their faith in prophetic Scripture. These people, and any serious readers of prophecy, are confronted with two challenges. First, am I willing to believe that the prophetic message is true? A step of faith and a knowledge that many biblical prophecies have already been fulfilled should lead us to affirm that God does not lie, that His word is true and that they can interpret their newspapers and experiences in light of Scripture. They must dare to believe that in doing so they are on solid biblical and intellectual grounds.

The second challenge of accepting biblical prophecy is, How is my belief reflected in the way I make life decisions and respond emotionally to my personal circumstances? I know Christians who affirm their belief in biblical prophecy and God's sovereignty over people's affairs, yet plan and react to events as if God is sitting in heaven biting His nails, wondering what on earth people will do next. The certainty that God's promises are true has not made an emotional or practical impact on their lives.

At the present we are living between the time of prophecies concerning Christ's Second Coming that have been given and the time of their fulfillment. As we interpret events of our day in the light of Scripture, we can see evidence of God's plan unfolding. This should spur us on to participate in bringing hope to those who currently stand outside of the joy God has designed for His people by sharing the gospel with them. As we do this we must realize that Satan is actively working to keep as many souls out of God's hand as he can (see 1 Pet. 5:8).

Throughout Scripture efforts to thwart God's plans have had the smell of Satan's involvement. At one time, the lineage from which the Messiah would be born was threatened by Jezebel's daughter, Athaliah (see 2 Kings 11). After Christ's birth Herod tried to eliminate the Messiah by massacring all the boys in Bethlehem and the surrounding area who were two years old or younger (see Matt. 2:13—18). And immediately following Jesus' baptism (see Mark 1:9-12), Satan tried to tempt Jesus to follow his plans instead of God's (see Matt. 4:1-11; Luke 4:1-13). After Satan entered Judas at the Last Supper, Judas immediately left the gathering to participate in the betrayal of Jesus

(see John 13:27). What irony that in attempting to cancel God's plan of redemption, Satan participated in its fulfillment. At Calvary Satan might have thought he had finally succeeded in his battle with God. Yet Colossians 2:15 says, "And having disarmed the powers and authorities, he [Jesus] made a public spectacle of them, triumphing over them by the cross."

Every generation, from Bible times until today, has been subject to an effort to disclaim the promises of God that are yet to be fulfilled. It is Satan's purpose to lead as many people into unbelief as possible (see 2 Cor. 4:4). The Christian's battle is to remain faithful to the gospel, share it with others and watch for Christ's coming (see Matt. 24:42-44; 28:19,20; 1 Cor. 4:2). This is difficult in a world filled with the allure of lust, the rationalization of human evil into normal behavior, theories of human behavior and personality that proclaim that a fulfilled person is one who is in control of his or her life, and the onslaughts of Satan against public Christian personalities. Under such conditions nominal Christians abandon their faith for the New Age movement and Eastern mysticism or often resort to atheism. All of these are symptoms of Satan desperately struggling to overcome an enemy he can never defeat: God.

As Christians, in these times of international stress and upheaval, nuclear threat and the undermining of positive moral values, our response to historic and current events must be built on a strong basis of faith and knowledge of God's Word—not on human perceptions. Negative humanists deal only in human perceptions and not in Christian hope. They dismiss this hope as implausible. Positive humanists create false hopes in their message. They look at man, ignore his lawlessness and carnage, and pronounce hope without dealing with man's spiritual condition.

By His Spirit

On the day I was married, a pastor friend sent my wife and me a telegram. In it he quoted 1 Corinthians 2:9,10. This passage speaks of the wisdom and insight that God gives to those who have His Holy Spirit. It is a wisdom and insight by which Christians can understand God's ways. The passage says, "However, as it is written: 'No eye has seen, no ear has heard, no mind has conceived what God has prepared for those who love him'—but God has revealed it to us by his Spirit. The Spirit searches all things, even the deep things of God." It is through the Spirit of Christ living in our hearts that we can face the future with a true hope. And as we are obedient to the Holy Spirit and seek to understand and identify God's control in human events, we will be rewarded with insight and a vision for the future. We will be like the servants in the parable who were charged to be dressed and ready to respond, watching for the moment the master returns (see Luke 12:35-40). Our waiting and watching must consist of our work at the tasks to which the Lord has appointed us (see Matt. 24:45,46; Mark 13:34-37; Luke 19:13), knowing that once He appears it will be too late for such labors. "It will be good for those servants whose master finds them watching when he comes" (Luke 12:37).

A B C PLAN FOR THE SESSION

Materials needed:
- Your Session 13 Leader's Guide Sheet;
- One copy of the Session 13 Lesson Outline for each group member;
- Index cards listing the three views of perspectives on history;
- Chalkboard or overhead transparency of the Session 13 Lesson Outline (optional).

Advance preparations:
- Invite two group members to present four-minute talks. Assign one of the following Scripture passages to each member. Encourage both to use a study Bible and/or Bible commentary for resource material. The answers to the questions accompanying the references will serve as a guide for their presentations.
    1. 1 Corinthians 2:9,10. How can this gift be used to understand current and future events, and how can a person have access to this gift?
    2. Matthew 24:36,42-51. While we are waiting for Christ's return, what are we instructed to do? What are some ways we may do this?
- Write the following three views regarding perspectives on history on three large index cards, one on each card:
  View 1:
  "History is what we make of it. Of course people have made some mistakes. But, basically, we're a good bunch. If we work at it, we can create a history that will be wholesome and helpful to future generations."
  View 2:
  "History is a result of people's actions. The best we can hope for is to learn from our past mistakes so that we can avoid repeating them in the future."
  View 3:
  "The past as well as the future are in God's hands. He works everything according to His plans. If we belong to Him, there is nothing to worry about. God has shown us in His Word that He has wonderful things in mind for His people. I am trusting that He will be faithful, as He has been in the past, and do everything that He has promised."

 PPROACH (5 minutes)

Ask, *As people today contemplate the future, what do you think may be some of their hopes and fears?* As members think about the question, mention that people's hopes and fears will probably vary with their ages. After several moments, ask for responses. List the hopes and fears suggested in two columns on the chalkboard or overhead transparency and briefly discuss them.

Move to the Bible Exploration by saying, *We all have certain hopes for the future, and we all struggle with fears of not knowing what will happen. On our own, our insights into the future are very limited. In today's study we will look at history and the future through God's eyes, and we will consider God's plan—past and future.*

B **IBLE EXPLORATION** (40-50 minutes)

Step 1 (7-10 minutes): Move members into three groups and appoint group leaders. Give each leader an index card listing one view relating to a perspective on history. Say, *Each group will consider one of three views relating to perspectives on history. You are to consider the view or quote assigned to your group and then list words that you feel would properly describe this view of the outcome of historical events.*

Allow four to five minutes for groups to work. Then regather into larger group and ask each group leader to share his or her group's suggestions. Share Lloyd Ahlem's comments from "Insight for the Leader" under the heading "History: A Divine Drama" concerning the positive and negative humanist views of the outcome of history.

Move to Step 2 by saying, *Two of these quotes— Views 1 and 2—represent views of historical events that are held by many people in our society today. View 3 represents a believer's view of history from a biblical perspective. Let's take a closer look at what God says about the future.*

Step 2 (8-10 minutes): Distribute the Lesson Outline to everyone. Encourage learners to take notes on their outlines as the lesson progresses. Do the same on the chalkboard or Lesson Outline transparency.

Next, divide the group into two sections. Assign the Scripture references, listed in point *A* of the outline under "Principles for Considering the Future," to one section and references in point *B* to the other section. Then ask everyone to work with a partner to discover, in the verses assigned to his or her section, one principle for examining events through God's eyes. After several minutes of working, ask for responses from each section. Include the following information and questions in the discussion:

A. Jeremiah 29:8,9; Matthew 24:24.

- Present a brief background of the setting for Jeremiah 29:8,9: The Jews in captivity in Babylon; the false prophets, with the key figure being Hananiah (see Jer. 28:10-17; also see information in "Insights for the Leader" under the heading "Hope for the Future").
- Be careful about believing what some people say about the future; measure their words against God's Word; be aware that people will appear, making predictions for the future, with the intention of deceiving their hearers.
- How is it possible for a false prophet to confuse a person's insight into God's plans for the future? (Inaccurate but convincing opinions about the future can make it difficult for the person who does not have a proper understanding of God's Word. Because of his or her lack of Bible knowledge, this person is unable to discern what is true and what is not. As a result, he or she becomes easy prey to the false prophet's message. And this person is unable to recognize God's actions when God's plans for the future are fulfilled.)
- Can you think of religious groups that make certain

claims regarding the future that are not in agreement with the Bible? Mention that groups such as the Jehovah's Witnesses and Mormons claim that certain things will happen in the future that are not biblically based. They also claim that their beliefs contain additional information beyond that of God's Word. (For further information, read *The Kingdom of the Cults*, by Walter R. Martin, Zondervan Publishing Co., Grand Rapids.) These groups use Christian-sounding words, but their beliefs and views are not supported by our only written source of information for God's point of view: the Bible.

B. Jeremiah 29:11; Matthew 10:29; Luke 21:25-28.

- Because the future is in God's hands, those who belong to Him can have hope, not despair.
- Point out that God was with the Jews during their exile; He did not forsake them (see Jer. 29:12,13).
- Mention that Jesus was honest in sharing about difficult times and situations that will transpire as signs of the end of history (see Matt. 24-25; Mark 13; Luke 21:5-36). But He also promised to be with those who love Him to the end. Read aloud Matthew 28:20.

Say, *The end of history is often referred to as "the end of the age." Now that we have discussed several principles that we should keep in mind when considering the future, let's take a look at several prophecies about Jesus and what He will accomplish at the end of history.*

Step 3 (15-20 minutes): Direct everyone to "The End of History" section on the outline. Invite volunteers to share in reading aloud the verses listed in this section. As the Scriptures are read, lead a discussion of the verses using the following guideline and questions, as well as additional information from "Insights for the Leader":

A. Zechariah 14:9; 1 Corinthians 15:24,25; Philippians 2:10,11; Revelation 1:5; 19:16.

- What titles are used for Jesus in these verses? (Christ, Lord, King.)
- Mention that the term "day of the Lord" is often used to refer to the time when Jesus will return and all things will be put in submission to Him (see Acts 2:20; 1 Cor. 1:8; 1 Thess. 5:2).
- How will people everywhere demonstrate that they recognize Jesus as Lord? (They will bow in submission to Him and verbally acknowledge His authority over everyone and everything.)
- What do these verses say Jesus will do when He returns as Lord and King? (Put His enemies under His feet by destroying their authority, power and

influence in the world; reign forever.)

- Who are Jesus' enemies? (Satan and all those who align with him in his evil deeds; all forms of evil; and those who have rejected Him—see Matt. 10:32,33; John 3:19,20; Rev. 19:19-21; 20:7-14.)

B. Daniel 10:5,6,14; Revelation 1:12-18.

- These verses describe Jesus as He will appear when He returns from heaven at the end of the age.

- Invite learners to suggest adjectives describing Jesus from these verses. List suggestions on the board as they are given. What impression do these descriptions give you about Jesus?

- Share that the prophecies following these descriptions include accounts of the rise and destruction of many earthly kingdoms as well as spiritual battles. The Bible clearly states that the events leading up to Jesus' return as King will be difficult and often accompanied by tragedy. How can a person's knowledge that these are signs of Jesus' return and that God has control of history affect the way he or she views current events or his or her personal experiences?

C. Isaiah 63:1-3; Revelation 19:13-19.

- What do these verses say Jesus will accomplish when He returns? (He will dispense judgment for sin that the world deserves.)

- Read aloud 2 Peter 2:1-6, Romans 8:1 and 1 Corinthians 1:8,9. When Christ returns, how will He respond to the ungodly? (He will judge them and give them the punishment they deserve.) How will He respond to those who belong to Him? (They will not be condemned; they will be blameless before God.)

D. Revelation 21:1-8.

- When Jesus has returned and sin and evil have been removed, what will the situation of those who belong to God be like? (They will be in God's presence; they will no longer experience death, pain, sadness, thirst or other hurts that we experience in our world today.)

E. Genesis 2:8,9; Revelation 22:1-6.

- What was present in the garden of Eden that will also be present in God's future, eternal Kingdom? (The tree of life.) Mention that Genesis 3:22 implies that eating from the tree of life would result in experiencing eternal life.

- Share that before Adam and Eve sinned, they enjoyed a perfect relationship with God. However, when they sinned this close relationship with God was broken; death was the penalty. Adam and Eve were cast out of the garden of Eden in order to pre-

vent them from eating from the tree of life and thus avoiding the penalty of death (see Gen. 3:22,23). At the end of history, after sin has been dealt with, the perfect relationship God had intended to have with people will be fully restored. (Invite a volunteer to read aloud Rev. 21:3.) The tree of life in the New Jerusalem (see Rev. 21:2; 22:2) represents the restoration of a perfect relationship between God and people. Those who belong to God will live forever, enjoying the relationship with Him that was originally intended in Eden.

- Point out that a significant difference between Eden and the New Jerusalem is that in the future, when Satan and evil have been obliterated, the possibility of sin will no longer exist.

Move to Step 4 by saying, *Those who belong to God have many wonderful things to look forward to. But until that time comes to pass, we still have to deal with living today—during the time between the prophecy and the fulfillment.*

Step 4 (10 minutes): Announce that two members will present a four-minute talk each on passages of Scripture that will assist us in understanding current and future events and that will inform us what we are to do while we are waiting for Christ's return.

Members present talks on 1 Corinthians 2:9,10 and Matthew 24:36,42-51.

Briefly summarize the presentations by saying that wisdom to understand current and future events comes from God's Spirit that is given to us, and that we are commanded to be watchful and faithful servants in telling others about Christ, in standing firm in faith and in serving the Lord.

Move to the Conclusion by saying, *A Christian's response to historic, current and future events must be based on a knowledge of God's Word, not human perceptions. A Christian who is obedient to God's Word and nurtures his or her relationship with God can face the future with hope, knowing that the outcome of history is certain and is in God's hands.*

C ONCLUSION (5 minutes)

Ask, *Do you believe that all God has spoken in His Word regarding future events will one day come to pass? Are there prophecies that you have difficulty accepting?* Encourage those who are struggling in this way to allow the Holy Spirit to reveal the reality of the prophetic passages to them and to minister faith to their hearts.

Remind believers, who may be fearful of current

and future happenings, of Christ's promise to be with us to the end of the age (see Matt. 28:20) and of the hope of one day being present in heaven with our victorious King (see Rev. 21:3).

Close the session in prayer thanking God that He is in control of the future and that those who belong to Him do not need to be afraid of what the future may bring. Also pray that those who do not belong to the Lord will consider what the future holds for them and the opportunity they have for hope in the future if they accept the salvation God has provided through Jesus Christ.

Encourage members to read chapter 13 of the Regal book, *Christ B.C.*, which will assist them in their time of daily devotions. Each day's devotion is based on the theme of a *victorious future*.

LEADER CHECKPOINT

Are Your Lectures Alive?

Lecture is by far the most often used method by Bible study leaders. If you use this method correctly your Bible study group will flourish under your guidance. But if you lecture regularly while ignoring some important guidelines for the lecture method, your Bible study group may lose interest.

Use the exercise below to help you evaluate yourself as a lecturer. Give yourself a numerical rating for each statement (1=always, 2=ofteen, 3=sometimes, 4=seldom, 5=never). Then select one or two of your lower rated qualities and begin to develop them into positive strengths.

1. My lectures are pointed and purposeful, free of rambling.

   1   2   3   4   5

2. My lectures focus on one main idea rather than several points.

   1   2   3   4   5

3. I use verbal illustrations (anecdotes, stories, personal examples, etc.) to keep my lecture practical.

   1   2   3   4   5

4. I use visual aids (chalkboard, overhead projector, charts, maps, diagrams, objects, etc.) to help my group "see" what I'm saying.

   1   2   3   4   5

5. At least once in a 20 minute lecture I stop to allow for group comments and/or questions.

   1   2   3   4   5

6. I provide worksheet for group members to record insights or questions while I talk.

   1   2   3   4   5

7. I know my material so well that I maintain good eye contact with group members, not being tied to my notes or outlines.

   1   2   3   4   5

8. I ask family members or trusted friends to evaluate my lectures and offer constructive criticism.

   1   2   3   4   5

9. I generously integrate other Bible study methods with my lectures to keep the group interested and involved.

   1   2   3   4   5

10. I am alert to minimizing distracting "ums," "ahs" and "you knows" from my lectures.

   1   2   3   4   5

SESSION 1
The Road to Emmaus

LEADER'S GUIDE SHEET

Materials needed:

- Copies of the Regal book, *Christ B.C.,* for group members to purchase;
- One copy of the three Lesson handouts for each group member;
- Large posters, felt pens and masking tape;
- Blank sheets of paper;
- Index cards or Post-it Notes with Scripture references;
- A *King James Version* of the Bible;
- Chalkboard or overhead projector with transparencies;
- Transparency of the Lesson Outline (optional);
- Name tags for group members (optional).

A PPROACH (10 minutes)

- Distribute name tags and introduce new members.

- Ask, "In the Old Testament, what foreshadows something that took place in Jesus' life or ministry, or that is yet to take place?"

- Members write suggestions on posters.

- Review suggestions. Say, "In this course we will explore Old Testament people, things, events or prophecies that prefigured events in Jesus' life, ministry and future. Today's study will show how Christ explained these types, symbols and prophecies about Himself to two distraught disciples."

- - - - - - FOLD

STEP 4 (10 minutes):

- Regather and ask for feedback.
  1. The Holy Spirit teaches us, since Jesus is no longer physically present. There are also teachers in the Church.
  2. A close relationship is an effective learning situation.
  3. Mature Christians serve as role models in social situations.
  4. Sharing reinforces our beliefs.
  5. Insight often occurs after pondering.
  6. God's Word presents and defends itself.
  7. Realize that God always takes the initiative.

C ONCLUSION (5 minutes)

- Review how the risen Savior restored the dreams of Cleophas and his friend.

- Add, "We have discovered principles of learning to apply to our lives so that we may experience: an acceptance of Christ as Savior; the restoration of shattered dreams; the healing of damaged areas in our lives; and/or the strengthening of our spiritual experience."

- Close the session in prayer, asking God for a greater understanding of His Word and His help to live out these principles in our lives.

- Direct members to read chapter 1 of the Regal book, *Christ B.C.,* which will assist them in their time of daily devotions. Each day's devotion is based on the theme of *understanding.*

Alternate Approach (5 minutes)

• Write the question listed under the Approach on the chalkboard or overhead transparency.

• Members form clusters of three and discuss the question. Distribute paper to appointed recorders for note-taking.

• Ask for feedback.

• Share the closing statements under the Approach.

B **IBLE EXPLORATION**
(35-45 minutes)

STEP 1 (5-10 minutes):

• Distribute the session handouts to learners and encourage note-taking.

• Share Augustine's words, "The New is in the Old contained; the Old is by the New explained." Ask, "What does this mean?"

• Explain the meaning of types and symbols.

• Share about the two types of prophecy. Explain that some prophecies are yet to be fulfilled.

• Member reads aloud Deuteronomy 29:29.

STEP 2 (10-15 minutes):

• Several people share in reading aloud Luke 24:13-27.

• Ask the following questions:
   1. How would you describe the mood of the setting of this event?
   2. What were the reasons for this mood? Share the rabbinic teaching concerning the coming Messiah.
   3. Why should they have understood the Scriptures?
   4. Would Jesus have reason to chide us today for similar reasons? Why or why not?

• Several learners read aloud verses 28-32.
   1. Read aloud Revelation 3:20.
   2. What do these verses say about our relationship with Jesus?
   3. How did Jesus assume the role of master/father of the household? What were the results?
   4. How do we deprive ourselves of spiritual enlightenment and God's rich blessings?
   5. Why are we prone to look to spectacular settings for spiritual enlightenment?
   6. Members share about moments of enlightenment during ordinary circumstances.

• Several members read aloud verses 33-35. How important is it to reaffirm spiritual truth? Say, "There are important principles of learning and understanding to be found in this narrative. Let's discover them."

STEP 3 (10 minutes):

• Move members into groups of four to six and appoint group leaders.

• Distribute numbered notes listing references.

• Groups research Scriptures and list one principle of learning and understanding each.

SESSION 2

God Covers Adam and Eve's Nakedness

LEADER'S GUIDE SHEET

Materials needed:

- One copy of the Lesson Outline for each group member;
- Small index cards or Post-it Notes with Scripture references;
- Chalkboard or overhead projector with transparencies;
- Transparency of the Lesson Outline (optional).

A PPROACH (5 minutes)

- Distribute index cards or Post-it Notes to members for reading of Scriptures in Step 1.
- Write and display the following statement: "Sin is almost always shared."
- Learners consider the statement and neighbor-nudge the person next to them whether the statement is true. If so, in what way?
- Group shares their conclusions.
- Say, "We will examine humankind's initial sin known as the Fall, and God's provision of the animal skins to cover Adam and Eve's nakedness. We will also see how God's act was a foreshadowing of a greater provision to be made centuries later."

------FOLD

- Follow with a brief discussion and point out the additional study in the lower section of the Lesson Outline.

C ONCLUSION (5 minutes)

- Review the fall of humankind.
- Point out Adam and Eve's futile efforts to cover their sin; they needed a Savior.
- Say, "Before creation, God set in motion a plan to redeem fallen humankind; God chose His Son to one day redeem the world through His shed blood" (see 1 Pet. 1:18-20).
- Mention that the shed blood of animals foreshadowed the shed blood of Christ.
- Ask, "Are you applying Christ's blood to your life for daily cleansing, or are you covering your sins by excusing them or blaming others?"
- For those who may not know Christ as their Savior, give them an opportunity to accept Him and His forgiveness.
- Close the session by asking, "Will it be fig leaves or forgiveness?" Then encourage learners to form clusters of three members and pray for one another, asking God's help to accept His greater provision of cleansing and forgiveness.
- Encourage members to read chapter 2 of the Regal book, *Christ B.C.*, which will assist them in their time of daily devotions. Each day's devotion is based on the theme of *righteousness*.

B BIBLE EXPLORATION
(40-50 minutes)

STEP 1 (5-10 minutes):

• State that Satan played a major role in humankind's initial sin, and he continues to fill that role today.

• Assigned persons read aloud Scriptures about Satan. The group identifies characteristics of Satan and his activities as Scriptures are read. List these on chalkboard.

• Say, "We will get a good look at Satan in action in today's study as some of his traits are revealed."

STEP 2 (10-15 minutes):

• Distribute the Lesson Outline and encourage note-taking.

• Learners open their Bibles to Genesis 2. Present a brief synopsis of this.

• Invite a learner to read aloud verses 16,17. Say, "Adam and Eve were given a will; they could obey or disobey."

• Several members share reading aloud Genesis 3:1-6. Discuss this passage and ask the following:
  1. What characteristics of the serpent are seen in this passage?
  2. How did Satan undermine God's command in verse 3?
  3. How does Satan seek to undermine God's Word today?
  4. How did Satan appeal to human reason and pride in Eve's life?

5. What other Bible characters fell because of pride?
  6. How does Satan mix the truth with a lie today?
  7. What three mistakes did Eve make in Genesis 3:6?
  8. How should the Christian handle sin that is flaunted in today's media?
  9. How was sin shared in Genesis 3:6?

• Invite a learner to read aloud verses 7-11. Ask:
  1. What did Adam and Eve learn about Satan?
  2. Do people realize their sinful state today?
  3. What did Adam and Eve lose and gain by disobeying God?
  4. What is implied in Adam's reasons for hiding from God? In what ways are people running from God today?

STEP 3 (15 minutes):

• Say, "As Adam and Eve tried to cover their sin with fig leaves, people continue today to hide their sin."

• Move members into small groups. Appoint leaders.

• Group researches verses 12-13, listing on the Lesson Outline the following:
  1. Excuses Adam and Eve made for sinning;
  2. Excuses people make today to cover their sin.

• After seven minutes, regather for feedback from small group leaders. Write responses on board.

• Say, "God provided a covering for Adam and Eve's sin, and He has made provision for our sin as well."

STEP 4 (10 minutes):

• Member presents a lesson on verses 14-21.

SESSION 3

Noah Finds Refuge in the Ark

LEADER'S GUIDE SHEET

Materials needed:

- One copy of the Lesson Outline for each member;
- Small index cards or Post-it Notes with Scripture references;
- Chalkboard or overhead projector with transparencies;
- Transparency of the Lesson Outline (optional).

A APPROACH (5 minutes)

- State that there is much talk today about high stress and the fast pace of living in our technological age.

- Ask, "How do people without Christ deal with this stress and cope with difficulties?"

- Write responses on chalkboard.

- Say, "Sometimes believers respond to stress in the same way unbelievers respond. Our Bible study today, about Noah finding refuge in the ark during the Flood, will help us to discover where we can find rest and refuge during the storms in our lives."

B BIBLE EXPLORATION (45-50 minutes)

STEP 1 (10-15 minutes):
- Distribute Lesson Outline to everyone and encourage note-taking.

------ FOLD

- Say, "We will focus on the ark as a type of Christ as our rest during times of stress and as our refuge from life's storms."

STEP 4 (15 minutes):
- Ask everyone to form groups of four to six and appoint group leaders. Distribute index cards.

- Invite groups to look up Scripture references on their cards and list ways Christ can be a refuge.

- Regather for feedback and discussion. State, "We can see that God has more than provided for life's storms. We do not need to take the escape routes that many in the world take." Refer to the suggestions in the Approach. Say, "Our rest and refuge can be found in Christ."

C CONCLUSION (5 minutes)

- Ask, "How are you coping with day-to-day stresses or critical trials? Are you responding the same way many unbelievers respond?"

- Refer to the list of suggested ways Christ can be our rest and a refuge.

- Ask, "Which one do you need to apply to your life? Which avenue will bring you rest in your trial?" Allow several minutes for thinking.

- Members form groups of four and pray for one another.

- Encourage members to read chapter 3 of the Regal book, *Christ B.C.*, which will assist them in their time of daily devotions. Each day's devotion is based on the theme, *refuge*.

- Members open Bibles to Genesis 6. Several share reading aloud verses 1-7, 11-13.

- Read aloud Luke 17:26,27 and lead a discussion of this and the above passages using the following:
  1. What were the moral conditions of the people at the time of the Flood?
  2. What similar conditions are seen in today's society? Point out that God hates sin and we should hate it, too. Add, "As God wanted to destroy humankind because of their sin, even so we should want to destroy sin in our lives."

- Several share reading aloud Genesis 6:8,9.
  1. In what ways was Noah blameless?
  2. What other Bible characters led godly lives?

- Present a brief synopsis of Genesis 6:14-22.

STEP 2 (5 minutes):
- Member presents report on specifications of the ark and displays any sketches or pictures.

STEP 3 (15 minutes):
- Say, "God provided for humankind's escape from the judgment of the Flood by instructing Noah to build an ark. Let's consider other ways God extended His mercy to humankind."

- Ask several learners to share in reading aloud Hebrews 11:7, 1 Peter 3:18-20 and 2 Peter 2:5. Ask:
  1. What do you think was the content of Noah's preaching?
  2. Are we responsible to warn people today of God's coming judgment on their sin?
  3. If you had never seen rain, what would your thoughts have been to see the building of such a large boat so far from water?

- 4. Why do you think the people did not respond to Noah's preaching? Present Josephus' writings about Noah.
  5. Can we always expect to receive the favor of people? Why or why not?
  6. In what ways are people's rejection of the gospel today similar to those of the people in Noah's time?
  7. How does sin deaden one's conscience?

- Invite several people to share reading aloud Genesis 7:6-12,15,16. Mention the following:
  1. The animals came to Noah on their own. Similar to God bringing animals to Adam.
  2. The Lord, not Noah, shut the door of the ark.

- Read aloud Genesis 8:6-14. Share the following:
  1. The dove is the basis of the modern symbol of peace. This told Noah God's judgment was over. The dove is a type of the Holy Spirit.
  2. Of what does Noah's act of reaching out his hand to return the dove to himself and into the ark speak to us?

- Invite several members to share reading aloud Genesis 8:15,20,21. What can we learn from Noah's actions?

- Draw learners' attention to Genesis 9:8-17 and point out that this passage gives details of the first covenant between God and humankind. The rainbow made its first appearance at this time.

- Mention that Noah is a type of Christ.

- Point out that Noah was offered a new beginning as we are when we receive Christ. Add, "And new beginnings are ours when we fail in our Christian walk."

- Ask, "How is the ark a type of Christ?"

SESSION 4
Melchizedek
LEADER'S GUIDE SHEET

Materials needed:

- One copy of the Session 4 Lesson Outline for each group member;
- Large index cards with questions and Scripture references;
- Chalkboard or overhead projector with transparencies;
- Transparency of the Lesson Outline (optional).

 **A** PPROACH (10 minutes)

- Write on the board, "Every person seeks redemption whether he or she understands it or not."
- Ask, "Do you agree or disagree?" Learners may move to designated "agree" or "disagree" sides, changing as the discussion takes place.
- Say, "Our study today will shed more light on this subject. We will consider, from God's Word, how Christ offers to all humankind perfect redemption in the order of Melchizedek."

 **B** IBLE EXPLORATION (40-45 minutes)

STEP 1 (10 minutes):

- Distribute the Lesson Outline and encourage learners to take notes.
- Announce the basis for today's study: Genesis 12:1—14:20; portions of Hebrews 5 and 7. Members open Bibles to Genesis 12.

----- FOLD

- State that during our discussion of the savior-substitutes, we have reaffirmed the completeness of redemption offered humankind through the perfect sacrifice of Christ, our Priest and King after the order of Melchizedek.

C ONCLUSION (5 minutes)

- Say, "The Levitical priesthood was inadequate to bring salvation to the world. The necessity to first offer sacrifices for their own sins, the need for repeated sacrifices day after day, and the filling of an office when a priest died, were all abolished when Christ came on the scene. Christ only needed to offer Himself once to redeem humankind, and He lives forever to make intercession for us."
- Ask, "Have you received the only One who is able to save you?"
- Learners compose a paragraph on reverse side of outlines stating why they accepted Christ, if they have done so. Those who haven't list reasons why they have chosen another savior.
- Give an opportunity for anyone who has not accepted Christ to do so. Challenge believers to keep Christ central in their lives.
- Close in a corporate prayer, thanking God for the gift of His Son, who alone can offer us complete redemption.
- Encourage members to read chapter 4 of the Regal book, *Christ B.C.*, which will assist them in their time of daily devotions. Each day's devotion is based on the theme of *redemption*.

- Say, "What do you know about Abraham's call?"

- Several members share reading aloud Genesis 12:1,5 and Acts 7:2-4. Mention God's promise to Abraham, Abraham's journey to Canaan and that Lot moved with him.

- Say, "Next we see Abraham traveling to Egypt." Ask, "What does verse 10 say is the reason for his going to Egypt?"

- Mention problems that caused Abraham to return to Canaan and share Dr. Lloyd Ahlem's comments about Abraham's detour.

- Learner reads aloud Genesis 12:16 and 13:1,2. Say, "Abraham left Egypt wealthier than when he arrived."

- Mention God's blessing upon Abraham as seen in his army and his influence.

- Review Genesis 13:1-13 and the circumstances of Lot's capture and rescue by Abraham.

- Several people share reading aloud Genesis 14:17-20 and Hebrews 7:1,2. State that there are varying opinions as to whether Melchizedek was a theophany or a real man.

- Ask, "How does Jesus fulfill the meaning of Melchizedek's name, 'king of righteousness' and 'king of peace'?"

STEP 2 (15 minutes):
- Say, "We have discussed how Melchizedek is a type of Christ as a king of peace, a righteous king and a king of Salem. Now let's consider how Jesus is our High Priest in the order of Melchizedek."

- Move members into groups of four to six. Assign leaders and give leaders an index card with their group's assignment. Next, regather for feedback.

- Ask the following questions:
  1. Why was the superior priesthood of Christ needed?
  2. Why was Christ able to meet this need?
  3. In what way is Christ's sacrifice complete?

OPTIONAL STEP 3 (5 minutes):
- Ask, "When you were a child, did you ever hear the story, 'Little Boat Twice Owned'?" Have someone else or yourself share the story and its application.

STEP 4 (15 minutes):
- Draw attention back to the Approach statement.

- Allow discussion, then ask for feedback from the whole group. List suggestions.

- Share that everyone, everywhere, at all times is seeking a savior and an object of worship. Include the four possibilities from Toynbee.

- Ask, "With which of the four saviors would you equate humanism, secularism, materialism and New Age beliefs?"

- Explain the deficiencies of each substitute—savior.

- Ask, "How would you enlighten someone who is basing his or her salvation on one of these saviors?"

- Ask, "What are the reasons an individual would embrace one of these saviors?"

- Say, "In a moment we will deal with this statement more definitively. Discuss with the person next to you ways, other than Christ, that people seek to receive or attain redemption."

112

SESSION 5

Abraham and Isaac

LEADER'S GUIDE SHEET

Materials needed:

- One copy of the Session 5 Lesson Outline for each member;
- Small blank index cards and large index cards with Scripture references;
- Chalkboard or overhead projector with transparencies;
- Transparency of the Lesson Outline (optional).

 **A** PPROACH (5 minutes)

- Distribute one blank index card to everyone and say, "If God were to ask you to give up three things in your life, what three things would be the most difficult for you to give up?"

- Learners write answers on the index cards, then share the answers.

- Say, "In today's Bible study God called on a patriarch to give up something very dear. To the average person this would be a difficult and confusing request. However, one divine purpose in making this request was to typify an event that would take place centuries later and change the history of humankind."

————————————————————————————— FOLD

- Review Genesis 22:8,13,14 and Romans 8:32.
  1. Share the name *Jehovah-jirah*—"the Lord will provide" and ask how the term can be applied to all our needs.
  2. Point out that the remission of sins is only the beginning of God's provision.

- Say, "We have seen many types of God's love and of Christ's death in today's study. The beautiful truth that God took the first step to reconcile sinful humankind to Himself only points up God's immense love for the world."

C ONCLUSION (5 minutes)

- Ask, "Have you been trying to offer your own substitute to God for your salvation? Or have you endeavored to meet the needs in your life through your own schemes, instead of receiving from God's provision through His Son?"

- Encourage everyone to form a large circle, or smaller circles, for closing prayer. Several learners pray sentence prayers, thanking God for His gift of Christ and asking His help to receive of His abundant provision, available through His Son.

- Encourage members to read chapter 5 of the Regal book, *Christ B.C.*, which will assist them in their time of daily devotions. Each day's devotion is based on the theme of *provision*.

B IBLE EXPLORATION
(45-50 minutes)

STEP 1 (5-10 minutes):

- Distribute outlines and encourage note-taking.
- Say, "Scripture is filled with improbable things God has done. Today's study includes just such an improbable act. First, a member will present a report on the Theory of Probability."

- Member presents report.

- Share the national hero story and mention the estimate of probability.

- Ask, "What are some improbable events in Scripture that God performed?"

- Say, "The setting of our lesson today involves a very improbable act carried out by God."

STEP 2 (15 minutes):

- Group opens Bibles to Genesis 12:1-4 and learner reads aloud this passage. Point out that Abraham was 75 at the time of this promise.

- Share God's promise by reading aloud Genesis 18:9-12. Say, "Another improbable event. But that promise was fulfilled 25 years after it was first given" (see 12:4; 21:5).

- Ask, "If such an event would happen today, how do you think it would be handled by the media?"

- Say, "God, who does the unusual and who has no equal, continued to do the improbable by making a very difficult request of Abraham."
  1. Member reads aloud Genesis 22:1,2.
  2. Explain the meaning of the word *tested*.

3. Point out that all of the other tests did not release Abraham from this great test.
  4. Add, "We, too, can expect our share of trials."
  5. Ask, "Why does this request appear to be a contradiction?"
  6. Ask, "Had you been Abraham, what would your feelings have been regarding God's request?"
  7. Read aloud Hebrews 11:19.

- Volunteer reads aloud Genesis 22:3-5.
  1. What can we learn from verse 3?
  2. Why do you think the servants were left behind?

STEP 3 (10 minutes):

- Write and display the following questions and Scripture references:
  1. The story of Abraham offering Isaac as a sacrifice is a type of what New Testament event? Genesis 22:1,2; John 19:16-18.
  2. What other types and lessons do you see in the details of the story?

- Members work alone to answer Question 1. Ask for the answer.

- Learners move into groups of four to six. Appoint leaders and give them Scripture references on index cards to answer Question 2 on board.

STEP 4 (15 minutes):

- Regather for feedback from leaders (A-J).

- Next, discuss Isaac's apparent willingness to be sacrificed. Ask, "Do you believe Isaac allowed himself to be bound without a struggle? Why or why not? What do his actions teach us?"

SESSION 6

Joseph

LEADER'S GUIDE SHEET

Materials needed:

- One copy of the Session 6 Lesson Outline for each group member;
- Chalkboard or overhead projector with transparencies;
- Transparency of the Lesson Outline (optional).

A PPROACH (5 minutes)

- Distribute Post-it Notes with Scripture references to volunteers.

- Write on the chalkboard: "1. A person who refused to obey God's Word and as a result does not enjoy the fulfillment of God's purposes for his or her life; 2. A person who obeyed God's Word and as a result realizes the fulfillment of God's purposes for his or her life."

- Members consider the above and think of a person who fits each category. Move into clusters of three and share thoughts.

- Say, "Obedience is the key to realizing God's purposes for our lives. Our lesson will reveal two people who lived this principle."

--------- FOLD

- Say, "Christ is the ultimate example of obedience for us."

STEP 4 (5-8 minutes):
- Partners work together to determine three results each of Joseph and Christ's obedience to God.

- Partners list results on their outlines under heading "Results of Obedience."

- After several minutes ask for feedback.

OPTIONAL STEP 5 (5 minutes):
- Member shares about a trial that fulfilled God's purposes because he or she was obedient to God.

C ONCLUSION (5 minutes)

- Say, "God has a purpose for the testings we experience. As we continue to obey Him in our trials, we will one day realize God's ultimate plans for our lives. And we will receive the 'crown of life' promised to those who persevere" (see Jas. 1:12).

- Close by encouraging pairing up for prayer. Members share with prayer partners about struggles they may be experiencing.

- Encourage members to read chapter 6 of the Regal book, *Christ B.C.*, which will assist them in their time of daily devotions. Each day's devotion is based on the theme of obedience.

B IBLE EXPLORATION (40-50 minutes)

STEP 1 (10-12 minutes):

● Mention that most of us are probably familiar with the story of Joseph. Say, "He is the first person we will consider today who was obedient to God."

● Two members present summaries of Joseph's life. Volunteers read aloud key Scripture verses at designated times.
   1. Genesis 37,39—41:40.
   2. Genesis 41:41—50:26.

STEP 2 (10 minutes):

● Follow with a question/answer discussion of the key points in Joseph's life where obedience was demonstrated.

1. What special relationship is revealed in Genesis 37:3?

2. What negative attitudes were evidenced in Jacob's home? Cause?

3. What does Joseph's response to Jacob's command in Genesis 37:13 reveal about Joseph?

4. What did jealousy lead to in the lives of Joseph's brothers?

5. What lessons of obedience can be learned from Genesis 39:1-12?

6. What can we learn from Joseph's continued obedience in Genesis 39:11-20?

7. Do trials tend to strengthen or weaken us? What makes the difference?

8. How are people today paying a price for refusing to compromise their Christian beliefs and principles as did Joseph?

9. How do you react when you are unjustly treated?

10. How would the cupbearer's memory lapse have affected you, had you been Joseph?

11. What do we learn about Joseph from his reply to Pharaoh in Genesis 41:16?

12. Why did Joseph deal with his brothers as he did?

13. What risks were taken by Joseph in confronting his brothers regarding their sin?

14. What can we learn from Joseph's response to his brothers' fears when their father died?

● Say, "We will now consider the greater purpose of Joseph being sold into slavery as we consider the greater example of obedience as demonstrated by Christ."

STEP 3 (15-20 minutes):

● Distribute a Lesson Outline to everyone.

● Move members into groups of four to six and appoint group leaders.

● Assign each group one or several groups of Scriptures (A-I) listed on the outline.

● Regather into larger group and ask for feedback from group leaders. As responses are given ask how Christ's obedience to the Father is evidenced.

A.

B.

C.

D.

E.

F.

G.

H.

I.

SESSION 7

The Passover

LEADER'S GUIDE SHEET

Materials needed:

- One copy of the Session 7 Outline for each member;
- Chalkboard or overhead projector with transparencies;
- Small index cards or Post-it Notes with references;
- Transparency of assignments and references (optional);
- Transparency of Lesson Outline (optional).

A PPROACH (5 minutes)

- Ask, "In your opinion, what is the most important historical event in the history of our country?"

- Jot down members' ideas and mention that nations build their identities out of important events in their histories.

- Say, "In today's Bible study we will focus on what was probably the most important event in Israel's Old Testament history. We will then examine how this event was a type of a later event that changed the course of history."

B IBLE EXPLORATION (45-50 minutes)

STEP 1 (10 minutes):

- Ask, "What do you remember about the reasons for the move of Jacob and his children to the land of Egypt?"

---FOLD

Bitter Herbs

1. Share more fully concerning Paul's previous life that he counted as rubbish.

2. What should this say to us?

Unleavened Bread

1. Believers need to rid themselves from sin.

2. What are some of the areas in a believer's life where godliness should be in evidence?

3. How may a believer deal with a particular sin in his or her life?

OPTIONAL STEP 4 (5 minutes):

- Invite volunteers in the group to give brief testimonies of their conversion experiences.

C ONCLUSION (5 minutes)

- Ask, "Are you still in bondage to sin, or are you free to fulfill God's designs and purposes for your life? If you have not realized His deliverance, you may by believing that Christ's shed blood can cleanse you from all unrighteousness. Confess your sin to Him today and accept His forgiveness. Let Him free you to a new life in Him.

- Close in small group prayer and encourage learners, who want to share their areas of need with one another, to do so.

- Invite those who have special prayer or counseling needs to meet with you following the session.

- Encourage members to read chapter 7 of the Regal book, *Christ B.C.*, which will assist them in their time of daily devotions. Each day's devotion is based on the theme of *remembrance*.

- Invite several volunteers to read aloud Genesis 46:2,3,26,27; 47:27.

- Say, "This appears to be a nice environment for building a great nation. But God had other plans for His people, and these plans did not include their remaining in Egypt. Let's discover what these plans were."

- Move to groups of four to six. Distribute the outlines and encourage note-taking.

- Appoint group leaders and give one assignment (1-3) to each group.

STEP 2 (15 minutes):
- Regather for leaders' feedback.

Assignment 1
Describe the situation in Egypt, reasons why situation existed and how people responded.

　1. What lessons can we learn from Exodus 2:23,24?

　2. What steps did Moses' parents take that went beyond crying out in distress? What can we learn from their actions?

　3. How did Moses demonstrate that he identified with the sufferings of his people? What does his example teach us?

Assignment 2
Describe the meal and event of the Passover.

　1. What were the three elements of the Passover meal and what were their distinctions?

　2. In Old Testament times, why was it required that the lamb be perfect?

　3. Share what the bitter herbs represented.

　4. Why was the bread unleavened? What can we learn from Israel's immediate obedience to God's

command to leave Egypt?

　5. Of what does Israel's dress code speak? What can be obstacles to our readiness to obey God?

Assignment 3
What special instructions did God give the people through Moses regarding the day and event of the Passover? What was the purpose of these instructions?

　1. Discuss the importance of preserving memories by deliberate and authentic means.

　2. Why is it sometimes easy to forget the painful events in our past and remember only the pleasant ones? Share how quickly the Israelites forgot their suffering.

　3. Why do you think many Jewish survivors of the Holocaust struggle to keep an accurate memory of this event?

STEP 3 (20 minutes):
- Distribute the Scripture references to volunteers. List the following headings as they are discussed:

Day of the Feast—Tenth Day of Abib
　1. Discuss the principle of freedom. How is freedom more anxiety-provoking than bondage?

　2. How was this seen in the religious systems of Jesus' day? Today?

A Perfect Lamb
　1. Without defect.
　2. Represented perfection.

Blood on the Doorframes
　1. Substitutionary sacrifice.
　2. A life laid down for another.

Deliverance Through Death
　1. God's judgment withheld.
　2. Life granted, instead of death.

SESSION 8

The Tabernacle Curtain

LEADER'S GUIDE SHEET

Materials needed:

- One copy of the Lesson Outline for each member;
- Blank paper, felt markers, masking tape;
- Small index cards or Post-it Notes with Scripture references;
- Large index cards with questions and Scripture references;
- Chalkboard or overhead projector with transparencies;
- Transparency of Lesson Outline (optional).

[A] PPROACH (5 minutes)

- Distribute paper and make markers available.

- Say, "Think of a person who has had an opportunity to accept Christ as his or her Savior but, for one reason or another, has hesitated to do so. Then print one or two words that describe the reason you believe this person will not respond to the claims of Christ." Allow several minutes for writing.

- Collect papers, post and review.

- Say, "As we have seen, there are many reasons why a person will not accept Christ as Savior. Many knowingly reject God's way of salvation while others may be unaware that a way has already been made. Our Bible study today will reveal that way, why all may come and how they will be made acceptable to God."

FOLD

- After five minutes, regather for leaders' feedback.
  1. In what way is the curtain covering the Most Holy Place a type of Christ?
  2. What did Christ's death accomplish? Abolish?
  3. What is required to be acceptable to God?

- Say, "In the Approach to our study, you suggested reasons why people you know do not accept Christ as their Savior." Review suggestions given.

- Point out the risk involved with accepting Christ.

- Ask, "Why do believers sometimes hesitate to approach God's throne in prayer during times of need?"

[C] ONCLUSION (5 minutes)

- Ask, "Are you trying to gain access to God other than through Christ's redemptive work on the cross?" Say, "Christ said that He is the way and that no one can come to the Father but through Him. Take a risk and trust Him first, and then you will understand the full benefit of His grace."

- Challenge believers to approach the throne of grace with their needs because Scripture says that we may enter with confidence.

- Give opportunity to receive Christ.

- Close in prayer, thanking God for Jesus who made possible our access to God's throne anywhere and anytime.

- Encourage members to read chapter 8 of the Regal book, *Christ B.C.*, which will assist them in their time of daily devotions. Each day's devotion is based on the theme of *reconciliation.*

B BIBLE EXPLORATION
(45-50 minutes)

STEP 1 (10-15 minutes):
- Say, "The most complete type of Christ in the Old Testament is the Tabernacle with its holy places, priesthood and sacrifices. We will study about the Tabernacle and the curtain before the Most Holy Place that foreshadowed an important New Testament event."

- Distribute outlines and encourage note-taking.

- Member presents overview of the Tabernacle.

- Share Exodus 25-27 about the Tabernacle:
  1. Center of life for Israelites.
  2. Carried everywhere they traveled.
  3. Resting place for the ark that contained the Ten Commandments. Judicial function.
  4. Where God communicated with His people; where information given out. Also called the Tent of Meeting.
  5. All of Israel's life was God-related by means of the Tabernacle.

STEP 2 (10 minutes):
- Say, "Moses received the instructions for building the Tabernacle on Mount Sinai."

- Volunteer reads aloud Exodus 25:1-8.
  1. Offering voluntary.
  2. Why would they have the materials for building the Tabernacle, after quick exodus?
  3. Do you think it was difficult for them to part with these possessions? Point out the gift-from-God element.
  4. What lessons can we learn from their spirit of giving? What Scripture passages encourage us to give? Share benefits of giving.

- Read aloud Exodus 26:31-34.
  1. What brought about the distance between God and His people (symbolized by the curtains)?
  2. What do the cherubim depict?
  3. What is symbolized by a tightly woven, heavy curtain?
  4. Who could enter the Most Holy Place? How often and for what purpose? (refer to Lev. 16:1-34.) What was the consequence of entering the Most Holy Place carelessly? Why was the penalty so severe? What other Bible characters were severely dealt with because they didn't obey God? What can we learn from these incidents?

STEP 3 (10 minutes):
- Distribute small cards for looking up references.
  1. Inner lining for curtain that surrounded Tabernacle and the other two curtains were made of linen. Linen was reserved for holy purposes in Old Testament. Type of Christ's holiness and righteousness. (Member reads aloud 2 Cor. 5:21; Heb. 7:26.) What should linen curtains speak to in the lives of believers?
  2. Cherubim speak of Christ's divinity. (Member reads aloud Isa. 9:6; John 1:1.)
  3. Hair and skins depict Christ's humanity. (Member reads aloud John 1:14.)
  4. In Jewish tradition, blue associated with heaven, purple with royalty, scarlet with earthly glory. Present picture of Christ's character in the colors. (Members reads aloud John 3:13; Rev. 19:12,13,16; Mark 15:17,18,20; Heb. 9:12; 1 Pet. 1:18,19.)

STEP 4 (15 minutes):
- Say, "There is a greater type of Christ that can be seen in this curtain that separated the Holy Place and the Most Holy Place." Move everyone into small groups, appoint leaders, give leaders index card.

SESSION 9

The Ark of the Covenant

LEADER'S GUIDE SHEET

Materials needed:

- One copy of the Lesson Outline for each group member;
- Index cards with Scripture and question/assignments;
- Chalkboard or overhead projector with transparencies;
- Overhead projector transparency of the Lesson Outline (optional).

A PPROACH (5 minutes)

- At the top of one column on transparency or chalkboard write "wrath." On the other write "mercy".

- Ask for synonyms of "wrath" and "mercy" and jot down in columns.

- Learners think of an incident when they felt God dealt with them in His judgment or in disciplinary action and one when they realized God's mercy. Volunteers share.

- Say that in today's study we will consider how God's mercy was demonstrated to the children of Israel and why His wrath was invoked. Add, "And we will see how His extension of mercy to the Israelites is a type of the mercy that is extended to everyone who, in faith, accepts the atoning work of Christ."

Alternate Approach (5 minutes)
- Sing together *Redeemed*.

—————— FOLD

STEP 2 (10 minutes):
- Move everyone into groups of four to six members and appoint leaders. Give each leader a large index card. Groups research and then complete assignments.

STEP 3 (15 minutes):
- Regather for leaders' reports.

- **Zacchaeus**—Is it always possible to make restitution? What can we learn from Jesus' acceptance of Zacchaeus?

- **Thief on the Cross**—How does this incident demonstrate that salvation is not by works? Deathbed conversion stories.

- **Immoral Brother**—What preceded mercy? What else comes with Christian disciplining?

C ONCLUSION (5 minutes)

- Ask, "Have you put your faith in Christ's finished work on the cross and received God's mercy and the forgiveness of your sins? If not, you may by asking God to forgive you of your sins and by believing that Christ's blood will cleanse you from all unrighteousness."

- Ask, "As a believer, are you allowing God to use you as a channel of His mercy?"

- Refer to the synonym list of *mercy*. Say, "All that mercy embraces is available through Christ's atonement as God's abiding presence is enjoyed."

- Invite brief sentence prayers, thanking God for His mercy and abiding presence and asking for help to extend mercy to others.

- Encourage members to read chapter 9 of the Regal book, *Christ B.C.*, which will assist them in their time of daily devotions. Each day's devotion is based on the theme of *mercy*.

• Say, "Today we will see how God's mercy and presence were demonstrated and displayed to the Israelites and how these acts are a type of the mercy that is extended to everyone through the atoning work of Christ."

B BIBLE EXPLORATION (45-50 minutes)

STEP 1 (20-25 minutes):

• Distribute Lesson Outline and encourage note-taking. Say, "God designed a place in the Tabernacle to meet with His people. His instructions regarding the furnishings began with the most important piece—the Ark of the Covenant."

The Ark of the Covenant

1. Volunteer reads Exodus 25:10-16. The ark was 3¾ feet long, 2¼ feet wide, 2¼ feet deep.

2. "Ark" means chest or box.

3. Wood and gold symbolize the humanity and divinity of Christ.

4. Acacia was a common material and readily available. God sent Jesus with common flesh. In what ways is He readily available to us?

5. Can you think of an incident when the ark was not carried as instructed? What can we learn from this?

The Atonement Cover

1. Volunteer reads Exodus 25:17-22. Atonement cover also called the mercy seat.

2. Why was gold used and not wood?

3. Cherubim symbolized throne of God and represented God looking upon the blood as satisfying the need for forgiveness and sufficient to restore broken relationships with God. In what other event in Israel's prior history did God see the blood and withhold judgment?

4. Atonement sacrifice offered yearly.

God in Our Midst

1. Volunteer reads Leviticus 16:2. What was the consequence of entering the Most Holy Place in an improper manner, without the proper preparations?

2. Share that Scripture infers that God's glory had to be shielded from view (see Num. 4:5,6). Volunteer reads Leviticus 16:12,13.

3. What do the rules, regulations and precautions tell us about the presence of God?

4. Volunteer reads John 1:14. What does this reveal to us about Jesus?

5. Share the statement by C.E. Fuller. Neighbor-nudge and tell if agree or disagree.

6. What have people constructed over the centuries to represent the awesomeness of entering God's presence? People who have visited cathedrals share. Do these structures represent how God chooses to relate to humankind?

7. Solomon's Temple was magnificent. Yet God came to Israel the second time to a simple manger.

8. What does the place of Christ's birth tell us about God coming to us?

9. What should this truth tell us personally?

God's Mercy and Wrath

1. How was God dwelling in the midst of the Israelites a picture of Christ's mercy and grace?

2. Volunteer reads Romans 3:25,26. What is the key to being justified?

3. How were God's people recipients of God's mercy instead of His wrath in Old Testament times?

4. To assist the Israelites in obeying God's commands, He put in the ark three objects whose meanings should help them stave off His wrath. The Ten Commandments—truth; Aaron's rod—direction; manna—sustenance.

5. Three things given to help us obey God?

SESSION 10

The Bronze Snake

LEADER'S GUIDE SHEET

Materials needed:

- Your Leader's Guide;
- One copy of the Lesson Outline for each member;
- Index cards with questions and Scripture references;
- Chalkboard or overhead projector with transparencies;
- Overhead projector transparency of the Lesson Outline (optional).

 **PPROACH** (5 minutes)

- Print horizontally on chalkboard or overhead transparency, "God's." Using the "G" from the word "God's," print vertically the word "grace."
- Members create an acrostic by suggesting words or phrases related to God's grace.
- Discuss suggestions made by learners.
- Say, "Today we will examine a particular incident in the history of the Israelites when they desperately needed God's grace. And we will discover the means God used to extend His grace to them and how it is a type of a greater grace extended to all humankind."

 IBLE EXPLORATION (45-50 minutes)

STEP 1 (10 minutes):

- Present the setting for the study: The Israelites wandering through the desert; refused passage through Edom; attacked by forces of King Arad; low morale.
- Distribute outline; encourage note-taking.

————————— FOLD

Discussion:

- How was Satan defeated by God? (see John 3:16; Gal. 4:3-5; Col. 2:13-15; 1 John 3:8).

- Christ became sin for us on the cross and became the fulfillment of the serpent (representing sin) who was lifted up on the pole and through whom healing was provided (see Rom. 5:9-11; 6:5-10; 10:9; 1 Pet. 2:24).

- Say, "While the bronze snake offered only physical healing, Christ's death offers forgiveness of sins and eternal life to all who put their trust in Him."

 **ONCLUSION** (5 minutes)

- Say, "Today's society offers many false options for the healing of troubled souls or the fulfillment of empty lives."

- Encourage anyone who has been looking for healing from sin through other avenues beside Christ, to receive His provision of salvation.

- Challenge believers to evaluate the object of their worship. Ask, "Where do you need to put God first in your life?"

- Close the session by inviting everyone to pray with another learner and to agree with him or her for God's help to keep the Lord central in their lives.

- Encourage members to read chapter 10 of the Regal book, *Christ B.C.,* which will assist them in their time of daily devotions. Each day's devotion is based on the theme of *grace.*

- Invite learners to open their Bibles to Numbers, chapter 21. Volunteers read aloud verses 4-9.

Grumbling Israelites

- What do you think caused the people to become impatient?
- How can we deal with circumstances that try our patience?
- Volunteer reads aloud 1 Samuel 15:23 and Proverbs 17:11. What do these verses teach us about rebellion?
- Can grumbling and complaining ever be justified? Why or why not? How about attitude?
- Share about God's provision of manna and water. How did the Israelites show ungratefulness? What can we learn from their poor example?

STEP 2 (10 minutes):

- Member presents five-minute report on serpents.
- Say, "We will see how the practice of serpent worship by heathen nations influenced the Israelites."
- Learner reads aloud 2 Kings 18:1-4. Share that it is uncertain as to when Israelites began worshiping the bronze snake. Some believe it began during reign of Hezekiah's father Ahaz (see 2 Kings 16).

STEP 3 (10-12 minutes):

- Move everyone into groups and appoint leaders. Give one index card to each group.
- Groups research and then answer questions.

STEP 4 (15-18 minutes):

- Regather for leader's reports.

Group A

1. How was the lifting up of the bronze snake a type of an important event in Christ's life?
2. How did the Israelites sin in worshiping the bronze snake?
3. What forms of idolatry exist in our society today?

Discussion:

- How are idols that we have today disguised? How can we know that something in our lives is an idol?
- Why is God alone worthy of our worship?

Group B

1. The view of the serpent was an individual look. What does this tell us about our acceptance and relationship with Christ?
2. Had the plague not been arrested, the entire nation would no doubt have been afflicted. In what way can sin be compared to the serpent's bite?
3. What are some philosophies and teachings people embrace when they refuse to accept the biblical truth that they need a Savior?

Discussion:

- Does church membership or being raised in a Christian family insure salvation? Why, why not?
- Share about people embracing other philosophies and teachings in an effort to gain salvation.

Group C

1. The means for healing from the serpent's bite was singular; one merely looked at the serpent. What is the similarity to salvation in Christ?
2. How do people today complicate the gospel message or endeavor to add to it?
3. What do you believe is the bottom line for saving faith?

Discussion:

- Read Ada R. Habershon's writings regarding healing being singular (see "Insights for the Leader" under heading "Lessons for Life," fourth point).

Group D

1. How were the serpents that bit the Israelites a type of Satan?
2. How do we know evil is personally dominated by Satan?
3. What did Christ become for us on the cross, and how is this related to the bronze snake?

SESSION 11

Prophecies of the Messiah

LEADER'S GUIDE SHEET

Materials needed:

- Your Leader's Guide;
- One copy of the Lesson Outline for each member;
- Small index cards with Scripture references;
- Chalkboard or overhead projector with transparencies;
- Transparency of Lesson Outline (optional).

A **PPROACH** (5-8 minutes)

- Before session, write on board or transparency the steps used by scientists to test a theory (keep it hidden).

- Ask, "What criteria do scientists use to prove if something is true or not?"

- Share the scientific tests.

- Say, "Today we are going to look at Old Testament prophecies of Christ's birth, life on earth, death and resurrection. These prophecies were written long before Jesus was born, and they predicted certain events that would take place in His life. Let's examine these prophecies to see if they were accurately fulfilled, if they prove the trustworthiness of the Bible, and what effect they may have on our faith in the Word of God."

———————————— FOLD

- After discussion, share Lloyd Ahlem's comments from "Insights for the Leader" concerning the Christo-center approach to Scripture.

C **ONCLUSION** (5-7 minutes)

- Say, "If you have not received Christ as your personal Savior, could you be one who because of a lack of understanding of *all* Scripture refuses to accept any part of it as truth, especially that which deals with the claims of Christ? Could you be using these intellectual doubts to avoid taking the leap of faith?"

- Encourage any unbelievers to receive Christ.

- Ask, "As believers, how may the fulfillment of Old Testament prophecies strengthen our faith in the Word of God today?"

- Point out that God's trustworthiness in fulfilling prophecies reassures that He will fulfill prophecies not yet fulfilled.

- Add, "And His promises concerning our spiritual growth and details of our personal lives can surely be realized as we obey His Word and meet the requisites of these promises."

- Close the session in prayer, thanking God that He has given us so much evidence that proves Christ is the Savior promised in the Old Testament. Ask God to help learners put their faith in the truth given in His Word.

- Encourage members to read chapter 11 of the Regal book, *Christ B.C.*, which will assist them in their time of daily devotions. Each day's devotion is based on the theme of *truth*.

B IBLE EXPLORATION
(40-45 minutes)

STEP 1 (15 minutes):

- Distribute outlines to everyone. Move members into small groups and appoint leaders.
- Distribute the index cards and point out that the Roman numerals and letters correspond to the outline.
- Groups research Scriptures to discover accuracy of prophecies.
- Learners list on their outlines the content of prophecies and fulfillments.
- Tell learners they have 15 minutes for research.

STEP 2 (15 minutes):

- Regather for leaders' feedback.
- Encourage note-taking. Use the following to complete outline:

I. A. Jesus was from the lineage of Jesse, King David's father.
   B. A virgin gave birth to Jesus.
   C. Jesus was born in Bethlehem.

II. A. Joseph and Mary fled for a time to Egypt with Jesus.
   B. Herod had all baby boys slaughtered in Bethlehem.

III. A. The way prepared for Christ's ministry.
   B. Christ preceded by messenger, John the Baptist.

IV. A. Many Jews rejected Jesus' message.
   B. Jesus was rejected by His own people.

V. A. Jesus suffered greatly, especially during time between trial and death.
   B. Jesus is the Lamb of God slain for our sins; silent before His accusers.
   C. Falsely accused but found faultless; crucified between two criminals; committed no sin.
   D. He healed the sick and possessed; was pierced in the side by soldier's sword; died for our sins; buried in tomb of wealthy man; bore our sins so we can be healed of sin.
   E. Arrested and crucified as a criminal; rose from the dead to intercede for those who come to Him; died for our sins as part of God's plan of salvation for the world.

VI. A. God raised Jesus from the dead.
   B. Jesus ascended into heaven.

STEP 3 (10-15 minutes):

- Refer to the scientific criteria and ask the following questions:

1. In evaluating spiritual matters to see if they are true, what problems do you see in applying only a scientific approach to your study?

2. In what ways can a scientific approach to studying Scripture help you in understanding some facts about the Bible? What areas of Scripture cannot be understood scientifically?

3. What are some ways you can evaluate if your understanding of something in the Bible is correct?

4. At what point do you think a person needs to place his or her faith in Christ in order to understand what the Bible says?

5. In what ways does faith in Christ help a person understand what God is saying in His Word?

SESSION 12

The Suffering Servant

LEADER'S GUIDE SHEET

Materials needed:

- Your Leader's Guide;
- One copy of the Lesson Outline for each group member;
- Large poster, felt pens and masking tape;
- Chalkboard or overhead projector with transparencies;
- Transparency of Lesson Outline (optional).

A PPROACH (5 minutes)

- On arrival, members write on poster worldly attributes for an important person.

- Say, "Today we will consider God's qualifications for the One He appointed to fill the position of Savior and Lord of all people: Jesus Christ, God's only Son. We will do this by lookng at several Old Testament passages that foretold Jesus' character and the suffering He would experience as God's chosen Messiah."

B IBLE EXPLORATION (40-50 minutes)

STEP 1 (15-20 minutes):

- Say that we are going to examine Old Testament prophecies commonly called the "Servant Songs." Add, "They foretold events that would happen during the Messiah or Savior's life on earth and also give a clear picture of His character and sufferings."

————————————————————————————— FOLD

STEP 4 (10 minutes):

- Say, "Many ask, 'If God is loving, why does He allow suffering?' How would you answer this question?" Mention that this is a complex question often asked with no easy answers.

- Share Lloyd Ahlem's points from "The Question of Suffering" section. Also suggest resources that deal with this topic.

C ONCLUSION (5 minutes)

- Say, "What painful experience have you realized that yet needs Jesus' healing touch? Or perhaps you are struggling with the 'big' question of why a God of love allows suffering."

- Challenge members to allow the truths of this study to minister to their needs.

- Learners form small prayer groups and share areas of need relating to suffering and pain. Close in a corporate prayer thanking God that we are not alone in our pain because He has provided One who understands our difficulties and the pain we experience.

- Tell learners that next session's study will deal with a very different side of Jesus' character—His role as mighty victorious King.

- Encourage members to read chapter 12 of the Regal book, *Christ B.C.*, which will assist them in their time of daily devotions. Each day's devotion is based on the theme of *compassion*.

- Distribute outlines. Volunteers read aloud verses under "His Qualifications." Group discusses:

A. Isaiah 50:6; 52:14; 53:1,2/Matthew 27:27-30; John 12:37,38.
1. Isaiah 53:2 describes Jesus' everyday appearance.
2. Other verses: Jews' rejection; Jesus beaten.
3. How are these traits different from what the world looks to in a leader?
4. Jesus was not what Jews expected from a Messiah.

B. Isaiah 42:2/Mark 7:31-36.
1. Jesus did not draw attention to His deeds.
2. How is this different from power-seeking people?
3. Share Lloyd Ahlem's comments from "The Unacceptable Image" section.

C. Isaiah 42:3/Matthew 12:15-21.
1. What aspects are part of Jesus' purpose as the Messiah?
2. What kinds of people are the words "bruised reed" and "smoldering wick" describing?

D. Isaiah 42:6,7; 53:4/Matthew 8:16,17.
1. What needs did Jesus minister to in these verses?
2. How does Christ minister to these needs today?

E. Isaiah 49:1/Luke 9:34,35.
1. What do these verses tell you about Jesus?
2. By what authority has Jesus been appointed as Messiah?
3. What about those who try to compete with Christ for the role of Savior?
4. Share Lloyd Ahlem's comments under "God's Concept of the Messiah" section.

F. Isaiah 53:9/Matthew 26:59-61; 27:13,14.
1. What is said about Jesus' character?
2. Why is integrity crucial for the Messiah?

STEP 2 (5-8 minutes):
- Ask, "How are God's qualifications for Jesus as Savior and Lord different from what people might think are necessary qualifications?
- Share Lloyd Ahlem's characteristics of human ideas under "Unlike Any Human Idea" section.
- Say, "Let's look at how Jesus' experience of suffering has qualified Him to understand our suffering and help us in times of painful need."

STEP 3 (10-12 minutes):
- Move members into pairs or trios and direct to "His Experience of Suffering" section on outline.
- Say, "The passages in Isaiah you have been studying portray Jesus as One who suffered greatly. Because of the content of these verses, Jesus is often referred to as the 'Suffering Servant of Isaiah.'"
- Groups review passages and list on outlines (A-C) ways Jesus suffered.
- After several minutes, regroup. Volunteers share.
- Several volunteers read Hebrews 2:18 and 4:15.
- Ask, "In the light of these verses and others you have studied today, why is Jesus able to understand people's suffering?"
- Say, "What a blessing to know that because Jesus suffered for us, He is able to understand our sufferings today. But this truth raises an important question."

128

SESSION 13

The Victorious King

LEADER'S GUIDE SHEET

Materials needed:

● One copy of the Lesson Outline for each group member;
● Index cards with history views;
● Chalkboard or overhead projector with transparencies;
● Transparency of the Lesson Outline (optional).

 **A** **PPROACH** (5 minutes)

● Ask, "As people today contemplate the future, what do you think may be some of their hopes and fears?" List responses and discuss.

● Say, "We all have certain hopes for the future and struggle with fears of not knowing what will happen. On our own, our insights into the future are very limited. Today we will look at history and the future through God's eyes, and we will consider God's plan—past and future."

 B **IBLE EXPLORATION** (40-50 minutes)

STEP 1 (7-10 minutes):

● Move members into three groups, appoint leaders and give each leader an index card with one perspective on history.

● Say, "Each group will consider one of three views relating to perspectives on history. You are to consider the view or quote assigned to your group and then list words that you feel would properly describe this view of the outcome of historical events."

────────────────────── FOLD

● Summarize by saying, "Wisdom to understand current and future events comes from God's Spirit. We are commanded to be watchful and faithful servants in telling others about Christ, standing firm in faith and serving Him."

● Say that a Christian's response to historic, current and future events must be based on God's Word, not human perceptions. Add, "A Christian can face the future with hope, knowing that the outcome of history is certain and is in God's hands."

C **ONCLUSION** (5 minutes)

● Ask, "Do you believe that all God has spoken in His Word regarding future events will one day come to pass? Are there prophecies that you have difficulty accepting?"

● Encourage those struggling in this way to allow the Holy Spirit to reveal the reality of the prophetic passages to them and to minister faith to their hearts.

● Remind believers of Christ's promise to always be with us and of the hope of heaven.

● Close the session in prayer thanking God that He is in control of the future and that believers need not fear what the future holds. Also pray that unbelievers will consider what the future holds for them and the opportunity for hope.

● Encourage members to read chapter 13 of the Regal book, *Christ B.C.*, which will assist them in their time of daily devotions. Each day's devotion is based on the theme of a *victorious future.*

- After five minutes, regather for leaders' comments.

- Share Dr. Ahlem's comments about "History: A Divine Drama" from "Insights for the Leader."

- Say, "Two of these quotes—Views 1 and 2—represent views of historical events held by many people in our society today. View 3 represents a believer's view of history from a biblical perspective. Let's take a closer look at what God says about the future."

STEP 2 (8-10 minutes):

- Distribute outlines; encourage note-taking.

- Divide the group into two, one section researches Scriptures in point A of the outline under "Principles for Considering the Future," the other in point B. Work in partners to discover one principle for examining events through God's eyes.

- Ask for responses. Include in discussion:

A. Jeremiah 29:8,9; Matthew 24:24.
1. Present background of Jeremiah 29:8,9.
2. Measure prophet's words against God's.
3. What religious groups present unbiblical prophecies?

B. Jeremiah 29:11; Matthew 10:29; Luke 21:25-28.
1. The future is in God's hands; people can have hope.
2. God was with the Jews in their exile.
3. Jesus told of difficult times, but promised to be with us. Read aloud Matthew 28:20.

- Say, "Let's look at what Jesus will accomplish at the end of history."

STEP 3 (15-20 minutes):

- Volunteers read aloud verses in "The End of History" section of outline. Include the following in the discussion:

A. Zechariah 14:9; 1 Corinthians 15:24,25; Philippians 2:10,11; Revelation 1:5; 19:16.
1. What titles are used for Jesus?
2. The day of the Lord is when Jesus returns.
3. How will people acknowledge Jesus as Lord?
4. What will Jesus do when He returns?
5. Who are Jesus' enemies?

B. Daniel 10:5,6,14; Revelation 1:12-18.
1. Learners suggest adjectives describing Jesus.
2. How does knowing God is in control affect view of current events and personal experiences?

C. Isaiah 63:1-3; Revelation 19:13-19.
1. What will Jesus accomplish on His return?
2. Read aloud 2 Peter 2:1-6; Romans 8:1; 1 Corinthians 1:8,9.

D. Revelation 21:1-8.
1. What will it be like when Jesus returns?
2. Who will not inherit heaven?

E. Genesis 2:8,9; Revelation 22:1-6.
1. What from Eden will be in the Kingdom?
2. Perfect relationship with God to be restored.
3. In New Jerusalem, no possibility of sin.

- Say, "Until Jesus returns, we have to deal with living today—during the time between the prophecy and the fulfillment."

STEP 4 (10 minutes):

- Members present talks on 1 Corinthians 2:9,10 and Matthew 24:36,42-51.

The Road to Emmaus

Lesson Outline

I. Unlocking the Scriptures Today
Deuteronomy 29:29

   A. Types and symbols.

   B. Prophecies.

II. Two Travelers on Emmaus Road
Luke 24:13-35

   A. A long walk home (see vv. 13-27).

   B. An evening meal shared (see vv. 28-32).

   C. A return trip to Jerusalem (see vv. 33-35).

   D. Principles of learning and understanding.

     1.

     2.

     3.

     4.

     5.

     6.

     7

Further Application and Study

During the week read Luke 24:13-35 again.

Are there areas in your life where you are confused and need to rely on Jesus more?

What steps can you take to relinquish these areas to His guidance?

Do research about the town of Emmaus and whether it exists today.

The Road to Emmaus
Bible Chronology

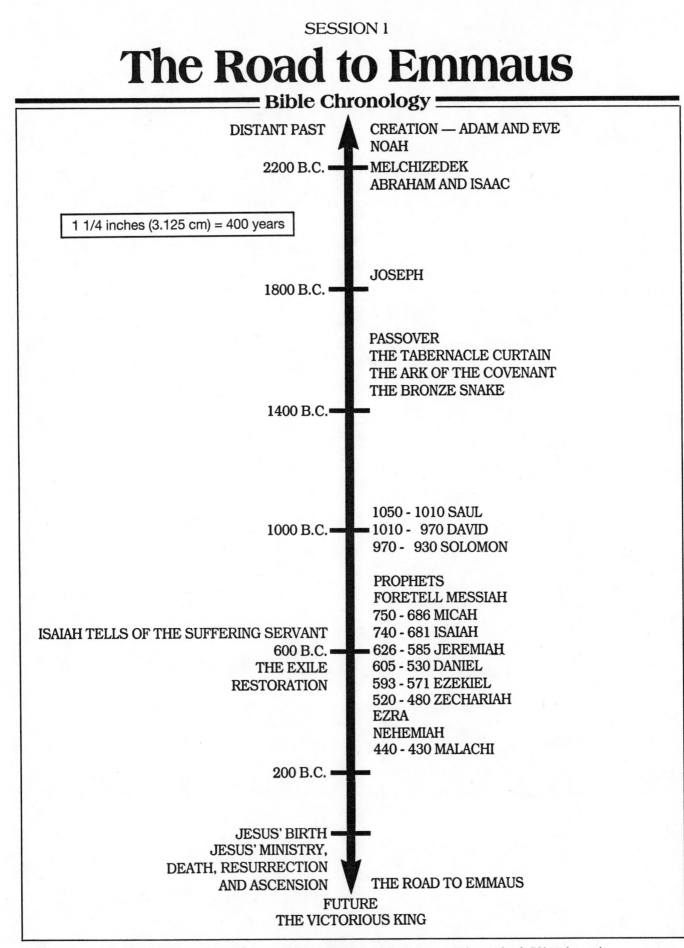

DISTANT PAST — CREATION — ADAM AND EVE
NOAH

2200 B.C. — MELCHIZEDEK
ABRAHAM AND ISAAC

1 1/4 inches (3.125 cm) = 400 years

JOSEPH

1800 B.C.

PASSOVER
THE TABERNACLE CURTAIN
THE ARK OF THE COVENANT
THE BRONZE SNAKE

1400 B.C.

1050 - 1010 SAUL
1000 B.C. — 1010 - 970 DAVID
970 - 930 SOLOMON

PROPHETS
FORETELL MESSIAH
750 - 686 MICAH
ISAIAH TELLS OF THE SUFFERING SERVANT — 740 - 681 ISAIAH
600 B.C. — 626 - 585 JEREMIAH
THE EXILE — 605 - 530 DANIEL
RESTORATION — 593 - 571 EZEKIEL
520 - 480 ZECHARIAH
EZRA
NEHEMIAH
440 - 430 MALACHI

200 B.C.

JESUS' BIRTH
JESUS' MINISTRY,
DEATH, RESURRECTION
AND ASCENSION — THE ROAD TO EMMAUS
FUTURE
THE VICTORIOUS KING

The Road to Emmaus

Word List

allusion: an implied or indirect reference; a hint.

antitype: the fulfillment of a type.

apocalypse: an unveiling; see revelation.

figurative: expressing one thing by another; using exaggeration or mataphor; not literal.

foreshadow: to represent beforehand.

illustration: to make clear by giving an example or a picture; clarification.

literal: actual; obvious; in relation to Scripture, the meaning of a passage may be both literal and figurative. For instance, the offering of Isaac as a sacrifice may be seen literally as a historic event and figuratively as a foreshadowing of God's sacrifice of His Son.

messianic psalms: psalms that point to the Messiah or that contain prophecies about Him (see Psalms 22; 69; 110).

picture: an event or object that gives a mental image or accurate idea about something else.

prefigure: to picture beforehand.

prophecy: divine declaration of divine will and purpose; a divinely inspired utterance; a prediction of something to come.

revelation: to make known something that was hidden.

theophany: a visible manifestation of God.

type: a type is a divinely purposed illustration of some truth. It may be (1) a person (see Romans 5:14); (2) an event (see 1 Corinthians 10:11); (3) a thing (see Hebrews 10:20); (4) an institution (see Hebrews 9:11); (5) a ceremony (see 1 Corinthians 5:7). Types occur most frequently in the Pentateuch, but are found more sparingly, elsewhere. The antitype, or fulfillment of the type, is found usually in the New Testament (C.I. Scofield).

typology: a study, analysis or system of classification based on types.

God Covers Adam and Eve's Nakedness

Lesson Outline

I. Adam and Eve in the Garden of Eden
Genesis 2:1-25
A. A perfect setting.
B. A command given by God (see vv. 16,17).

II. The Fall of Humankind
Genesis 3:1-6
A. Satan's methods (see vv. 1-4).
B. Eve's mistakes (see v. 6).
C. Sin shared (see v. 6).

III. Loss of Innocence
Genesis 3:7-11
A. Adam and Eve's enlightenment (see v. 7).
B. Adam and Eve's fig-leaf coverings (see v. 7).
C. Adam and Eve hide from God (see v. 8).

IV. Humankind's Fig-leaf Coverings
Genesis 3:12,13
A. Excuses made by Adam and Eve.
B. Excuses made by people today.

V. God's Provision for Humankind's Sin
Genesis 3:14-21
A. Results of the Fall (see vv. 14-19).
B. Covering of skins (see v. 21)
C. Covering of Christ's righteousness (see v. 15; John 3:16; Romans 3:22; 13:14).

Further Application and Study

During the week read Genesis 2:1—3:21 again.

Are you making excuses or rationalizing concerning a sin in your life?

Determine to confess this sin to God and allow Christ's blood to cleanse you from sin.

Research the many provisions of salvation through Christ by checking a Bible concordance for Scripture references listed under the following words:

eternal life;
gift(s);
grace;
salvation;
saved.

Noah Finds Refuge in the Ark

Lesson Outline

I. The Days of Noah
   Genesis 6:1-7,11-13; Luke 17:26,27; Genesis 6:8,9
   A. Wickedness abounds.

   B. Noah found blameless.

II. The Ark Is Built
   Genesis 6:14-22
   A. God's specifications (see vv. 14-16).

   B. Who will enter the ark (see vv. 18-20).

III. The Preacher of Righteousness
   Hebrews 11:7; 1 Peter 3:18-20; 2 Peter 2:5
   A. Content of Noah's message.

   B. People's response.

IV. Noah Finds Refuge in the Ark
   Genesis 7:6-12,15,16
   A. Noah's family and the animals enter (see vv. 7-9).

   B. The door is shut (see v. 16).

V. God's Judgment Ends
   Genesis 8:6-14,20,21; 9:8-17
   A. Noah sends out a raven and a dove (see vv. 6-12).

   B. Noah builds an altar and offers a sacrifice (see vv. 20,21).

   C. The first covenant between God and humankind (see 9:8-17).

VI. Types of Christ
   A. Noah.

   B. The ark.

Further Application and Study

During the week read Genesis 6:1—9:17 again.

Who or what do you seek out as a refuge to run to in times of trial and stress?

List several ways you can respond to Christ's invitation to receive His rest and peace during difficult times.

What other types can you discover from Scripture that may be made from the story of Noah finding refuge in the ark? A Bible commentary and concordance will assist you in your research.

Melchizedek

Lesson Outline

I. Abraham's Call and Journeys
Genesis 12:1—13:1
A. Leaves Mesopotamia and enters Canaan (see Gen. 12:1,5; Acts 7:2-4).
B. Detours to Egypt (see Gen. 12:10).
C. Returns to Canaan a wealthy man (see 12:16; 13:1,2).

II. Abraham Rescues Lot
Genesis 14:1-16
A. King Kedorlaomer and his allies conquer Sodom (see vv. 8-11).
B. Lot taken captive (see v. 12).

III. Abraham Greeted by Melchizedek
Genesis 14:17-20
A. King of righteousness (see Heb. 7:2).
B. King of Salem—king of peace (see v. 2).
C. Receives tithes from Abraham (see Gen. 14:20).

IV. Jesus and the Order of Melchizedek
Hebrews 4:14; 7:1-28
A. As King (see Ps. 23; Ezek. 37:24-28; John 14:27; 19:19; 2 Tim. 4:1; 1 John 2:1; Rev. 19:1-16; 22:3-5)
B. As Priest (see Heb. 4:14; 7:1-28).

V. Complete Redemption
John 19:30; Hebrews 7:27; 9:12; 10:4
A. Levitical priesthood inadequate (see Lev. 9:7; Heb. 5:1-3).
B. Christ's priesthood adequate (see 2 Cor. 5:21; Heb. 7:26,27).

VI. Man-made Saviors

A.   C.

B.   D.

Further Application and Study

During the week read Genesis 12:1—14:20; Hebrews 5:5-10; 7:1-28 again.

If you have not accepted Christ's complete redemption, consider doing so today.

If a believer, are you seeking other "saviors" to meet your needs? Determine to seek Christ's provisions.

Research the various views regarding Melchizedek. Was he a theophany or a man who once lived and died?

Abraham and Isaac

Lesson Outline

I. An Improbable God
   Genesis 12:1–4; 17:15-19; 22:1,2
   A. The Theory of Probability.

   B. An improbable promise (see 12:1-4; 17:15-19).

   C. An improbable request (see 22:1,2).

II. A Three-day Journey
   Genesis 22:3-5
   A. The preparations (see v. 3).

   B. The destination in view (see v. 4).

   C. The servants left behind (see v. 5).

III. Old Testament Types
   Genesis 22:6-18

   A.   F.

   B.   G.

   C.   H.

   D.   I.

   E.

IV. Christ Our Sufficiency
   Romans 8:32
   A. As the sacrifice for our sins (see 3:23-25; 8:32).

   B. As the supplier of all our needs (see Romans 8:32; Ephesians 3:8,19,20; Philippians 4:19)

Further Application and Study

During the week read Genesis 22:1-18 and Hebrews 11:17-19 again.

Examine your life to determine if you are performing good works in an effort to make peace with an offended God? How can you better accept the substitutionary death of God's Son, Christ, on the cross for your sins?

Research in Scripture the word *provision*. A Bible commentary will assist you in your investigation.

Joseph

Lesson Outline

I. Joseph's Life and Obedience—a Type of Christ
Genesis 37,39—47
A. Genesis 37:3; Matthew 3:17; 17:5.

B. Genesis 37:2,5-9; Matthew 24:30,31; Mark 8:31; John 8:31-58.

C. Genesis 37:19-28; Matthew 26:14-16; Luke 20:19

D. Genesis 39:7-10; Matthew 4:1-11.

E. Genesis 39:19,20; 40:1-22; Matthew 26:59-65; Luke 23:32,33,39-43.

F. Genesis 41:14,41-43; Matthew 28:18; Acts 2:24; Ephesians 1:19-23.

G. Genesis 42:1,2,6,25; 47:25; Luke 24:50-53; John 20:24-28; Philippians 2:9-11.

H. Genesis 41:55-57; John 3:16; Acts 4:12; 1 John 5:11,12.

I. Genesis 44:16—45:14; John 20:17; 2 Corinthians 5:18; 1 John 1:9.

II. Results of Obedience
A. As demonstrated by Joseph.
1.

2.

3.

B. As demonstrated by Christ.
1.

2.

3.

Further Application and Study

During the week read Genesis 37, 39—50.

Are you struggling to be obedient to God in a trial you are experiencing? Begin to pray about how you may respond to God's will in your trial.

Also list ways God is with you and helping you in spite of your circumstances.

Research Bible people who remained obedient to God during difficult times in their lives. Then list ways God used them to fulfill His plans and purposes.

The Passover

Lesson Outline

I. Israel's Bondage in Egypt
Exodus 1; 2:1-8,23,24; Hebrews 11:23-27
   A. Conditions (see Exodus 1:8,10,11,14-16,22).

   B. Reasons (see vv. 8-10).

   C. People's response (see Exodus 2:1-8,23; Hebrews 11:23).

   D. God's response (see Exodus 2:24).

   E. Moses' response (see Hebrews 11:24-27).

II. The First Passover
Exodus 12:1-13,21-23,29-50
   A. Elements of the meal and their distinctions (see vv. 3,5,8,9,46).

   B. Instructions regarding the lamb's blood (see vv. 7,22).

   C. Dress code (see v. 11).

   D. Event (see vv. 23,29,30).

   E. Exodus (see vv. 31-41,51).

III. Commemoration of the Passover
Exodus 12:14-20,24-27; 13:1-16
   A. Instructions (see 12:14-20,24,25; 13:1-7,10).

   B. Purpose (see 12:26,27; 13:8,9).

IV. Christ in the Passover
   A.   D.

   B.   E.

   C.   F.

Further Application and Study

During the week read Exodus 12 and 13.

What sin or bondage is affecting your life? Are you ignoring it, or are you struggling to overcome it?

Consider what you must do to deal with it. Then take definite steps to be cleansed and/or freed from its hold on you.

Look to Christ, the Passover Lamb, whose blood will free you from sin's bondage.

Research in Scripture, admonitions to godly living. Check a Bible concordance for Scripture references listed under the following words:

alive	perfect
free	pleasing
godly	renew
good	righteous
holy	spiritual

The Tabernacle Curtain

Lesson Outline

I. The Tabernacle
   Exodus 25—27
   A. Its furnishings

   B. Center of Israel's life.

II. Freewill Offering
   Exodus 25:1-8; 36:6,7
   A. Items people were to bring (see 25:3-7).

   B. People's response (see 36:6,7).

III. The Most Holy Place
   Exodus 26:31-34; Leviticus 16:1-34
   A. Its curtain (see Exodus 26:31-34).

   B. Its ministry (see Leviticus 16:1-34).

   C. The consequence of entering carelessly (see v. 2).

IV. Jesus as the Curtain
   A. As seen in the linen (see 2 Corinthians 5:21; Hebrews 7:26).

   B. As seen in the cherubim (see Isaiah 9:6; John 1:1).

   C. As seen in the hair and skins (see John 1:14).

   D. As seen in the colors of yarn (blue—see John 3:13; purple—see Revelation 19:12,13,16; Mark 15:17,18,20; scarlet—see Hebrews 9:12).

   E. As the curtain dividing the Holy Place and Most Holy Place (see Mark 15:38; Hebrews 9:11; 10:19,20).

V. Results of Christ's Death
   A. Accomplishments (see John 1:12; Ephesians 2:8,9; Hebrews 9:12,15; 10:14,22).

   B. Abolishments (see Hebrews 9:1,7,11,12).

Further Application and Study

During the week read Exodus 25—27; Leviticus 16:1-34.

Do you need to take a risk and come to God by putting your faith in Christ's redemptive work? Ask God in simple faith to reveal Himself to you, and He will!

Believer, list the things you need to approach God in prayer about. Go to Him today; the door is open.

Make a further study of the rules and requirements the priests, and especially the high priest, had to keep and meet in order to minister in the Tabernacle.

This study will give you a richer understanding of the full impact of Christ's death that did away with the old covenant.

The Ark of the Covenant

Lesson Outline

I. The Ark of the Covenant
Exodus 25:10-16
A. Its size (see v. 10).

B. The materials (see vv. 10-13).
1. The wood and gold (see vv. 10-13).
2. Type of Christ (see John 1:14; 4:6; 1 Tim. 1:17; Rev. 15:3).

II. The Atonement Cover
Exodus 25:17-21
A. The materials (see v. 17).

B. The cherubim (see vv. 18-20).

C. The sprinkling of blood (see Lev. 16:14-17).
1. Once a year (see v. 34).
2. Type of Christ (see Rom. 3:25; Heb. 10:10,12,14; 1 Pet. 1:18,19).

III. God in Our Midst
Exodus 25:22
A. God's presence and glory (see Exod. 25:22; Lev. 16:2).

B. God's glory shielded from view (see Exod. 26:31,33; Lev. 16:12,13; Num. 4:5,6).

C. Type of Christ (see John 1:14; Eph. 2:13; Col. 1:19,20).

IV. God's Mercy and Wrath
A. Mercy (see Lev. 16:11,14-17; Rom. 3:25,26).

B. Wrath (see Num. 13:1,2,26—14:45).

V. New Testament Examples of Mercy.
A.

B.

C.

Further Application and Study

During the week read Exodus 25:10—22.

Write down the name of one person to whom you may extend mercy in the coming week.

If it is impossible to do this in a tangible way, determine to pray for this person that God's mercy will be realized in his or her situation.

Do a further study about the three objects—Ten Commandments, Aaron's rod, pot of manna—God placed in the ark. Using a concordance and Bible commentary, discover how these objects are also types of Christ as they relate to truth, direction and sustenance, respectively.

The Bronze Snake

Lesson Outline

I. Grumbling Israelites
   Numbers 21:4-9

   A. Reasons for impatience (see Exodus 16:2,3; Numbers 14:1-3; 21:4,5).

   B. Venomous snakes (see Numbers 21:6).

   C. A cry for help (see v. 7).

   D. God's response (see v. 8).

II. Worship of the Bronze Snake
    2 Kings 18:1-4

   A. By the Israelites (see vv. 1,4).

   B. Bronze snake destroyed (see v. 4).

III. Lessons on Life

   A. Type of Christ (see Numbers 21:8,9; John 3:14,15).

   B. Individual view and universal sin (see Numbers 21:8; Romans 3:23).

   C. Healing through one means (see Numbers 21:9; Acts 4:12).

   D. Venomous snakes—type of Satan (see Numbers 21:6; John 10:10; Revelation 12:9).

Further Application and Study

During the week read Numbers 21:4-9; 2 Kings 18:1-4.

Are you looking to other means of salvation apart from faith in Christ? Receive Him into your life, today, and be saved.

Believer, examine your life for idols that may be hindering you from giving God His rightful place of worship. Confess them to God, seeking His help to destroy them.

Research the words *patience* and *obedience* in your Bible as they relate to the children of Israel. A Bible concordance will assist you in your research.

Your findings will reveal the level of the Israelites' spirituality.

SESSION 11

Prophecies of the Messiah

Lesson Outline

I. Christ's Lineage and Birth
   A. Isaiah 11:1; 53:2—

   B. Isaiah 7:14—

   C. Micah 5:2—

II. Christ's Flight into Egypt
   A. Hosea 11:1—

   B. Jeremiah 31:15—

III. Christ's Ministry Prepared
   A. Isaiah 40:3-5—

   B. Malachi 3:1—

IV. Christ's Message and Ministry Rejected
   A. Isaiah 53:1—

   B. Isaiah 53:3a—

V. Christ's Trial and Death
   A. Isaiah 52:14; 53:3—

   B. Isaiah 53:7,8—

   C. Isaiah 53:9—

   D. Isaiah 53:4-6—

   E. Isaiah 53:10-12—

VI. Christ's Resurrection and Ascension
   A. Psalm 16:9-11—

   B. Psalm 68:18—

Further Application and Study

During the week read Isaiah 53.

List at least one point or area of Scripture where you may be struggling with doubts. Using the criteria of fact and faith, endeavor to deal with these doubts. You may want to enlist the help of your group leader or minister.

Do an overview of Isaiah 40—66 and list prophecies relating to the ministry of Christ (apart from His sufferings) that were not considered in the session.

Using a concordance and Bible commentary, discover if the prophecies have been fulfilled, or if they await a future fulfillment.

The Suffering Servant

Lesson Outline

I. His Qualifications
   A. Isaiah 50:6; 52:14; 53:1,2; Matthew 27:27-30; John 12:37,38—

   B. Isaiah 42:2; Mark 7:31-36—

   C. Isaiah 42:3; Matthew 12:15-21—

   D. Isaiah 42:6,7; 53:4; Matthew 8:16,17—

   E. Isaiah 49:1; Luke 9:34,35—

   F. Isaiah 53:9; Matthew 26:59-61; 27:13,14—

II. His Experience of Suffering
   A.

   B.

   C.

III. Why He Is Able to Understand Our Suffering
   A.

   B.

IV. Why God Allows Suffering
   A.   D.

   B.   E.

   C.

Further Application and Study

During the week read the Scripture references listed on this outline.

If you continue to struggle with hurts received from a painful experience, complete the following statements:

■ Jesus understands my pain because . . .

■ Because Jesus understands my pain, I can . . .

Check a dictionary or thesaurus for synonyms of the word *compassion.*

Next research the word *compassion* and its synonyms in your Bible as they relate to Christ's ministry. A Bible concordance will assist you in your research.

This further study will reinforce your understanding of Christ's compassion for you during times of pain.

The Victorious King

Lesson Outline

I. Principles for Considering the Future
   A. Jeremiah 29:8,9; Matthew 24:24—

   B. Jeremiah 29:11; Matthew 10:29; Luke 21:25-28—

II. The End of History
   A. Zechariah 14:9; 1 Corinthians 15:24,25; Philippians 2:10,11; Revelation 1:5; 19:16—

   B. Daniel 10:5,6,14; Revelation 1:12-18—

   C. Isaiah 63:1-3; Revelation 19:13-19—

   D. Revelation 21:1-8—

   E. Genesis 2:8,9; Revelation 22:1-6—

III. Today's Situation
   A. 1 Corinthians 2:9,10—

   B. Matthew 24:36,42-51—

Further Application and Study

During the week read the Scripture references listed on this outline as well as Revelation, chapters 21 and 22.

List present and future events that cause fear or concern in your life. In the light of today's study, write two steps you plan to take to deal with the resulting fear or concern.

Research the following passages regarding fearful and troublesome situations and discover how the Lord proved faithful to those involved.

Genesis 21:1-20
Exodus 14
1 Kings 17:7-16
Luke 1:26-38; 2:1-7; Matthew 2:1-15
Mark 4:35-41
Acts 27